The Joker's Wild

Other books by the same author

King of Fools
The Princess Royal
Five for Hollywood
The Trial of Rock Hudson
Prince Philip

THE JOKER'S WILD

The Biography of Jack Nicholson

John Parker

Anaya Publishers

LONDON

First published in Great Britain in 1991 by
Anaya Publishers Limited
49 Neal Street, Covent Garden
London WC2H 9PJ

British Library Cataloguing in Publication Data

Parker, John *1938–*
The joker's wild.
1. Cinema films. Acting. Nicholson, Jack, 1937–
I. Title
791.43028092

ISBN 1-85470-035-9

Typeset in Monotype Bembo
Printed and bound in Great Britain by
Butler & Tanner Ltd, Frome and London

Contents

Acknowledgements

My research for this biography has been made especially rewarding by the cooperation I have received from a large number of people who have given of their time, and I would especially like to thank those personalities in Los Angeles, New York and London, who provided me with invaluable recollections and showed me their kind hospitality in inviting me into their homes. Thanks also to journalist Kenelm Jenour and Karen Mayo-Chandler in Los Angeles for the signed transcripts of her recollections of her association with Jack Nicholson, and to Douglas Thompson for his interview with Anjelica Huston. Also to Mr Hugh Hefner and *Playboy* magazine for permission to quote from interview transcripts.

I received tremendous assistance from many others in Hollywood, and from the archive centres which kindly provided me with splendid help and access to their documentary files, as well as to their video and film library facilities. I express my thanks to the staff at the Academy of Motion Picture Arts and Sciences, Los Angeles; the American Film Institute Library and Archive, Los Angeles; the Special Collections Department at the Doheny Library of the University of Southern California; and the Performing Arts Library at the Lincoln Centre, New York and the Tasiemka Archive, London. Special thanks to Professor Ronald L. Davis and his staff at the Southern Methodist University of Dallas, Texas, for access to the vast selection of tape-recorded interviews from the Oral History Collection on the Performing Arts, which forms part of the university's DeGolyer Institute for American Studies, and provides transcripts from conversations with leading show-business personalities, amounting to some 20,000 pages; thanks to the university for permission to use extracts.

John Parker,
Northamptonshire, August 1990

Prologue

'Now listen, pal.'

The voice is threatening and his choice of the word pal is not meant as a term of endearment. He uses it when he is angry or sarcastic, otherwise it is 'babe'. The eyebrows go up in an arch that would make a complete circle if they carried on down, the lids over those eyes, likened by to a cobra's by Candice Bergen, narrow to a slit; the gleaming white teeth flash through the pursed lips in what *Vogue* editor Diana Vreeland called a 'killer smile'. He shows his annoyance with some intimidating facial expression, backed up by a sparse selection of adjectival punctuation invariably using the 'f' word, which he uses with considerable effect. He is capable of rages near to those on-screen moments when he can scare the living daylights out of a cinema audience. Then the anger subsides, as quickly as it flared. His speech goes back into a relaxed drawl, eyebrows half-cocked this time, and a mischievous glint makes the instigator of this flash of temper wonder whether he meant it in the first place. He did. He's talked enough about drugs. That's it. Why talk about it any more?

The scenes switches. He's at a party in Toronto to honour his pal Warren Beatty; someone is always giving a party for Beatty and when they don't he gives one for himself.

There's a blonde approaching. Beatty thinks he's got it made, but she turns to Jack. She's a reporter and Jack knows it. She tilts forward slightly, revealing an ample cleavage and brazenly says to Nicholson, 'Hi Jack, would you like to dance?'

He pauses before answering, eyes going up and down, mouth narrowing to a leery smile. 'Wrong verb, honey. Wrong verb.'

That's the image. Womanizer. Is it true? Of course, but exaggerated. Does he encourage it? Yes, or did once when it was important to him professionally, when there was still the lurking doubt that no one would call any more to offer him a great new role, an insecurity built on the fact they no one did call in the first fourteen years of his professional life. It was always the other way round, and when he found overnight fame, he clung to it with both hands and worried sometimes that it would go away again. And so the image is important: it keeps the punters on the hook. What has also developed is a kind of unofficial contest between himself and Warren Beatty which is all about women, i.e., their famous conquests and their alleged insatiable quests to make it with the world's most attractive women, or some alluring beauty either may have encountered in a bar or restaurant. For Nicholson, success in this quarter is doubly gratifying – displaying his ability to attract women by means other than looks. Unlike Beatty, who always had the advantage of being the living image of the role-model Hollywood leading man with dark, mysterious eyes, classic features and a huge mop of hair, Nicholson is the unlikely romantic hero. But then, it was not his good looks that made him famous. When stardom struck, he was already in his thirties, the hair showed signs of receding and because it was brown Beatty taught him a trick with make-up shadow that reduced the emphasis of an enlarged forehead. He was already having to watch his weight. He could not be described as handsome, and, in later years, with his weight fluctuating to in excess of fifteen stone through his appetite for junkish food between pictures, he showed signs of a middle-aged spread; not being tall, at five feet, nine inches, it tends to be obvious. Although there will be plenty of examples of his deep love of women, not merely for their sexual attraction but for their companionship, conversation and intelligence, he can be struck by an infatuation for women he has never met. He invariably falls in love with his leading ladies. Yet, while he considers his relationships to be 'personal' and not a matter for newspaper talk, he played the public role of superstud for years. He, like Beatty, manipulates women just as they do the media. Example: One day an interviewer is holding forth about Jack's latest film when the door opens and an aide calls in, 'Jack, there's a girl on the phone. Says her name is so-and-so. Says you'll remember her.'

Jack says, 'I don't remember the name.'

Aide says, 'She met you in Aspen and you told her to give you a call when she got back into town.'

Jack says, 'I don't remember. I've met a lot of girls in Aspen. Take her name and number and tell her I'll call her back.'

The reporter puts that little exchange into the first five paragraphs of his story. Some time later, Jack's at home, for another interview to publicize a couple of films, including his appearance in Warren Beatty's *Reds*, at a time when Beatty was in a heavy romantic alliance with their co-star Diane Keaton. The mood is relaxed. Coltrane is blowing softly in the background. The secretary interrupts and says, 'Telephone Jack, will you take it now?'

Jack says, 'Who is it?'

Secretary whispers indiscreetly, 'It's Keaton.'

Jack says, 'What does she want?'

Secretary says, 'Dinner.'

Jack says, 'Say yes . . .'

The interviewer knows a secret and naturally imparts it to his million or so readers in the next issue.

Jack the lad is jolly and jovial. Life is good. Every day of every week he becomes richer by more money than he made in his first ten Sixties films put together and then some. But the Sixties gave him a background to emerge from; in fact, he wrote part of the script for the age and it never left him; he didn't allow it to leave him.

'He is more hip than any man I know,' says film executive Mark Canton, who helped to make Jack as rich as he is today, by persuading him to play The Joker in *Batman*. 'I've never known anyone who enjoyed being himself more than Jack. He brings out the child in himself and everyone else.'

Women have viewed him differently, and, even at fifty-three, his *Batman* co-star Kim Basinger gives witness that he is 'the most highly sexed individual I ever met . . . he's just *the* devil.' Women have also brought him trouble. He's had a lifelong fight with feminists who accuse him of extreme male chauvinism and damaging their dignity. His one-night stands and his expansive appetite for fun in the night clubs of Los Angeles, New York and London have been charted in the gossip columns for two decades. Occasionally, there are other setbacks, though none as spectacular as the mess he got himself into during 1989.

Having only just made peace with his companion of fifteen years, Anjelica Huston, he was struck by the first kiss-and-tell in his entire life, and he was angry. He knew it was coming because the girl who sold her story to *Playboy* magazine in America and the *Sunday Mirror* in London – British model and actress Karen Mayo-Chandler – warned him. Her story was plastered all over the December issue of *Playboy* and every time he switched on the television, she was there repeating it all as a multitude of chat-show hosts clamoured to get her on their programmes.

Jack was mad and even madder with the American scandal magazine the *National Enquirer*, too, although that was nothing new. Three weeks earlier they had devoted a page to the story that another of his girlfriends, actress Rebecca Broussard, aged twenty-six, was expecting his baby, revealing that he was 'excitedly looking forward to playing daddy, but the bed-jumping Joker has flatly told Rebecca that he had no intention of marrying her.' (This latter fact appears to be incorrect; at the time of writing his plans to marry Rebecca were announced.) And Anjelica Huston returned to her own home saying that she had been humiliated for the very last time. No wonder. Karen Mayo-Chandler's allegations made lascivious reading: 'When girls are asked what they look for in a man, they always talk about sensitive things, like intellect, kindness and a sense of humour. Well that's all very nice, very nice indeed, but what I also want is a guaranteed non-stop sex machine and that's exactly what I got with Jack. He's into fun and games in bed, all the horny things that I get off on like spankings and Polaroid pictures. Now that's a man to die for!'

Nicholson registered his disapproval with a call to his pal, Hugh Hefner, owner of *Playboy*. Then, there was nothing else to be done except get back to work in the cutting room at Paramount where he was working around the clock on *The Two Jakes*, for which the world of movie entertainment was waiting with bated breath; because even though all of the above makes fascinating reading for everyone intrigued by Hollywood's pop royalty, especially one so colourful and mercurial as Nicholson, it is the mere trivia, the overcoat of gloss and glitz that hides the real Jack Nicholson....

1

Relative Values

There was always a danger that the legend would become larger than the man, just as it certainly has with his close friend Warren Beatty and thus it is easy to see why Jack Nicholson now guards himself well and repels invaders. He likes his secrets and was impressed by his mother for the way she kept hers for years, that he was not her son. He will happily talk about his films and what makes Jack the performer that he is, but now he rarely allows interviewers into his private territory. But when, as his friend and director Mike Nichols asserts, an actor has inscribed upon popular history a character who has influenced the modern male personality, as did Henry Fonda, James Cagney, Spencer Tracy and Humphrey Bogart, his personal idiosyncrasies are worth more than a cursory glance. That is especially so when the actor in question can be viewed as a contender for the title of number one in a profession well populated with aggressively chauvinistic egocentrics.

The search for the inspirational sources of Jack Nicholson the artist, and Jack Nicholson the man, takes us on a far more diverse journey than some of his contemporaries, like Robert Redford, Warren Beatty and Dustin Hoffman, who were born in the same year – 1937. No one can deny that he is more exciting, excitable and unconventional, with a mix of old and new Hollywood rolled up into a package that mixes James Dean with Humphrey Bogart, though Nicholson insists that he does not want to be compared with anyone. His range of roles has crossed many more adventurous and challenging boundaries, from the devil himself through to perhaps his now most famous portrayal of The Joker in *Batman* and when Nicholson insists that everything he does on screen is in some way

autobiographical, delves into what makes him tick find con-
tradictions and confusion at almost every turn. In fact, when his
colourful personal life is added into the equation, the line between
reality and fiction becomes very blurred indeed, though that is
nothing new amongst the elite in Hollywood history.

In Nicholson's case, however, it is more interesting and quite
important to characterize the age in which he found fame – the
drug infested anti-establishment set of the Vietnam era – as one of
the advance guard leading the underground movements of the
Sixties to the surface of American life in a cloud of head-spinning
smoke, at a time when marijuana was the best cash crop in Southern
California. He stole the show and became the epitome of the
American anti-hero, the spit-in-your-eye champion of counter-
culture whose irreverence captivated and finally liberated his audiences from the time warp in which they had been trapped since
Montgomery Clift, Marlon Brando and James Dean began it in a
rather less volatile manner in the early Fifties.

The very starting point of his story, his birthdate of 22 April
1937, provides instant clues to the mystique and the aura. Anyone
with a passing knowledge of astrological influences will realize that
he was born on the cusp, a Taurus caught in the influence of Aries,
which makes him bullish and a bit of a ram. Curiously enough, if
we add in the Chinese system of horoscopes, he is an ox, which also
rings true: 'as stubborn as ...'

All of this provides an imagery of a person who has lived his
entire life with feelings of a split personality, to such a degree that
Nicholson was moved towards a study of 'cusp people' in his own
search for explanations. Never one to occupy the psychiatrist's
couch, he preferred deep, theoretical and practical explorations,
even to experimentation with LSD. And as students of the star signs
will verify, the cuspate divisions help explain his ability to carve the
characters he plays into different personality fragments to give them
added depth. With the careful selection of the roles, he is also one
of the few major screen actors able to alter his identity from part to
part – and one Jack Nicholson performance is usually vastly different
to the next – yet retaining the kind of personal stamp that often
attracts the criticism: 'Oh, it's just Jack Nicholson playing himself
again.'

Opposing traits in his make-up were already evident during his last year at school, when he was voted both class optimist and class pessimist, though, at that time, he had yet to appreciate certain complexities of character on which he would draw for his screen creations. It led him also to the study of existentialism, a popular discourse among Fifties youth, made popular by the interest of James Dean, and whose definition seems to sum up what Nicholson has become: 'a free agent answerable to no one in a deterministic and seemingly meaningless universe'.

Pre-determined astrological influences may have provided the outline. Existentialism and all those other topical philosophies of the past three decades, which seemed important at the time, may have given him some guidelines. Life itself added the boldest brush strokes and when, finally, he, Jack Nicholson in person, confronts the world, there is the most awesome feeling of encountering a man of unquestionable charm, intelligence and friendship, yet who possesses an indefinable menace that can only be compared with some of the roles he has acted. And who was it who said that when he agreed to play the Devil in the *Witches of Eastwick*, it was because he had been practising for the role all his life? He did!

★   ★   ★   ★   ★

His identity was a confusion even from conception. His sister was his mother, only he did not know it until he was thirty-eight years old. He appeared philosophical on being informed of this startling revelation but it wounded him, more than he would show. According to his friend Peter Fonda, it gave him a 'real deep hurt inside; there's no way of resolving it, ever'. It also may have answered a few queries over which he may have pondered in his youth and then discarded to the rear of his mind for later consideration.

The boy Jack – it was John in those days – was born into an uncertain and rather gloomy world. He was just another statistic, as was another recent arrival and pre-destined best friend, Henry Warren Beatty, who arrived not far away in Richmond, Virginia, precisely three weeks earlier. The developing influences around them had bearing on their futures; there was evil and unhappiness in the air. Hitler was breaking out and at the time his bombers, summoned up by Franco, were in the process of wiping out the Basques' spiritual and cultural home of Guernica. The exiled Leon

Trotsky was calling for the overthrow of Stalin, then engaged in his most murderous of purges. A new king was about to be crowned in England, the previous one having decamped with an American divorcée. George Orwell was warning everyone of the plight of poverty-stricken masses, whose only salvation was socialism and not the sort recommended by vegetarian cranks in sandals. Churchill was telling everyone of the dangers in Europe but no one would listen. And, Germany suffered a massive blow to its pride when the *Hindenburg* crashed in a ball of flames just a few miles from Nicholson's home town, Neptune, New Jersey soon after he was born.

★   ★   ★   ★   ★

The arrival of this bonny bawling boy had caused considerable consternation. A baby born out of wedlock was a great sin, then, and a huge embarrassment to the family. Jack appreciated that thirty or forty years later he might never have been born. He would have become just another abortion statistic, and speaks almost bitterly of having his 'own downtrodden minority. The bastard. I tell myself I've got the blood of kings flowing through my veins.'

Ethel May Nicholson, the woman Jack called 'Mud', short for mother which she wasn't, was a broad-shouldered woman, though not physically, who carried the family and occasionally her husband when he was too drunk to stand without support. Hard times in the lower middle-class regions confronted her and she doggedly fought back to make sure her young family never suffered. She was from strong and wealthy Dutch Protestant stock, a religious family from Pennsylvania who virtually cut her off when she met, fell in love with and married a handsome Roman Catholic, a rakish sign painter of Irish descent named John Nicholson. He was initially a good provider and noted for his smart clothes in the post-depression days. He won the local Easter parade a couple of times as the best-dressed man which, in the depressed Thirties, must have put him in the mould of something of an exhibitionist. His liking for convivial company, found only in the male-dominated bars of New Jersey, a throwback from his forebears of County Cork, eventually forced them into a difficult matrimonial situation from which he occasionally evacuated himself and went off on a drifting reconnaissance of the world outside.

There were two daughters of the marriage: June, who was seventeen when Jack was born, and Lorraine who was two years younger. They had proceeded through childhood and into their adolescence just like a thousand and one other families in the community. In those days, it was a community and most people knew their near neighbours well. Ethel May was well known and well liked, which stood her well when she was forced to support the family single-handedly, by opening a beauty shop in her own home. Everyone came to her for advice, as if she did not have enough of her own problems to solve. Daughter June had inherited some of her father's wanderlust and had a yearning for show business.

★   ★   ★   ★   ★

A one-time Italian band singer, Donald Forcillo-Rose, came out of the woodwork in October 1980 to claim that he and June were lovers when she was just sixteen and he was twenty-six, and that she became pregnant. In 1980, Jack already knew the family secret but he had never known his real father, not even his name, and since June was no longer around to confirm Donald Rose's story, having died of cancer in 1965, his version of events remains a mere matter of record.

Jack's sister Lorraine said she knew that June had dated Don Rose around that time but no one could confirm that he was the father, or his secondary claim that he had married June before the baby was born (he said they had separated quickly and she'd later got a Mexican divorce, though apparently no papers are available to support his allegations.) Jack, by then very famous, called him for a chat and asked if he needed anything. It might be true that Rose was the father. It might not. Nicholson appeared to accept that it was possible, but no special relationship was formed between them. By then, time and sadness had dulled the need for any new discoveries about the past.

In the spring of 1937, June went to Bellevue in Manhattan to have the baby, and returned quietly and resolutely to begin the charade that had been pre-determined, that the child had been born to her mother and father, Ethel and John. If Donald Rose was the father, he was no longer around to become involved in his son's upbringing, and even June, masquerading as the sister, left home four years later to become an Earl Carroll showgirl in Miami. Lorraine stayed in New Jersey and married a local boy, George Smith, to whom she remained devoted for the rest of his life, until he died in 1986.

At some point or other, though Jack has never discussed the possibility in public, he appears to have suspected that all might not be as it seemed in the Nicholson household. He developed what psychologists might describe as a reluctance to address members of his family by their given names or titles. Mother became 'Mud', father became 'Jack', Lorraine was 'Rain' and her husband George, the man who became the father-figure in his life, was nicknamed Shorty. This continued into adult life and he had a habit of creating nicknames for his closest friends: Anjelica became Tootie, Beatty became the Pro, John McEnroe was Johnniemac, etc.

John Nicholson wafted in and out of their lives and Jack's recollections of the man he imagined was his father are tinged with a certain sorrow that he had become an alcoholic, with memories of scenes on the home front, and of the young Jack cooling his heels outside one bar or another with a fizzy drink while his 'father' stood inside drinking neat brandies. And then he would be off again. He remembers him as a melancholy figure. Even schoolfriends in Neptune remember that John Nicholson's drinking occasionally caused the family some worry. Salesman George Anderson, a classmate in high school, can recall a conversation about him, when Jack told him 'I saw my father yesterday' – as if it was an event to be noted – 'the poor old guy, I feel sorry for him because he can't help it.' The relationship was obviously not a close one. When he died in 1958 Jack, by then impoverished and attempting to gain a foothold in an acting career in California, did not fly east for the funeral.

There weren't many secrets in that neighbourhood and it is a wonder that Mud's own was kept for so long. Mrs Nicholson meanwhile was doing rather well in her beautician business and when Jack was five they moved from the less-salubrious surroundings of Sixth Avenue in Neptune to Fifth Avenue in Neptune City which was, as Jack recognized years later, a slightly better position for a young boy. In fact, he has continually made a point of recording that he was not a boy from the wrong side of the tracks, as some tried to indicate, but that his mother/grandmother made sure they were well provided for. They were never rich, but neither were they poor. He was still surrounded by women, of course, mostly fat ones receiving Mud's beauty treatment and so his early life was dominated by the female presence rather than the male which may help explain his future attitude to women for which flocks of emerging feminists, and a few of his friends, would berate him. In part, that may be explained by his own view of women formed from those days in Neptune: they should be independent, take their strengths from their inner self and not rely on men, except for moral support. Mud was like that ' . . . a tiny little elephant carrying everyone on her back'.

He was a fairly typical boy of his neighbourhood, well liked by his friends, and with facial features that remained pretty unaltered through youth and early life, except for a tendency towards puppy fat. No harm was done by the apparent lack of male influence. The heavy hand of a resident father would probably not have stopped him being suspended from school three times, once for smoking, once for swearing and once for self-confessed vandalism (breaking a rival basketball team's scoreboard because they played dirty, for which he took a part-time job to pay for the damage). Nicholson recognized later that Mud had given him his head; he appreciated the responsibility and did not do anything too foolish; irresponsibility came later when he was well outside of any parental influence. Stubbornness was an early characteristic, as was the way he would call a halt to any admonishment laid down by Mud. He would storm off upstairs, banging his feet on the steps as he went, groaning 'For cripes' sakes'. Later he was sorry, and much later he was appreciative. In one of his rare public reflective moments, he looked back on the three women in his early life, Mud, Lorraine and June, with gratitude because they gave him a good start, independence and the belief that he could always take care of himself, come what may.

Shorty was also a good guide and mentor for a growing lad, as good a father as any man could want. He was a man of simple tastes who had a down-to-earth view of life that he passed on in an almost unconscious way with an innate goodness that is found among the local pillars of the community who never stray far from their birthplace. True, he was an All-State footballer which gave him some excitement and fun; but he always stayed in Neptune with Lorraine and with Mud.

Jack progressed; school was no problem. He had a relaxed attitude towards his learning. He was one of those lucky children whose economy of effort never showed up in examination results which were invariably straight 'A's, and he was particularly good at dashing off a 1000-word essay while others were still biting their pen-ends. When he eventually became an overnight star after fourteen years of hard labour in Hollywood, the seekers of his past came knocking on the doors of his tutors and former friends. They usually disappointed everyone by recalling that he was remarkable for his unremarkableness, just another kid on the block; not a hero, not a superstar at sports, not especially remembered for outstanding feats of school bravado nor had he made any particular impression on the girls. One former teacher, Virginia Doyle who was to be discovered in retirement in Sherwood Forest, Toronto, remembered him as a clowning, cunning boy who was good enough to get high marks without apparently doing a lick of work. She thought him a most responsible and sensitive young man and then reflected that for all his fooling around, it probably masked his unhappiness and disappointment over his 'father'. The jollity was a cover for hidden sadness.

An echo: Once in fourth grade, he was sent to stand in the corner, next to the blackboard; whilst there, he powdered his face with white chalk and when he turned around he was a clown, beaming a smile at the class like The Joker in *Batman*. Jack's own assessment of his schooldays was covered in his own biographical notes as having 'deportment problems' which he later explained in more explicit terms as 'fucking up, not in line or as with adolescents nowadays, making a big show they they don't give a fuck, that's bad deportment.'

Harry Morris, Jack's principal tutor in his senior year, also remembered his clowning and had a vivid memory of him as always being late for history class, which followed games. He was, said Harry, always interested in entertaining fellow students and he was a good dancer, always involved in after-school events.

Jack disagreed. He only joined the drama group because the best chicks were in plays; he didn't especially like dancing in his mid-teens because he had become too fat; sports interested him, and he was fanatical about basketball. He was never good enough to make the team, but he was always there on the sidelines cheering and managing. He joined the Air National Guard in high school and just after his fifteenth birthday, became a part-time life guard at the beach; Mr Cool, with mirrored sunglasses and oxide on the nose. Cool was the thing. The DA and Tony Curtis haircuts were making their debut. The beebop era was just fading, Presley had not quite arrived and the advance guard of popular Fifties music that the kids in Neptune listened to were Johnnie Ray, Ray Charles and Chuck Berry. Somewhere off in the distance, the sound of Bill Haley was heard. The rock 'n' roll years were just beginning.

That was the home-town boy.

He arrived at his final year at high school in good fettle and with enough good grades to get to university if he wanted. His old classmate, Gil Kenny, who later became a local police chief, said no one thought Jack would set the world alight. 'He was a clown, he wasn't serious about anything.' He was offered a Dupont chemical engineering scholarship and might have become a captain of industry somewhere in middle America, balding, bloated and with a houseful of his own children, anonymously having pursued a largely uneventful career in that worthy but slightly boring structure of management in a giant US conglomerate. He took a certain route leading to another kind of life and ended up famous.

★   ★   ★   ★   ★

Fame? 'So what can I tell you?' said Shorty to the umpteenth magazine interviewer who came to call, looking for the definitive analysis in the search for Jack Nicholson, once he had become a star. 'You know, he was just a fine kid. Loved his mother. Loved peanut butter and jam sandwiches. To be honest, I'm getting pretty goddamned tired of talking about Jack. What more is there to say? ...'

There was plenty, not about the past but what was to come in the future. To get to that point, there was a quantum leap to be achieved, the proverbial turning point in a young man's life when fate or some other thing takes a hand, and it was at this point in time that June — whom he says he still believed was his sister — reappeared in the story as a catalyst to a decision that would ultimately prove to be the most important in his life.

In the seventeen years since his birth she had stopped being a

dancer in Miami, become the straight lady to entertainer Pinky Lee
for a time and, during the war, done her bit for the American effort
in the control tower at Willow Run, the central domestic sending
centre for the military. Through this work she met and married a
dashing test pilot who was the son of a wealthy Boston brain
surgeon, had two children and lived in some style on Long Island
where Jack spent many holiday breaks, lapping up the upper-class
luxury. The marriage ended because of her husband's drink problem
so June came back to Mud's house at Neptune with her two children
and went back to work as a dance instructor, at Arthur Murray's
highly popular dance centre in New York. In the early Fifties she
decided to branch out on her own; she moved west and drove with
her two children across America to Los Angeles, where she became
a secretary in an aircraft factory and later a fashion buyer at J.C.
Penney's. To complete June's story, she remained to see Jack, her
son, move into the higher echelons of Hollywood and stardom but
she would never witness his greater achievements.

In 1963, she was diagnosed as having cancer, and died two years
later. But it was not until ten years later that Jack discovered she
was his mother. A magazine was preparing a cover story on the
emergence of Jack the star and in their background investigations,
which took them to Neptune in search of old chums, discovered
the secret that Mud had kept from him since birth. A reporter from
the magazine telephoned him in Mexico where he was filming *The
Fortune* with Warren Beatty.

Nicholson said he was stunned; he never knew and thus the
magazine article did not include this item.

Only a few weeks before, he had said in response to a publicity
interviewers' assertion that his father, John, had abandoned the
family when he was born: 'My father and mother separated when
I was a baby. I saw him extremely intermittently. He was a nice
man. He's been dead for some time. My mother is also dead, so I'm
an orphan.'

He called Lorraine. She confirmed he was June's baby. Only June
and Ethel knew who his father was and now they were both gone
and they had not told anyone. He appeared to shrug off the news
but there is no question that it interjected some kind of identity
crisis into his life. There was also one piece of the jigsaw that now
slotted into place: before June died, he took LSD in controlled

circumstances with a therapist: 'I became conscious of very early emotions about not being wanted – feeling that I was a problem to my family as an infant.'

★   ★   ★   ★   ★

It was quite coincidental that June, by her search for a new life in California, drew him towards what would be the hub of the rest of his life and it was touch and go whether he stayed or went back to Neptune. Also, coincidentally, other rebels were gathering in that same year.

Jack went west for a holiday in the summer of 1954 while he contemplated his future. James Dean had just arrived there for his first major role, having been brought from New York by the famed director Elia Kazan to star in *East of Eden*. If Nicholson had strolled down Sunset Strip, he would have caught sight of Dean at Googies or one of the other coffee joints where Dean would meet with Natalie Wood and Dennis Hopper. The Strip, at the westerly end of Sunset Boulevard and closest to the hub of the film industry, was the avenue for poseurs where every young hopeful – and plenty not so young – hung out to be discovered in one of the dozens of coffee bars that eventually gave way to rock 'n' roll clubs and then strip shows of the Sixties and Seventies. Dean, an early influence on anyone of Jack's age, had little more than a year left of his life and was in regular attendance in 1954, which was also the year Marlon Brando made it very big indeed in another Kazan film, *On the Waterfront*. They were both notorious for racing up and down the Strip on their motorbikes or in flash sports cars. Warren Beatty was flitting in and out for visits, because his sister, Shirley MacLaine, was also there. But that was a world that Nicholson had no thoughts about and nor prospect of joining.

In fact, Los Angeles scared him a little and for the first six months he barely ventured out of the house alone. He was then still slightly shy in company, though sharp and confident in other areas and among his equals, like the pool halls where he would hustle for a few dollars. In his late teens, there were still signs of puppy fat, and his rounded face sat under an unruly head of hair trimmed to the current style, though not especially trendy, and he could be lost in a crowd as being just another boy on the block; unassuming and unspecial.

What he did decide, and June did not try to dissuade him, was that he would not go back to school. He'd had enough of learning. A self-styled lazy student and with no wealth in the family to support a college boy, he decided that summer to quit. Emerging in his mind was the thought that he might become a writer. In the meantime, he earned his keep with a part-time job in a toyshop. Nothing more exciting than that appeared on the horizon in his first six months in California, and he was already talking to June about going back to Mud and Neptune.

Out of the blue he had got a job as a mail boy in the MGM studios at thirty dollars a week, twice as much as he was paid in the toy store. He was attached to the office dealing with Tom and Jerry, the MGM cartoon characters who were at their peak, and they needed an assistant to help handle their fan letters.

Well, it was a start.

More than that, it gave him the opportunity of laying on the grass at lunchtime, trying to catch sight of Lana Turner's legs. . . .

2

Starting Out

At MGM, he saw all the famous movie stars that populated that most famous of studios, and to his friends he name-dropped a few like Grace Kelly, with whom he fell in love from afar before she ran off to marry her prince. It was Hollywood's most glamorous studio. Louis B. Mayer used to boast that there were more stars in MGM than in heaven and nowhere had they shone more brightly. Garbo, Garland, Gardner, Garson and Gable were there – and that was just the Gs – but the old grey Mayer wasn't what he used to be, and he had been ousted from MGM by the time Nicholson arrived as a messenger boy. The turmoil that emerged both immediately before and after Mayer's departure epitomized, perhaps more than in any other of the major Hollywood studios, the convulsions of change that were sweeping through the film capital, eventually spawning an underground of new, raw and raucous talent of which Nicholson was to be part. A new Hollywood was being born, but no one realized it at the time. New arrivals on the street scene were to be the stars of tomorrow and the mink-lined coffins that were the grand old studios were about to disappear for ever.

The money men, the purveyors of soft drinks, the bankers, the lawyers, the agents and the wheeler-dealers were taking over; the stars themselves, those in a strong enough position to negotiate strident new financial benefits, were demanding a bigger slice of the cake. As Harry Cohn, head of Columbia, said shortly before a heart attack killed him in 1958: 'The lunatics have taken over the asylum.' There were many in the Screen Actors' Guild who would have agreed with him. At least under that system hundreds of young actors and actresses found regular employment under contract which meant they were paid whether they worked or not, whereas in 1990 the figures from the guild showed that at any one time as many as eighty-five per cent of its Los Angeles membership were not working. For better or for worse the studio system the moguls created, dubbed by its detractors as the slave trade, which had discovered and nursed the greatest names of Hollywood of three decades, and probably ever, was on the verge of collapse, though as Elizabeth Taylor put it so succinctly: 'The death rattle seemed never ending.'

By the mid-Fifties, many of MGM's greatest stars were drifting away, either voluntarily or forced, as the accountants hacked away at costs. It was not a fun place any more and doors were already slamming shut to the hundreds of young hopefuls hanging around outside the studio gates about the time when Nicholson began his search for work. What emerged, as we now know, was a very different industry, less secure for the multitude, perhaps, but the replacement system was to provide the top stars with multi-million-dollar pay packets which they apparently feel disinclined to share with lesser-known mortals in their trade.

To discover the Hollywood roots of Nicholson and his con-temporaries, it is necessary to go back in time for a moment, to get a glimpse of the prevailing wind immediately prior to their era. One who had arrived there as the convulsions started was Charlton Heston who achieved almost instant stardom and became especially known for his appearances in the biblical epics. He had one foot in the old camp and one foot in the new, and, incidentally, became Nicholson's neighbour when Jack struck gold and bought a big house. 'When I came to Hollywood in 1950, the studio system was still in place but it was crumbling,' he told the author. 'I was only the second actor to get a non-exclusive contract. The first was Brando. Now, I didn't get it because I was the greatest thing since sliced bread. Hal B. Wallis, who hired me, was a very shrewd man who recognized that the studio system was over and in five years' time it would no longer be there.'

Apart from the fact that the McCarthy purges of alleged Com-munists had left a bad scar on the film industry, two other develop-ments were eventually to bear much of the blame for the demise of the glitterama of old Hollywood. The first was television and the Hollywood moguls' abject refusal to have anything whatsoever to do with it. The second was the decision of the American Supreme Court that they should divest themselves of monopoly control of the cinema chains which, as Heston said, was in hindsight a death blow which merely served to hasten the financial decline of each and every studio. One of the several results was that it was very beneficial to fifteen actors like himself and eight directors who were 'hot', and five good writers. For the rest, the good times were over. Until then, every studio had a cast list of thirty or forty top-billing actors and actresses and dozens of contracted young people who were provided with their acting lessons, their dance lessons, their speech lessons, and the young directors were given their directorial tests, and they all went into bat often. 'By the mid-Fifties,' said Heston, 'That was all coming apart at the seams. Soon everyone was on non-exclusive contracts, or no contracts at all. And with the advent of television, the cinema chains virtually abandoned the B-movies overnight; it was shattering for the younger actors and writers who cut their teeth on the second-string movies churned out by the studios. Without this kind of back-up, you can't learn your craft, you can't get audience exposure, you can't get practice and more importantly, you can't fail . . . . '

Jack Nicholson almost crept under the wire before the studio system was finally extinguished at MGM. As mail boy, he had picked up the habit of addressing everyone by their Christian name, whoever they were. Why not? Everyone else did. And when he saw producer Joe Pasternak, the renowned MGM star-maker, approaching him in the corridor one day, Nicholson spoke up: 'Hiya, Joe. What about giving me a film test?'

Pasternak was apparently impressed; far lesser actors than Nicholson would eventually become began their careers by similar bravado, and he arranged for him to be tested. In earlier days, even that formality might not have been necessary for a contract. Nicholson dreamed for a day or two. Then Pasternak's office called him and told him that he had flunked the test. He was not without talent, though, said Joe, and he advised him to join a local theatre group to get some experience now that the studio training scheme had been abolished.

* * * * *

Other things were happening in Hollywood that affected Nicholson, both in his outlook to the film business and to life itself. He had become interested in the culture of the place as he ventured out and made new friends, youngsters in the industry who talked nothing else but films and stars, and was suddenly struck with the notion that he might become an actor. There was much talk in the coffee shops about the new film James Dean was working on, called *Rebel Without a Cause*; Brando was stunning everyone with his performance in *On the Waterfront*. Talk was intense among the youngsters, and the young actors and actresses roaming Sunset Strip were no different to the youth of America, if not the world, in that they too were a disoriented bunch in search of idols; Clift, Brando and Dean were providing them with a whole new repertoire of sayings, postures, stances and gestures. They were also rejecting the Great American Dream that had gripped their post-war acquisitive parents, who were stocking their homes with every electric device provided in the Fifties consumer boom.

And what else? Rumour had it that if you went to a Norman Mailer party, you'd see people smoking marijuana, covertly passing around a joint behind the bushes at the bottom of the garden. Well, that's nothing, said the jungle telegraph; Jimmy Dean was smoking dope heavily and seemingly without fear of arrest. It was new. Only jazz musicians had smoked marijuana before, and everyone was astounded about Dean because open use of drugs was virtually unknown and still carried heavy penalties; regular offenders were sent to prison and any public knowledge of even marijuana usage brought furore in the headlines, as Robert Mitchum discovered.

Down on Sunset Strip, some weird friends of Dean cashed in on his death and began holding court, relating tales of the Jimmy they knew. Nicholson was now venturing into the haunts of the hopefuls and joined in. Everyone was into existentialism, along with the beginnings of meditation, Zen and some other odd philosophies practised and preached by one of Dean's advisers, a male witch named Samson DeVreer, who was often in company of another of Dean's odd acquaintances, the television hostess named Vampira, because she looked like one, of whom Dean once said – when asked by Hedda Hopper if he was seeing her – 'I don't date cartoons.' In a way they were the leftovers of the James Dean set, but a new pseudo culture was growing, and Nicholson became part of it, wearing the uniform of round-necked sweaters and jeans or corduroys.

DeVreer typified the kind of Los Angeles thinking at the time among the youngsters who listened to his vitriolic demolition of the Californian life. These grass-smoking disciples flocked to his open house like moths to hear him reciting his life story, or his predictions with the tarot cards, or discussing Camus, or analysing Jean-Paul Sartre. They were exotic, impoverished days for Nicholson and, above all, big experiences for the boy from Neptune who had by now left the protective custody of his sister/mother and was sharing an apartment with one of a group of friends who he met at the time and with whom he remained close when he became well known. It is a characteristic of Nicholson that he displays and hopes for loyalty from a friendship and thus most of those he met and formed relationships with in the late Fifties and early Sixties were still in his life at the turn of the Nineties. Several of them went to an acting class run by Jeff Corey, where other aspirants included James Coburn. Corey was not especially impressed by Nicholson's acting. He said it lacked poetry. Nicholson responded that perhaps Corey hadn't seen the poetry he was showing him.

★   ★   ★   ★   ★

They were gathering on the Strip, in the coffee houses like the Unicorn, Mac's, Luan's and the Renaissance. When they had no work, which was often, they'd spend all afternoon sitting over one coffee or one coke trying to write plays. Other new faces were arriving. Steve McQueen had followed Dean west from New York after three or four years of casting-call line-ups. Paul Newman had just secured his first major film role, with Pier Angeli in *The Silver Chalice* (which was so bad that when it was shown on television in the Sixties, he took out newspaper advertisements apologising to viewers for having to watch it).

Dennis Hopper, then a mere passing acquaintance of Nicholson's had, in comparison, made it big at nineteen, appearing with Dean in *Rebel Without a Cause* and *Giant*. The less fortunate among them, like Nicholson and Robert Towne, Charles Eastman, the writers, and Monte Hellman, the director, got together in a play group and literally built their own theatre, stealing timber from building sites for their scenery; they ripped a toilet from a petrol station and lighting and electronics were similarly acquired.

When Jack left MGM to make a serious foray into acting, he took the advice of the cartoonists Bill Hanna and Joe Barbera and joined the Players Ring Theatre and began acting lessons. The bug had caught him and he was a determined as anyone to make it. 'It was a time of freshness and discovery of what acting was all about,' he said. 'It was about meeting new people and being inspired by other people's work, or watching an actor or actress who could hardly talk come into a class and then six months later suddenly do a brilliant scene. That was part of the early days.'

Friends were important, if for nought else but moral support and sharing food and money. They shared their women, too. Jack reckoned he was known amongst his male friends of that era as the Great Seducer – his own words – but friend-for-life Robert Towne did not quite remember it that way. There were plenty of girls around in Hollywood but no Hollywood girl wanted relationships with nobodies, and that's what they were still. They worked occasionally and acted and wrote their plays and read Jack Kerouac like Dean had done a couple of years earlier. When someone in the group became temporarily wealthy through employment, there would be a red wine party. One day, in 1958, it was Nicholson's turn – and he had an acting job at last, and not just any part, but the lead in a new film. True, it was in one of the cheap, filmed-in-a-fortnight (and sometimes two days) type of movie for which producer Roger Corman was to earn the dubious title of master of exploitation movies; other nicknames likes Schlockmeister and King of the Bs also stuck. It was a start and a good one.

A word about Corman is necessary here because he became an important link in the Nicholson story; and not just Nicholson's either. Corman, a young independent producer born of the post-Superior Court ruling when studios were cutting back on their own B-movie productions, did not know it at the time, nor did anyone else, but he was about to make a significant contribution to what later became known as the 'new Hollywood' through the personalities he gave work to on low budget films, either acting, writing, directing or all three. Apart from Nicholson, Peter Fonda, Peter Bogdanovich, Francis Ford Coppola, Stephen Spielberg, Bob Rafelson, Martin Scorsese and Robert De Niro were among a long cast list of now famous names who found a toe-hold in Hollywood by working with him. A graduate of Leland, Stanford and Oxford universities, he was a sharp, intelligent man from Detroit, Michigan, who has all too often been dismissed as the maker of low-budget movies which exploited a particular mood or event in time, heavily criticized for their voyeurism. Such criticism was doubtless deserved at the time because his films were to Hollywood what some of today's tabloids are to the newspaper industry. He made films that were designed basically for the drive-in movie, to be glimpsed between clinches. In the course of the next three decades, however, he became a cult figure, though more for horror films with such titles as *Swamp Women*, *Attack of the Crab Monsters* and *Bucket of Blood*.

His work became the subject of college analysis and European film festivals which, incidentally, were recognizing his work with retrospectives as early as 1964. Nicholson, while rejecting Corman as his 'mentor' gladly acknowledges the start and subsequent ten years' work he gave him. Corman was not consciously in the business of developing talent. His job was to produce inexpensive movies for American International Pictures and, in doing so, hired cheaply, never paying more that the basic union rate. He made available to the newcomers he employed all the mechanism required to make films. They used it and prospered. So did he. And on that basis, the cult value of his early work was purely accidental. A lot of his films were unpretentious junk, but they made money and Nicholson and others came along in the slipstream. Corman admitted, 'I did one film really more as a joke to see if I could do it; filmed it in two days and a night. I did it, though I vowed I would never work that fast again.'

The film for which Nicholson was chosen as the lead was typical of the late-Fifties genre, called *Cry Baby Killer*, one of dozens that sloped in on the back of *Rebel Without a Cause*, exploiting the cause and increasing the violence. While parents and local burgermasters were complaining about Elvis' swirling hip movements, the jiving in the aisles at Bill Haley concerts, the sexual implications of Chuck Berry's movements and increasing violence in the American classroom as depicted more responsibly in *Blackboard Jungle*, the Corman film went straight for sensationalism with advertising which read 'From Teen Rebel to Mad Dog Killer.' The link with Dean's *Rebel* was deliberate, so that it could be seen almost as a sequel. Nicholson believed he had arrived: 'I said to myself, 'This is it. I'm meant to

31

be an actor. 'It was a thrilling feeling.' The movie, however, attracted such critique as 'vapid ... mob voyeurism to which the movie pandered.' It was so down-market that many cinema chains refused to take it. It was filmed in eleven days and cost $7000 to make. There would be many more to come when Roger Corman got into his stride in the early Sixties turning out back-to-back movies, using the same set and actors in two weeks or less, with self-imposed budgets of under $30,000.

Cry Baby Killer did not bring Nicholson any new offers and he did not work again in films for nine months. Nicholson returned to the bosom of his friends, somewhat dejected but still determined.

*   *   *   *   *

Martin Landau, friend of James Dean's when they were both in New York and again when they came to Hollywood, was running acting classes between jobs. Like Dean, Landau had studied the Method approach to acting devised by Stanislavski and modified for the Actors Studio by Lee Strasberg. With Brando and Dean mumbling their way through the currently most talked about pictures, it was very much in vogue, passionately discussed and used among the younger actors. Many more established figures were none too sure about it, probably because the exercises might involve the exposure of one's private parts, the display of secret and personal habits and the use of expletive expressions in the passionate search for one's inner self. When, for example, establishment actor Raymond Massey saw James Dean in action for the first time on the set of *East of Eden*, emitting as he did a stream of sexual and genital adjectives, Massey stormed off the set declaring, 'I have never experienced anything like this in my entire life. I just cannot work with this man.' Nicholson's exercises, devised by Strasberg and taught by Landau – who was nominated for an Oscar in the 1990 awards – were rather less shocking. He had to sing 'Three Blind Mice'. 'I sang that song in Marty's class for two years. It's an exercise Lee Strasberg invented, the song exercise, for what he called 'the diagnosis of the instrument'. I guarantee I can tell what kind of actor a person is if I hear them do "Three Blind Mice".' The exercise was designed to make a student stand in front of class, sing his song and force each syllable out in an elongated manner so that it had a beginning and an end; this, Landau explained, ought to enable the student to go into neutral, physically and mentally, so that tensions could be released and what was happening inside could be heard through the voice changes. It was one of many Method exercises taught to help the actor to reach inside of himself, unleashing personal emotions in an effort to heighten realism. Over the next few years, Nicholson went from one teacher to another in his quest for knowledge of all acting techniques. Eventually, he rejected the Method as a personal technique, developing his own style and approach, which he insisted had no set parameters such as those required if the Method was followed to the letter.

In between acting class and all-night parties at one of the homes of one or another of the inmates, Nicholson slotted in some compulsory service as a fireman, attached to an air-crash fire-fighting crew, which some have used to suggest was a draft dodge on his part. He, in turn, said it was not; he merely regarded national service as a waste of time. Back to acting, he found occasional work in television drama but nothing substantial came along, nor would it for some time to come. There were one or two escapees from within his group, however. Michael Landon was plucked from the Ring Theatre Group to instant stardom in the television western series, 'Bonanza'; Eddie Byrnes went into '77 Sunset Strip' and Robert Fuller was selected for 'Laramie'. Gradually most of the group began to get work, though for Nicholson it was, as he put it, still a time of preparation.

3

Emerging with Horror

'People who haven't seen my [early] movies are better off than I am ... but like all actors I needed the work. I did all those movies because they were the only work I could get,' Nicholson said in a frank assessment of his next few years of acting roles on the fringes of Hollywood, appearing almost entirely in low-cost, quickly made horror films, and what were then called teenage exploitation pictures, mostly with Roger Corman. They gave Jack the chance to practise some of the underhand humour that eventually became part of his mystique. Everyone needs practise and Jack got the opportunity for more than most. With the old B-movie system virtually gone, there was no other place for mediocre talent to apply and that was how he would be brutally classed. Overnight stardom was largely a myth, though some climbed higher up the ladder more quickly, and quite often suffered as a result. Dennis Hopper, who was to become an important figure in Nicholson's eventual break into major films, came in on James Dean's coat-tails and was devastated by Dean's death, as were Natalie Wood and their other close friend, Nick Adams. Nicholson saw them around Sunset Strip and for a time they were joined by Elvis Presley, who had seen *Rebel Without a Cause* forty-four times and could speak Dean's lines word perfect. They smoked marijuana and talked about suicide. 'No cancel that,' said Hopper. 'Jimmy wouldn't want that. Let's have an orgy instead.' Someone suggested they should all bathe in champagne beforehand and the bath was filled with some cheap bubbly. The orgy had to be aborted, however, on account of Natalie's screaming with pain in a tender place, inflamed by the alcohol. She had to be taken to hospital for treatment. That was a story Hopper liked to tell, to demonstrate how they were all good friends who were creating a new style of acting; later, when Nicholson arrived, they had long discussions about this era and the influences it had on all of them. Hopper thought he was another Dean, and then became outcast from Hollywood within three years because he acquired a reputation for being a Dean-like perfectionist. 'To me, Dean was the most talented and original actor I ever saw,' said Hopper. 'He was a guerilla artist. He once pulled a switchblade on his director because they couldn't agree on the way to do a scene. I imitated his style and it got me into trouble.' Notably, he ran up against director Henry Hathaway who was known as one of the toughest directors in the business, and Hopper had a minor role in *From Hell to Texas*. Hathaway wanted the scene played one way, Hopper wanted to do it another; they battled for seven hours and eighty-six takes before Hopper finally bowed to the director's wishes to do it straight. At that very moment, Jack Warner, having heard what was going on, walked on to the set and barred Hopper from ever working for Warners again. *Persona non grata* in Hollywood, he moved to New York, appearing in plays and television, and becoming a well-respected stills photographer; he would return later to make Nicholson a star.

Warren Beatty also discovered a route to instant fame, co-starring with Natalie Wood, one of the world's most glamorous young actresses in 1959, in Elia Kazan's *Splendor in the Grass*. It was Beatty's first movie and he was sprung from nowhere into the superstar bracket. As Hopper, a nice guy but slightly mad, discovered, there is always the danger that after such auspicious beginnings, it might be downhill. Nicholson on the other hand was taking the pretty route, basically because he had no choice; no one was making him any offers. He was looking and learning and perhaps there is no better early example of his ability for natural, laid-back humour than in *Little Shop of Horrors* in which Nicholson plays Wilbur Force – they all had names like that in Corman films – who is a sadomasochistic patient of a sadistic dentist.

'This is going to hurt you more than it's going to hurt me,' says the dentist in true written-in-ten-minutes dialogue.

Wilbur replies, 'No Novocaine; it dulls the senses,' and then, as the dentist begins his drilling and pauses for a moment, Wilbur screams out, 'Oh my God, don't stop now.'

At the end of the session, he thanks the dentist and says 'I can truly say I've never enjoyed myself so much.'

Corman's *Little Shop of Horrors* became a cult classic largely through its star – not Nicholson, but a plant that thrived on human flesh. It devoured demised or murdered human bodies, of which the sadistic dentist was one. Reviewers who took it all too seriously said Corman's movie and Nicholson's part in it was bad film-making, bad acting, bad taste and quite undeserving of consideration. But soon the colleges came to grips with *Little Shop of Horrors* as a topic for campus debate the world over, and they decided that Corman was telling them that he was not trying to hide the fact that it was a cheaply made film – this was the one he shot in two days – but he wasn't trying to pass it off as serious movie-making either. It was all intended as a subtle joke.

Corman naturally agreed with this assessment and is not saying whether or not it was the way he and Nicholson intended it. It matters not; within a few years and many fast and furious films later, he was being heralded not as the king of exploitation but as something of a genius, to which description he again did not object. It was true that as he progressed, with Nicholson and his soon-to-be-famous contemporaries on hand for adventurous collaboration, Corman did attack social issues involving drugs, homosexuality and the ever-popular parental generation gap. Only he truly knows whether they were cheap pictures produced with one aim, to make as much money as possible from the least amount of effort, or whether he had other more high-flown artistic notions in mind. It seems hardly worth posing the question.

★   ★   ★   ★   ★

The next few films in which Nicholson appeared, however, had none of *Little Shop's* subtleties. *Too Soon for Love* was, like *Cry Baby Killer*, straightforward sensationalism of the still current topic of youth rebellion and teenage violence, yet another sequel to *Rebel Without a Cause* with Nicholson playing a secondary role in a gang of second-rate, cut-price actors who had clearly been chosen to look like the originals in the Dean film. Two other roles secured in that year, 1960, held better promise but in the end brought him no further progression in his career.

The first is worth mentioning only because it gave him his debut in a major studio, for a United Artists production of *Studs Lonigan*, one more Dean-like character taken from a successful trilogy of novels by James T. Farrell. As with a number of similar literary-based projects around in Hollywood at a time when mainstream studios were trying to discover what to do next after the demise of musical and religious epics, it was not a success. *Studs Lonigan* dropped through the floor into a bottomless pit, never to re-emerge, even for a moment's campus debate; the United Artists film that was supposed to become the moving blueprint of life for the new decade of Sixties youth caused but a ripple in the thoughts of these sensitive young souls and vanished without trace. As Hollywood kept on discovering at its own expense – and this was a relatively costly movie compared with Nicholson's previous works – good and successful literature does not necessary transfer easily to the big screen. The recent box-office calamity of *Marjorie Morningstar* was another example; the big-budget Warner Brothers adaptation of Herman Wouk's best-selling novel, starring Natalie Wood and Gene Kelly, ended up so dismally after such a huge build-up that Natalie began seeing her analyst at lunchtimes as well.

Tail between legs, Nicholson returned to the Corman factory for another in the psychotic youth genre, *The Wild Ride*, with a cast of three and running a mere sixty-three minutes. Served up as B fodder, at least it provided him with a salary, albeit on rock-bottom union rates of around $300 for a full working week, which assured him a place barely above the poverty line.

Financial security became something of an issue at the beginning of the new decade. At the time, he was sharing a house with two friends, writer-to-be Don Devlin and producer-in-waiting Harry Gittes on Fountain Avenue, a few streets from Sunset Boulevard. It was, in his own description, the wildest house in Hollywood for a time, until he moved out to set up home with actress Sandra Knight, a slender, auburn-haired girl of striking appearance whom he met in Martin Landau's acting class. Sandra joined the Nicholson crowd in the B-movie circle and was to become something of a model for future long-term relationships. She was an actress who, like the rest of them, had high hopes. But she was not in the flighty, dumb-blonde mould. She was intelligent, quietly responsible and could hold her own in the group's endless meaning-of-life conversations.

Slightly dominant, she slotted admirably into the mother-substitute figure that Nicholson seemed to require for stability – as opposed to the more sexually desirable women who figured in his life with frequency. He was smitten not especially by Sandra's looks, but by her whole demeanour, and those who were around at the time must have thought he had understated his feelings when he said later, 'It was a no-big-deal act for me. I got married not thinking about it one way or the other; I just loved the girl.' It was actually something of a momentous decision – and one which it seemed thirty years later was never to be repeated.

Days of wine and roses, and wild, wild parties with Devlin, Gittes and fellow nightowl Harry Dean Stanton – another of his big buddies from acting class who remained a friend and co-star for ever – became temporarily less important to him and, for a couple of years, he settled into the life of a happily married man, with Sandra seemingly intent on becoming the loving wife at home. A year after their marriage she produced his only legitimate child, a daughter whom they christened Jennifer. In between minor television roles, in series like 'Divorce Court', Jack took to practising script writing for a time, while waiting for work. Nothing came along immediately and ahead were a couple of lean years. Sandra had virtually given up her career to devote herself to the task of keeping house and raising a family, though, in that respect, the relationship did not mature as she had hoped. The studious intensity of learning a craft together, the long and fanciful discussions about the philosophies of life that were prevalent topics, and the unorthodoxy of their nightlife did not easily transfer to a happy-families home. They grew apart.

Some blamed Jack for wanting to continue the way he had before marriage which, of course, meant occasional flings with the abundance of available women. It was also in this period of the early Sixties that he experimented with LSD and, like most of his contemporaries, used marijuana. Sandra, who once saw a bad LSD experience, became fixed to what he called a firm mystical path, seeking enlightenment even before it was fashionable. God was not a subject he could handle with any real heart, nor compete with. Her religious leanings and slightly Presbyterian view of life did not match Jack's own. And, towards the end of their marriage, he was also trying many things in his efforts to bolster his career, writing furiously and trying hard for the elusive break. The marriage had been good, he said, for two or three years and then they drifted towards the rocks until they were agreed on only one thing, their incompatibility. A mirror image of the way their marriage had developed was captured in that typically frightening Nicholson scene in *The Shining*, in 1980. He recalled, 'I was under the pressure of being a family man with a daughter, and one day I accepted a job to act in a movie in the day-time and was writing another movie at night. And I'm in the back in my little corner and my beloved wife Sandra walked in on what was, unbeknownst to her, this maniac, writing furious and tired. I told Stanley Kubrick [his director in *The Shining*] about it and we wrote it into the scene. I remember being at my desk and telling her, "Even if you don't hear me typing it doesn't mean I'm not writing. ... " Separation and divorce became inevitable; it was a 'good divorce – non-violent and non-tumultuous ... we had come to a real separating of the ways and it was obvious there was only one thing to do and we did it very simply.' Sandra moved away, eventually to Hawaii taking their daughter with her. Jack agreed on her having custody of the child, and an amicable arrangement was made regarding visiting. He continued to see Jennifer on a regular basis and over the years; she would come for holidays and weekends, and he did the loving-father duties, which he treated seriously, and never shirked his responsibilities. A strong bond based on a frankness about his own lifestyle was formed between father and daughter as she developed into a quietly studious girl who enjoyed her excursions to visit her father at work on the film sets.

*   *   *   *   *

At the time, though, the Nicholson legend was slow to take off, especially in comparison to that of his chum Warren Beatty, who became a Hollywood name even before his first picture was released. At local parties he was known not so much for his acting ability but for his great talent as a jazz pianist especially his impression of George Shearing. He also, through his sister, had the 'in' to some of the posher places in town, way ahead of Nicholson's current social station, which was still restricted to the cheap red-wine class. Nothing so common for Warren. He was already into the champagne and mansion bracket up in the hills and very soon began his first famous relationship, setting up home with Joan Collins.

But here, in these two contrasting worlds of Hollywood social strata – Beatty among the establishment and Nicholson well beyond the fringe – were the beginnings of two legends, Warren and Jack, leaders of the pack, whose stories would reverberate around this village community, overlapping and intertwining in their relationships and romantic conquests, for years to come. Beatty was rocketed to stardom by Elia Kazan – the director who brought Dean to stardom in *East of Eden* – and, unlike Nicholson, he had influential friends and relations. Anyone who suggested that his rise to fame was undeservedly achieved by nepotism and favouritism, would be referred by Beatty to a piece in *Time* magazine which read, 'With facial and vocal suggestion of Montgomery Clift and the mannerisms of James Dean, he is the latest in the line of hostile, moody, sensitive, self-conscious, bright, defensive, stuttering, self seeking and extremely talented actors who have become myths before they are thirty.' With acclaim like that, Beatty's agent immediately put a pricetag of $300,000 a picture on his head – and was getting it. Jack's average fee at the time was several noughts less. He had little of Beatty's on-screen charisma – yet.

The difference showed in other ways, too. Before and after his marriage, Nicholson could date happily without fear of a single solitary piece of salacious writing in any newspaper or magazine – 'complete anonymity in social exchange' was the way he described his situation – or, as a further succinct explanation, 'I was able to go around picking up stray pussy.' Beatty, as befitted his newly acquired status in life, was in the high profile dating league and prime fodder for the gossip columnists. Miss Collins spoke very highly of him, praising his prowess and insatiable three-, four- or five-times-a-day appetite for sex. Thereafter, he promptly ran off with Natalie Wood, his co-star in *Splendor in the Grass*. 'They became lovers whilst I wasn't looking,' said Kazan. Natalie's distraught husband, Robert Wagner, found temporary but platonic comfort with Miss Collins.

The young stars were all over the newspapers and fan magazines, and Nicholson loved to read and hear about their adventures. The full force of being public property and pop royalty had not hit him – whereas Beatty, who was being chased by the news hounds from New York to Florida to the South of France, with Natalie in tow, had suddenly become the talk of the town.

Beatty had a good five-year head-start on him, and most of the other male leads with whom they would both be compared in the forthcoming age of the anti-hero. Paul Newman, older, of course, and Steve McQueen arrived in the big time, too. Dustin Hoffman, Robert Redford, Gene Hackman and Robert De Niro were still a long way from making even their first films. Dennis Hopper came back to Hollywood in that year of 1961 and shocked everyone by marrying into one of the most exclusive Hollywood families. Brooke Hayward was the daughter of actress Margaret Sullavan, who had been Henry Fonda's first wife, and producer Leland Hayward. The omens were bad from the start. In the same year, the Hoppers' Bel Air mansion was all but burnt down in a fire and virtually the whole of Dennis's collection of poems and paintings were destroyed. Peter Fonda was, in that year, also heading towards Hollywood, without the slightest encouragement from his father. They were difficult times for all of them.

★　　★　　★　　★　　★

In 1962, Jack was surely wondering what it would take to get a bigger, more important film role. His next was a western, *The Broken Land*, for Roger Corman again. It did not light any new fires for Nicholson and died a quiet death. Even so, Jack was not ungrateful to Corman. 'He was giving me work when no one else would and without him I would not have survived. For that we would be eternally grateful. He also underpaid us and for that he will be eternally grateful.'

Corman returned to horror and Nicholson went with him. Some years earlier, Corman had inspired the onset of his cult following with idiosyncratic adaptations of Edgar Allan Poe classics like *The Tomb of Ligeia*, *The Masque of the Red Death* and *The Pit and the Pendulum*. Now, he came back to the theme with a script loosely based on Poe poem, *The Raven*, but the connection was so loose that no one could discover what it was. There were a number of horror stars looking for work who would not want the earth in salaries, and he assembled a notable team of players which included Vincent Price, Boris Karloff and Peter Lorre. Corman added Nich-

olson in the lead role and a couple of attractive females, and the
result was another Corman classic, a comic-strip horror tale, silly in
conception but wittily funny. And, with those arch-weirdos speaking their lines with magnificent mock-seriousness, poor Jack looked
sadly dull. But there was an interesting sequel, which gave him his
first, insightful, small stab at directing.

Corman called 'It's a wrap' on Friday evening, and realized that
he still had almost forty-eight hours' usage left on the warehouse
and sets he had rented for *The Raven*. That left two days of filming
available before the sets had to be taken down and returned to the
owners. He had a brainwave: to make another picture over the
weekend. He asked Karloff, who was on the payroll for another
three days, if he would do it. Yes. He cast Nicholson in the lead
role and all he needed was a female. What about Sandra Knight?
(She and Jack were still married at the time.) Jack called Sandra and
asked if she would appear in a Corman film that weekend. Yes.
'What is the play to be called?' Boris asked his producer. 'And where
is the script?'

There was no script. Not even a title. Overnight, Corman wrote
the start of a screenplay for a piece of nonsense entitled *The Terror*
and hurriedly the cast went to work the next morning to make use
of the sets before they were torn down. It was his intention to shoot
what they could, mostly the scenes involving Karloff because his
were the only words Corman had written. Karloff recalled the chaos
that was going on around him: 'When we started filming, the
removal men came to take away the sets. As they were knocking
them down, Corman was following me around with the camera
directing my speaking parts. It was a fiasco. But the film got
made.'

Corman directed most of the picture but then had stop because
union rules, to which he adhered religiously in terms of actors' and
technicians' payments, made it impossible to continue with a fully
fledged production team. He came to an arrangement with two
more actors, gave the camera crews some private pocket money
and turned the film over to his assistants. Francis Ford Coppola,
then an AIP assistant producer, directed some and Monte Hellman
did some more. On the last day of shooting, Nicholson chirped up:
'Look, everybody else in town had shot part of this picture. I want
to shoot the final sections.' He did and they all edited it together a

week later. The film was a mess, naturally, but Jack, Coppola and Hellman all had their first try at directing.

The saga of the *The Terror* was not yet concluded. In 1966, Peter Bogdanovich, by then an assistant director and part-time scriptwriter for Corman, was given his chance to direct a thriller called *Targets* in which Boris Karloff was cast because he still owed Corman two days' work. Bogdanovich shot the footage with Boris and booked other actors to complete the film, shooting over the succeeding ten days. Then, a print of *The Terror* was cut up and plagiarized to fill out *Targets*, which was made in fourteen days at a cost of $125,000 of which Karloff was paid $22,000 and Bogdanovich as director received $3000.

All of this racketing around with has-beens and yet-to-bes, filming on rented sets in disused warehouses, ought to have been doomed to failure, even laughed off the screen. Often they were. It was chaotic, true, but Corman's pictures always made money and that was the way everyone was judged. In his first eighty films, only two went into the red. Yet the chances of failure in the legitimate side of the business were even greater, as Nicholson discovered with a new role which on the surface seemed a godsent opportunity – to appear in *Ensign Pulver*, the much-discussed sequel to *Mister Roberts*. The original film, with Henry Fonda, James Cagney and Jack Lemmon based on Thomas Heggen's novel of the same name was applauded worldwide. Lemmon won an Oscar for his magnificent portrayal of the coward who becomes a hero.

Warner Brothers producer Joshua Logan and author Thomas Heggen wrote the play for the sequel, entitled *Ensign Pulver* (released in 1964). Jack Lemmon was asked to return but adamantly – and wisely – refused. The rest of the cast looked strong, with Robert Walker jnr., Walter Matthau, Burl Ives, Larry Hagman, Tommy Sands and, albeit a minor role, Jack Nicholson. It flopped, badly. Universally panned by the critics, the film fans who were already vanishing in their droves from the theatres by the mid-Sixties, were given further encouragement to stay away and heads rolled at Warners. Nicholson was left smarting and wondering why he had ever strayed to the glamour side of the business from the safe haven of Corman's mini-budgets and rented sets.

Although Nicholson's part in *Ensign Pulver* was small, being attached to such a poor movie depressed him intensely. It was also a bad time personally. It was while filming *Ensign Pulver* that he received news that June, the sister who was really his mother, had cancer.

It was a time for reflection in 1964, when the film was released. He was coming up to his twenty-seventh birthday and his face had already acquired some of the lived-in look that became one of his characteristics later in his career. He was not what might be described – in comparison with Robert Redford, say – devastatingly handsome or outwardly charismatic. His appearance and demeanour were fairly average and he was not a head-turner for female fans. He kept his hair – at this stage – fairly short and neatly trimmed across his forehead to hide the evidence of recession. He had filled out, too, with broad shoulders and strong though not overly muscular arms. In other words, he was still developing the characteristics that would eventually make him a character actor. In his move towards the latter, perhaps at that time he did not quite appreciate how influential to himself and others Roger Corman had become in providing the schooling for some of the most important filmmakers of the second half of the twentieth century.

Nicholson's interest in writing was re-awakened by his scriptwriting assistance on *The Terror*, and his next project was a screenplay in which he was encouraged by Roger Corman, who thought it was a good idea because though he personally felt Nicholson showed great potential as an actor, others around him did not always agree. Nicholson teamed up with his friend and former flatmate Don Devlin to write the script for a film called *Thunder Island*, a thriller which was to be shot with a tiny budget on a Caribbean island. The plot had a topical theme; it was about a corrupt dictator who had been exiled from his Latin American country. Once more, the critics placed his work where it honestly belonged, in the basement of B-movies, as were his next two, *Back Door to Hell* and *Flight to Fury*, both directed by Monte Hellman. They provided interim employment and on the second, a further chance for Nicholson to hone his writing talents, since he both acted in it, and wrote the screenplay. The collaboration between Nicholson and Hellman was to continue for two more pictures.

Hellman recalls that they were both toying with the idea of a western and talked to Corman about the finance. Naturally, he said, 'Well, if you are doing one western you might as well do two.'

They agreed and he agreed; so, with an advance cheque from Corman's company deposited in their bank, they formed their own company, Proteus Films, rented an office, bought a couple of typewriters and began work. Nicholson had an idea already; other friends were asked to submit outlines for a screenplay and one of those was Carol Eastman, who wrote under the pen-name of Adrien Joyce. None of their ideas were really in tune with what Corman had suggested – as Jack described it, 'plenty of tomahawk numbers and a lot of ketchup', which was the popular requirement of westerns then, especially with such popular television series such as 'Bonanza', 'Rawhide' and 'Bronco'. Nicholson's own idea was, in fact, to write the first existentialist cowboy story, which was something of a departure from the current genre; he was surely right in his assumption that Corman might not see the potential, if such existed. His tale was based on the Camus essay, 'The Myth of Sisyphus' which demonstrates man's 'dignity is his return down the mountain after pushing up the stone'. The title was *Ride the Whirlwind*.

Carol Eastman, meanwhile, had written her screenplay on the inspiration of a Jack London story, which was similar moody vein to *Ride the Whirlwind* and she called hers *The Shooting*. It was a slightly more complicated plot, with similar undertones of mythical melancholia which were written to drift off the screen rather than by means of an actual ending to the story. So they collected their actors and actresses, a film crew of twelve and their livestock and moved off to the Utah desert to begin filming. Nicholson had an acting role in both.

Eight weeks later, they returned with their two films in the can and Hellman began the cut, with Nicholson by his side. Eventually, they were ready for viewing by the backer, Roger Corman.

'Interesting,' said Corman, as he sat back in his chair and banged his feet down on the row of seats in front of him. 'You've done something with a western that I've never see before. You've made the characters intelligent, and life isn't like that. There's no beginning, and there's no end. Audiences won't like that.' And raising his voice, he shouted, 'There are no Indians. Where are the Indians?'

Hellman cautiously observed, 'Does this mean you don't like them?'

'Oh sure. They're different. I like them for being different,' said Corman. 'But who is going to buy them? Tell me that? They just aren't commercial enough. No theatre booker in the land is going to take them.'

That prediction was proved entirely correct. No one did want the films, not in America, at least; Nicholson and Hellman had tampered with the popular view of western history and had taken it to deeper levels, failing totally to appreciate that mass audiences enjoyed westerns purely because they provided escapism. They did not want arty philosophical essays. Three, four months went by until only two routes for selling them remained unexplored. One solution was to cut their losses and sell to television. The other was to try Europe, which Nicholson decided he would do. He arrived in Nice full of hope and, indeed, managed to secure a showing for both at Cannes. Almost immediately a French company made an offer for the European rights. Nicholson accepted and flew back to Los Angeles in better spirits. Bad news followed in his wake; the French company went bankrupt before it could pay out the cheque. So, even moderate fame still eluded him, and Nicholson remained unknown outside of a small Hollywood clique. He was now approaching thirty years old and, as the year turned, he wanted desperately to get an audition for the new movie they were all talking about, in which the star was to be a young man playing opposite an older woman. It was called *The Graduate* and, said Nicholson, they were 'auditioning everyone I was having lunch with'.

Another completely unknown actor, also thirty but looking much younger, named Dustin Hoffman, impressed director Mike Nichols so much in his off-Broadway plays that he was running favourite, despite his lack of experience. The night it was announced in *Variety* that Hoffman had the role, Nicholson swore violently and went out and got drunk.

4

Bike Trippers

He was working hard, yet he was hard up, and when he became an overnight star, he had appeared in close on twenty films, written six, co-produced three, and edited or assistant edited five. Numerically, it was an impressive record but it did not bear too much scrutiny. Nicholson's contribution to the film industry had been, to this point, almost entirely tied to Roger Corman's own eccentric career. There wasn't much to be proud of in a mixed bunch of movies which were largely exploitation of current trends, regardless of how Corman tried to disguise them with socio-explanations. But, at last, there was a light at the end of the tunnel.

It was the headlamp of a large Harley Davidson motorcycle roaring towards the cinema audiences of the mid-Sixties as the biker movies suddenly came into vogue, along with all the other fashions and fads of the emergent, decadent age. The underground revolution was coming up to the surface, although it was nowhere near breaking through. The beatniks, the bomb banners and campus peace groups were still a fairly intense crowd, dressed in their turtleneck sweaters and jeans, and using Jack Kerouac's *On the Road* as their symbol, their bible and guide to escapism and backseat sex. Kerouac himself, meanwhile, had resorted to alcohol to seek oblivion in his pursuit of Buddhism, nonviolence and love for all creatures. He was a disturbed man. Something was happening amongst the youth movement that so admired him and he couldn't quite put his finger on it. Neither, sometimes could his disciples understand their master, rambling when drunk, as observed one evening by British novelist Kingsley Amis when they shared a college platform in Boston debating new liberalism. Amis joined the the popular front of rising protest and who, in those days of rebellious literary figures, could have imagined that he would become a knight?

This was immediately prior to the Nicholson 'star' era; the wave of which he rode the crest was beginning to build and it is interesting to chronicle for a moment some of the events leading up to his 'discovery' as a major Hollywood personality – a hero of the age and one who, as we have seen, was much influenced by the existentialist prophecies of Kerouac, which were now, finally, coming home to roost in middle-class America and elsewhere. These early influences were to extend well into his career.

It was a vague but important time in the cultural and social history of the western world, a good time for those who were in it and enjoying themselves, a bad time for those who were dismayed at 'young people today'. *Time* magazine had long ago been berated by Kerouac and his compatriot American poet Allen Ginsberg for its repressive attitude to the surging movement of youth inspired by these literary figures and by the likes of Brando and Dean on screen. If society had been worried about the juvenile delinquency problem of the Fifties, as portrayed in *The Wild One*, *Blackboard Jungle* and *Rebel Without a Cause*, it was now on the precipice of sheer panic about drug-crazed beatniks and hippies whom the establishment and *Time* regarded with derision, as did its stablemate *Life*. It scorned the 'beat' movement with a staged photographic layout under the headline: 'THE ONLY REBELLION AROUND: But the shabby beats bungle the job ....' And Ginsberg wrote, 'Are you going to let your emotional life be run by *Time* magazine?' In other words, Ginsberg and his followers were campaigning against the establishment, the Luce family who controlled *Time* and *Life*, school, parents, the police – anyone in authority just as, in Britain it was emanating from Liverpool, the Marquee and Carnaby Street.

In a way, the revolution had been a long time coming and somewhat contained in America, despite the reactions of the mass media which had been – like all conservative America – horrified, if not titillated by the lurid images of beat youth. Britain was much less shocked by it. All that strange 'beat' talk of the late Fifties and the avant-garde personality of the earlier Sixties that had become the language of kids in the coffee bars and campuses throughout the English-speaking world, was giving way to a more cynical view of life and the much harsher realities of the rock 'n' roll years.

The coffee-bar era – twee and tame in hindsight – was all but gone, and the great new wave of stylism was heralded by rock stars, Indian mystics and Dr Timothy Leary, the high priest of the marijuana and acid society. The open air theme, eventually to become epitomized by visions of Woodstock and the Rolling Stones performing live in Hyde Park, was itself a throwback from Kerouac's *On the Road*: because the road became the central symbol of his disciples' lives – hitting it in search of new horizons when the local scene became dull. Dropping out meant taking to the road, hitchhiking or biking far away from home, and the landscape became dotted with the beat replacements, the hippies. By the end of 1965, the first beginnings of a mass shift, and movement, in the young was being signalled. The young Robert Zimmerman had changed his name to Bob Dylan and had been wailing away for a couple of years or so, and Nicholson was among the first of his fans who listened to and studied the words of his anti-establishment anthems, 'The Times, They Are A-Changin' and his 'Mr Tambourine Man' which was a taunting, haunting song with a very hard edge that white middle-class youth took to be an ode to a dope dealer, which Dylan denied. 'We listened to the song and drew our own conclusions, but it didn't matter what it meant,' Nicholson recalled, 'because everyone was so stoned they couldn't remember the words. This was it, babe. I mean this was the scene we were all at, to use the then terminology. Dylan, Shankar, the Stones. And it was terrific. Terrific.'

Finally, even *Time* magazine had to give some credence to the arrival of this remarkable undercurrent in the motivation of young people, but preferred to blame London influences rather than American. In its cover story of the 15 April 1966 issue of *Time* said, 'In this century, every decade has its city and for the Sixties, that city is London. In a decade dominated by youth, London has burst into bloom. It swings; it is the scene.' The era was further epitomized by the Beatles' number one hit at the start of the year, 'Day Tripper', and the Rolling Stones' new album, *Aftermath*. Dylan upset his traditionalist fans by adding electronic backing for his new tour in the wake of the weird and wonderful sounds being emitted by two underground bands called Pink Floyd and Soft Machine.

Underground?

Marijuana, liberalism, wild living and protestation had been around for a long time. The Dean crowd and their successors had been smoking as a regular habit ten years earlier but only now, at the height of the Vietnam crisis, when the futility of the war was beginning to dawn with the return of disillusioned young soldiers prepared at last to tell the truth, were drugs beginning to appear on the American campus scene and in London streets in any volume.

Encouraged by the words of the pop songs and those who were already well established users of various natural and manufactured mind-expanding substances, youth took a wrong turn – or the right one, depending on your stance at the time. The drug age was in its infancy; there would be many dead and injured in its wake and as we all now know in the wiser Nineties, the knock-on effects would reverberate in much more sinister and sordid terms not just for the rest of the decade but the rest of the century.

Users fell basically into two groups: there were the milder peace-loving 'Smile on your brother' types, whose philosophy was invoked by Jefferson Airplane's hit record using that phrase, or the far more violent set who were emerging with hard rock and the free-as-the-wind Hell's Angels, the unkempt, unwashed, tough and brutal rabble who were the built-in bad guys of the counter-culture; they made the gangs in *Rebel Without a Cause* and Brando's *The Wild One* look like a Sunday school gathering.

In the middle of this explosion of pop culture, Nicholson had also become a free agent again, having parted from his wife in 1966, and moved in with his actor friend Harry Dean Stanton at Laurel Canyon. The Great Seducer was on the loose and quietly and anonymously returned to a more vigorous social exchange. Money was still short and days were long, and parties were often and red wine was cheap. Thrill-seeking impulses led them to many momentary and immediate adventures, and it was this period of his life he referred to when he said he had never been in an orgy of more than three people, although he tried ineffectively to promote it a time or two. His parties certainly looked like orgies. 'I guess you could call them orgies in the strictest definition,' he admitted. 'There were a lot of rooms in my house and people could take their private little trips. I don't know what they were doing and I guess that could be called an orgy. But it wasn't where everybody's naked and fucking one another all over the place. I've never been into that scene.'

Meanwhile, he was writing and acting, but still he was dogged by the need to continue working in cheap exploitive films, in between do-it-yourself repair jobs on his beloved Karmann Ghia out on Stanton's front lawn (like a massive brake-job to save fifty dollars). Two films gave him temporary solvency and cast him straight into the seedier end of the youth market, the biker movies which were at the beginning of a craze that would last four or five years. Everyone was making bike movies after Roger Corman's runaway success with *The Wild Angels*, starring Peter Fonda, Nancy Sinatra, Bruce Dern and Diane Ladd, released in 1966. Corman brushed off accusations that it was total exploitation – which it was – of the California motorcyle gangs, full of disgusting gang bangs, orgies, sadism and drugs. He preferred to think of it as a meaningful social comment, which it certainly was not, otherwise the dialogue and plot might not have been so banal.

Friends of Fonda's father said Peter should be ashamed of himself for linking a 'great name in movies' to such disgraceful junk. The American critics quickly despatched it to the second-string scrapheap, but young cinema fans weren't put off. Nor were they in Europe, where it took off in a big way as the cult movie of the moment, especially in countries where the dire American dialogue could be dubbed over or subtitled with more viable prose. Fonda was rocketed to stardom, and posters of him astride his bike were quickly outselling star portraits of Brando, Newman and McQueen.

The film became the American entry, by invitation, into that year's Venice Film Festival and the *New York Times*' critic, Bosley Crowther, summed up his nation's embarrassment when he described it as a 'brutal picture which caused diplomats to mop their brows – a vicious account of boozing, fighting, pot-smoking, vandalizing and raping done by a gang of sickle riders who are obviously drawn to represent the swastika-wearing Hell's Angels, one of several disreputable gangs on the west coast. Mr Corman has shot the whole thing in colour and in a *cinema-verité* style that makes it resemble a documentary.'

Nicholson did not appear in the film and was used as a production assistant by Corman; but it is worth mentioning because it was a significant moment in Hollywood history, inspiring as it did a succession of similar films when other producers noticed that *The Wild Angels* grossed eight million dollars in no time at all, and had been made on a shoestring budget. Nicholson was caught up in the aftermath and became Hollywood's hottest property to emerge for two decades.

Unfortunately, his initial contributions to the biker craze were insignificant and forgettable. Two films, *Hell's Angels on Wheels* and *Rebel Rouser* were supposed to follow in the wake of *The Wild Angels*, even to the point of including some of the cast of that film, like Bruce Dern and Diane Ladd. Not much needs to be said about either, except perhaps to record two aspects: in the first film, a critic said Nicholson's acting consisted more or less of variations on a grin. In comparison to his contemporaries in 1967 he had completed a lot more films than most; the difference was that his were a succession of B-movies that paid him little. Beatty, on the other hand, was making $450,000 a picture by then and was shooting *Bonnie and Clyde* with Gene Hackman and Faye Dunaway which turned Beatty into a multi-millionaire overnight because he also prised some percentage points from the backers. McQueen had starred in such epics as *The Magnificent Seven*. Robert Redford and Paul Newman were about to start *Butch Cassidy and the Sundance Kid*. Hoffman was on the verge of international fame and $200,000 a picture after *The Graduate*.

Yet, when Nicholson crossed the street to the legitimacy of a major studio, 20th Century-Fox, to join an all-star cast for *The St Valentine's Day Massacre*, to be released in 1967, he had only a minuscule role, which had one speaking line consisting of twelve words, courtesy of Roger Corman who, for once, had landed a big-budget contract with a major studio and wanted Jack to share his momentary joy of being able to spend it. Bruce Dern said Corman did him and Nicholson a favour by getting them a part because they both needed the money at the time; Corman arranged it so that their shooting schedules would require them to be available for the first and last weeks of the four-week stint, thus, under union rules guaranteeing them a salary cheque for the full four weeks. Nicholson got nothing out of it except a few good pay days and suffered occasional touches of melancholia about his work; he was getting 'old' and anything substantial was nowhere in sight. He was his own critic. He kept telling himself that he was as good as anyone around. 'But unless someone else says that about you, there's no way of believing in it totally,' he said.

While working on the two biker films and his one sentence in *The St Valentine's Day Massacre*, undemanding as they were, Nicholson was also writing another film script for Corman who was once again ahead of the field in latching on to the latest craze sweeping through the world: the children of the post-war baby boom were coming out to play and nothing could stop them now. From the early Sixties break-out, psychedelia was upon them with Sergeant Pepper, painted VWs and Dr Leary, extolling the virtues of LSD and eating strange mushrooms.

The revolution was here at last, and social commentators spoke with alarm about the march of freedom, and said the youth of all nations appeared to be abandoning traditional values to embark on journeys into the unknown, pushing out into previously unexplored and destructive avenues of life. Even Dr Leary, after his highly publicized experimentation with the psychedelic mushrooms, said he was moved to agree with the arch right-winger of American politics, Governor George Wallace, on one thing, that nothing less than western civilization was at stake.

For the benefit of those who were not part of this scene, there was enormous and very real concern among the ruling classes that the whole of the young generation had fallen into a degenerative backslide which, of course, it had not. The media and politicians joined the bandwagon and lumped hippies, Hell's Angels, dope-takers and black militants together in a crescendo of reaction.

There were great discussions especially among show business and literary figures, about the legalization of pot. And politically, the young were becoming much more aware, and campaigning. In December 1966, police had to evict anti-war demonstrators from the Berkeley campus, and, as student leaders called for a campus strike, they started singing the old student favourite, 'Solidarity Forever'. Few knew the words, so they sang 'Yellow Submarine', instead. Thus the Beatles' song became the anthem for hippie activists, and a mock-up submarine was built to head a peace parade of 10,000 through New York City.

In January 1967, there was the famous Human Be-in at Golden Gate Park in San Francisco, and Allen Ginsberg, now suitably converted to Buddhism blew on a conch shell and chanted Hindu sayings and recommended that every healthy American over the age of fourteen should try LSD once. Timothy Leary led a chorus of 'Tune-in, Turn-On, Drop-Out'. This brief excursion through the advent of rock 'n' roll, drugs and sex – in that order – is an over simplification of serious underlying trends and tensions that gripped western youth, but more especially, American youngsters faced with the prospect of being drafted. It was certainly significant to the next stage of Nicholson's career, and indeed what was happening in Hollywood itself at a time of changing tastes which made it almost impossible to predict what next year's cinema audience would go into raptures about.

So Roger Corman said to Jack Nicholson, 'I want you to write me a screenplay called *The Trip*, about this psychedelic craze and LSD, put someone on an acid trip. No film has yet been made about LSD. It will be the first. Will you do it?' Jack said he would and twenty-three years later, in May 1990, Roger Corman named it as being among the best pictures he had made, and by then the total had exceeded 200.

Peter Fonda and Dennis Hopper were to co-star and Nicholson wrote a part in it for himself but Corman refused to cast him and Bruce Dern played the role instead. Dern said Jack was 'very pissed off' about not being allowed to play the role. In reflection, Nicholson remembers that apart from the task of writing a film about a new subject on which there was very little in the way of written research material, it also came at a time when he was going through his divorce. 'Most of the trauma I was going through at the time is written into that film,' he admitted reflectively. But there was also much more. Because of the subject matter, Nicholson could draw on his own experiences with LSD. It was familiar ground too for Fonda and Hopper – who were already good friends. They came to Corman's office to establish what would become a lifelong, though intermittent, friendship between them and Nicholson. Fonda was able to say that he had first tried LSD a couple of years earlier, and had also been a spasmodic user of marijuana – in between more prolific bouts of drinking vodka or scotch – since 1962 when he was turned on by Jim Mitchum at the Carlton Towers Hotel, in London. He was introduced to LSD in September 1965, when he was twenty-five. A friend administered the drug and supervised the trip 'because he knew my head was really fucked up.' Fonda claimed that this first experience began the halt of a downhill slide into alcoholism, acquisitive, habitual spending on fast cars, Cessna airplanes, fine suits and provided him with the insight to revoke his staunch conservative opinions and adopt a liberalistic, casual, 'don't-give-a-fuck approach to life'. These changes and realizations, he credited to his experiences with LSD though conceded that it might not work for others in the same way. He was able to pass on to Nicholson authoritative recollections of seeing huge worms crawl out of biscuits, eating a plum that was alive, seeing his wife sitting beside herself and all that kind of hallucinatory experience.

Hopper – crazy, mixed up, Dean-possessed Dennis – had already carried out a pretty full testing programme on several available substances and it was often a gamble to assess his behavioural pattern: lovable, sexual, violent or zonked out. Nicholson had taken LSD, but he had first done so, he said, as a quest – an adventurous actor seeking experiences to file away for the future. He went to a qualified medical practitioner for his first experience in 1963 and, according to himself, became one of the first people in the country to take the drug. He spent four hours with the therapist who administered it to him and supervised his acid trip, and he remained under a structured hallucinatory influence for a further five hours at home. He was blindfolded for part of the time, which had the effect of making him 'look inside of himself' and he admitted that he was not ready for the experience and some of the discoveries he made. At one point, he was screaming at the top of his voice; he also relived his own birth, met his fears of homosexuality and had the most terrifying fright 'that my prick was going to be cut off'. He said it was all highly graphic visually, especially the part when he was inside his mother's womb. When he got out, he had the feeling he wasn't wanted and that as an infant he was a problem to his family – a feeling which he expressed publicly long before he became aware that his sister was really his mother.

He began writing these experiences for a film and when he produced his manuscript it was partly autobiographical. The central character, Fonda's part, is a writer of television commercials who cannot stand the pressure of the effect it is having on his wife Sally (played by Susan Strasberg) and their marriage. He begins to experiment with LSD in an attempt to obtain more understanding of his problems. In the beginning, it is serene and peaceful, with lots of idyllic scenes and brilliant colours, but it ends with him being confronted by the nightmare of attending his own funeral. These elements were inspired by his own experiences during the break-up with Sandra after she had suffered a bad LSD experience in her search for enlightenment.

Fonda thought the play was brilliant.

He took it home with him that night and sat reading the words. Susan, his wife suddenly noticed he was crying.

'What's the matter, baby?' she asked.

'This script ... it's so beautiful, you have no idea. Listen to this ...'

Fonda read aloud a page of words to her and though his wife had never joined him in his LSD excursions, and marijuana made her sick, she understood from her husband's descriptions of expanded-mind experiences and images the intensity of his feelings.

He said, 'I don't believe it. I don't believe that I am really going to have the chance to be in this movie. This is going to be the greatest film ever made in America.'

The statement was probably a bit of an exaggeration but it demonstrated just how strongly Peter Fonda felt about the Nicholson play. In this he was joined by Dennis Hopper, who was equally ecstatic. So was Bruce Dern. 'The original script was just sensational,' said Dern. 'He injected into it some really way-out visual ideas that no one had ever tried before.'

Fonda finished reading and drove around to Nicholson's house.

They weren't yet close friends, more acquaintances. Nicholson was surprised to receive the visit, and more surprised when Fonda told him, 'Listen. That is the greatest script I have ever read. I think Fellini wrote it.'

'Are you serious?' Nicholson replied. 'You really understand it?'

'I understand every single word,' said Fonda. 'It's right on the nose.'

Corman, who was both producer and director of *The Trip*, was unsure about Nicholson's script. He wanted certain scenes spelled out; he could not understand some of the subtleties. Fonda, Hopper and Nicholson all knew what they meant and they knew that most of the youngsters in the audience would know what they meant. Corman remained unconvinced, especially in the way that the multi-coloured fantasy scenes were to be portrayed.

Fonda exploded. 'Now it's going to be just a predictable film with a beginning, a middle and an end. The ending's a cop-out.'

Corman wasn't arguing. That's the way he wanted it and his own bosses at American International Pictures made further changes through the difficulties they anticipated in getting the film distributed to the cinemas; it was quite probable that it would arouse backlash over its drug content, although, as John Baxter wrote in his review of Sixties films, it was one of those films that exposed with skill the psychological moral pressures vexing society. It was, nonetheless, a film that tried to solicit an understanding of the emerging drug culture, and, for good or evil, persisted with its apologist tone that acid was OK when used with caution. Corman, however, never permitted the final conclusion and left an ambiguous ending in which suicide seemed the only answer for the Fonda character.

Reviews were mixed but largely went the way of those who saw it as a one-and a-half-hour commercial for LSD. Even Corman publicity later admitted that *The Trip* attracted a 'small but loyal group of enthusiasts'. *Film and Filming* magazine said the film had given everyone an insight into the thinking of Corman and Nicholson. It appeared that the former was hung up on sadomasochism and the latter high on sex, leaving little for Fonda and Hopper to do but punctuate every word with 'man'. Nicholson failed to make a name for himself once again, though because of some inspired controversy he had at least achieved a wider circle of critics.

Fonda made his feelings about the picture known by blaming the producers. As he cleared off to lick his wounds in Canada he spoke of his displeasure – 'by trusting AIP (Corman's parent company) to make a beautiful flick, I put my balls on the table and they got lobbed right off.'

Then, in a light haze of vodka in a Toronto hotel room, came the moment that would finally lead to recognition for Nicholson as an actor. Fonda suddenly had the idea for another film. It came to him, just like a flash of lightning and he was so excited that he picked up the telephone and rang Dennis Hopper in Los Angeles.

'Wow, I'm glad you called, man,' said Hopper who thought his friend had telephoned to patch up a quarrel they'd had before Fonda left for Canada.

'Fuck that,' said Fonda. 'Listen to this, man.'

He outlined his idea for a movie plot, which was basically the story of two Californian friends who decide to make a once-and-for-all fortune by selling a consignment of cocaine, and then setting off across the country for a marijuana–cum–motorbikes adventure.

'Whaddaya think?' asked Fonda. 'We'll take the two leading roles.'

'Wow, man that's great. Jesus that's great, man.'

'I'm going to produce this movie and I want you to direct it.' said Fonda. 'Will you do it?'

'Gee whiz, man. Are you kidding me? Wow, babe. Jesus that's great. Of course, I'll fucking do it. What's the title?'

'*Easy Rider.*'

'Wow ...'

5

Easy Rider

In 1968 Jack Nicholson was thinking of giving up acting altogether. He was approaching thirty-two and the elusive big break and rainbow's end that is the goal of everyone who ever set foot in Hollywood seemed no nearer to achievement. He was like a gold miner, chipping away at the rocks and occasionally discovering tantalizing little nuggets that spurred him on towards his dream of striking a rich seam. The Klondike and Hollywood had much in common. True, the word star could be loosely applied to him on the basis that he had 'starred' in more than a dozen films. The reality was that he could walk into any bar or restaurant anywhere in the world and no one would give him a second glance.

Occasionally, there might be a glimmer of recognition by a student or a horror-film fanatic and in Hollywood itself he was known – according to his friend, the Polish director Roman Polanski – to about fifty people. This, for a man whose entire working life had been devoted to making it big in the movies, came as a depressing, frustrating fact as he surveyed his position that year. What was it all about? Why did he spend his life making films that would be forgotten almost as quickly as it took to make them? How could he change his life, which seemed irretrievably set on a course of obscurity? Admittedly, he was not driven by the same devoutly mercenary ambitions of some of his colleagues and sought artistic satisfaction wherever possible. At the end of the day, however, recognition as an actor was also inexorably linked to becoming rich and famous – Warren Beatty's words – and even a modest hope of that seemed as far away as ever. He had been talking about giving up and concentrating his efforts entirely on writing and directing

59

and, like the discovery of another little nugget, was spurred on by reaction to *The Trip* which, in spite of a critical mauling on the grounds of promoting drug abuse, was still seen as a gifted piece of writing. Two other similar projects were already lined up and, again, his career was being pulled in a certain direction by events of the moment.

In the months Nicholson had been involved in the writing and filming of *The Trip*, flower-power had reached its peak and the Haight-Ashbury district of San Francisco had become the Mecca of hippiedom, where all the children with flowers in their hair were at; naturally enough, this prevailing situation provided AIP with the backdrop for another psychedelic experience called *Psych-Out*. Only the title and script changed. The actors were pretty much the same as for *The Trip* – Susan Strasberg, Bruce Dern and, this time, there was a role for Nicholson, for whom that ever-popular name of Stoney was resurrected.

The central character in this story of the times is a seventeen-year-old runaway from New York City, who is taken by the whole current youth philosophy and ends up in California, where she tries to locate her brother who also headed for San Francisco. There, she is befriended by Stoney, a sexy rock 'n' roller who rescues her from a world of LSD that she has dropped into. It gave the producers the chance to create some enticingly colourful kaleidoscopes, largely by Lazlo Kovaks' cinematographic wizardry; otherwise there was little about the film that either Nicholson, Dern or Strasberg would admit to being proud of.

It was notable in one respect, in that it saw the development of Nicholson's romance with the stunningly attractive former model, Mimi Machu, who appeared in *Psych-Out* well down the list of credits under the pseudonym of I.J. Jefferson. He had met her previously when she was given a similarly small part in *Hell's Angels on Wheels* and now they were both unattached and deeply attracted to one another. An invigoratingly stormy relationship was in the making and if Nicholson had been gossip-column fodder at the time, the writers would have had a field day. She was tall, dark-haired and strong-willed, characteristics which were largely repeated in all of Jack's long-term relationships. She was a little like Sandra Knight in looks, and, in some respects, temperament. She was also slightly taller than himself. His friends viewed the affair with interest as it gathered a fair head of steam. Mimi's sexuality captivated The Great Seducer. Jack, they said, was in love again. As their relationship progressed, it was apparent that Mimi had the upper hand in terms of authority. He did pretty well what she wanted with their lives, which caused some occasional irritation. She was with him, also, at the very time his career began to take off and this, with her own hopes for fame as an actress, can be the cause of unintentional jealousy. As the year drew on, their affair became more and more fractious. ...

★　　★　　★　　★　　★

On the work front, he took a step nearer to what he thought would be a move towards transferring his energies to the other side of the camera and his next work was so outlandishly eccentric that perhaps in the year 1998 it will be rediscovered and offered as a superb example of long forgotten pop art of thirty years earlier. It was a film called *Head*, which he wrote and appeared in as himself; it deserves to be brought out and dusted down. It said a lot about the times and included some witty – but strangely unwieldy – material in Nicholson's script. Few saw it like that at the time. In fact, few saw it, period. It was dreamed up for the Monkees and its original conception was supposed to loosely parody the Beatles' films *A Hard Day's Night* and *Help!*. Nicholson's offering, in his first working partnership with director Bob Rafelson, was more than that. Between relentless, disjointed images of everything from cowboys and Indians to real–life Vietnam clips and even an off-colour star of a former age, Victor Mature as the Jolly Green Giant, he managed to write the obituary for that totally plastic group, created from nothing as NBC's teenybop answer to the Beatles and who were a pale shadow in terms of comparative talent. Bob Rafelson, whose later acclaimed directorial skills were – like Nicholson's acting – still largely undiscovered in 1968, had an interest in the Monkees. He and James Frawley had been their virtual creators for the television network and they had seen some excruciatingly successful years. By 1968, the clean-cut image of lads in suits and neatly trimmed hair was definitely for the birds, but not the Byrds, and the Monkees had all but swung from their last branch; the exploitation of four young men who were plucked from audition lines and manufactured into an internationally famous foursome was all but over. Their infantile antics were even making the perpetrators sick.

Still, they might have had a few more years left in them yet, and so in that respect, it was rather courageous of them to accept Nicholson's script and Rafelson's apparent decision that all good things must come to an end. It virtually put them out of business and had Mickey Dollenz calling out to Rafelson, who also appears as himself, 'Bob, I'm through with it.' Which he was; they all were. They themselves had been exploited for the purposes of exploitation and although they made a stab at the psychedelic scene, it hadn't really come off. In *Head*, Nicholson had kindly provided them with a suicide note for which Mike Nesmith was eternally grateful. Not many reviewers really saw the point he was trying to make. In fact, a lot of them could see little point in the movie at all. Renata Adler sat down at her typewriter at the *New York Times* and scolded Nicholson for a 'dreadfully written script'.

Nicholson was naturally defensive and protective of his own work: 'I saw it a thousand and one times and I loved it. It was the best rock 'n' roll picture ever made because it was anti-rock 'n' roll. It had no form, no structure and believe me that's a difficult, unique thing to achieve in movies.' And, by the way, it was also Nicholson's own goodbye to the Roger Corman school of movie-making. Jack could have no complaints. He had learned his craft and had lingered too long. The forked road which every star, perhaps every person, faces at least once in a lifetime lay dead ahead.

★　　★　　★　　★　　★

For one brief moment, it seemed as if there might be a conventional route to fame, through the young director Roman Polanski who had just entered the fast new Hollywood crowd of which Nicholson was a member, as was his friend Robert Evans, who had been recently appointed vice president of Paramount and in charge of all new production projects. Polanski arrived in Hollywood from Europe on the back of a spoof horror film, called *The Fearless Vampire Killers*, a parody of the horror genre, which he directed and in which twenty-three gallons of imitation blood were used. The film starred Sharon Tate, whom Polanski thought was only fourteen years old. He became besotted, and one day after filming, he asked her, 'Would you like to make love to me?' She smiled sweetly and replied, 'Yes. I would love to . . .' He discovered she was no teenager and Sharon moved into Polanski's mews house, just off Eaton Place, London. Polanski was also known to some of the Hollywood crowd through its inter-connection with the swingers of London and the skiing crowd who populated Gstaad and Aspen, notably his friendship of one of the men at the hub of the English scene, Victor Lownes, the cool, urbane and towering figure whom Hugh Hefner had appointed vice president of Playboy International and despatched to London to oversee the new Playboy Club in Park Lane. Polanski used the club as his base and as an access point to its abounding supply of beautiful women; just as Hefner's Playboy mansion in Los Angeles was a magnet for the bright young things of Hollywood, so Lownes established a social whirl that attracted the cream and the elite of off-beat London society, plus some very famous names, eventually to include Nicholson himself.

Robert Evans contacted Polanski in the London Playboy Club one afternoon and inconsiderately invited him to stop what he was doing and come to Hollywood immediately. Polanski replied that he could not rush matters of a sexual nature. However, he flew to Los Angeles and went to Paramount to discuss the new project, a horror–thriller called *Rosemary's Baby*. They selected Mia Farrow as the lead and Polanski asked Warren Beatty to read the script for the co-starring role of Rosemary's husband, Guy. Beatty turned it down as not being a big enough role, and so Polanski went for Robert Redford. In fact, he was already discussing it in his office when he discovered that Paramount were in the middle of a feud with Redford and were just about to serve him with a writ. Evans said they should get Jack Nicholson for the role and he was invited in for a try-out. Polanski's assessment was not encouraging. He recalled, 'Nicholson was a complete unknown at the time. He'd played in some eminently forgettable horror movies and I felt I could not seriously consider him. For all his talent, his faintly sinister appearance ruled him out. The part called for a clean-cut, conventional actor.' John Cassevetes got the part and thus ended Nicholson's brief hope of a major starring role, and provided further incentive to the prevailing thought that he should get out of acting. His friendship with Polanski developed, and he and Robert Evans were to have major roles reserved for them in Nicholson's life, personal and career.

*   *   *   *   *

Nicholson, by now, had already heard of *Easy Rider*. Who hadn't? Hopper and Fonda were looking for finance, although all that existed at the time was an eight-page outline for the plot, which Fonda had been toting around. Corman's AIP had already turned it down because although they liked the idea of another biker film, the prospect of Hopper – bearing in mind his recent reputation – bringing in the picture without problems hardly seemed worth the gamble. Their reaction was pretty typical of Hollywood. What's Dennis the menace up to now? There were other imponderables. They were talking about having no other actors apart from the three main characters to be played by Hopper, Fonda and Rip Torn – in between Hopper's directing and Hopper's scriptwriting and Fonda's production and Fonda's co-scriptwriting work. Apart from a few bit parts, the rest would be real people. Whoever heard of putting real people into a film? Spirits dashed, Fonda and Hopper came up with another idea for a picture called *The Queen*, starring themselves and Jack Nicholson as Robert McNamara, Dean Rusk and Lyndon Johnson apparently plotting the assassination of John F. Kennedy. They took this idea to BBS, a new production company formed by Bob Rafelson, Bert Schneider and Steve Blauner (thus BBS – Bob, Bert and Steve) to produce intelligent low-budget pictures – the thinking man's Roger Corman movies, someone said.

'Needless to say,' said Fonda, 'they wouldn't touch it, but Bert Schneider asked what else we'd got. I said "Well, we got this great story for a motorcycle picture. ...." And his eyes lit up.' Nicholson, who was spending a good deal of his time in the new BBS offices, which he hoped would be the starting point of his own aspirations towards directing, chipped in with the observation that his biker pictures had all grossed respectable money and made very handsome profits from a low outlay.

'How much will it take to make it?' Schneider asked.

'Half a mill, maximum,' said Fonda, but he was ready to negotiate because he desperately wanted to make the picture.

'OK. I'll give you $375,000. Go and do your picture and come back and show us,' said Schneider.

Dennis Hopper was even more determined than Fonda to make it work. He saw it as his main chance to regain some respect. They both had something to prove. Like most others who managed to remain – tolerantly and understandingly – friends of Hopper's, Fonda and Nicholson were well aware that he had suffered disappointment after disappointment during the mid-Sixties. He and his wife Brooke Hayward were on the verge of divorce – they finally split up in 1969. She had suffered during long bouts of Hopper's depression, rages and his obsession with James Dean. It tormented him and tested his sanity to breaking point. Through Brooke and his own contacts, he had entry to the cream of Hollywood parties and the cream of Hollywood society. It could and should have led him to great opportunities.

Dennis invariably ruined his own chances by his complete anti-establishment stance. He would start the evening in his quiet, sometimes moody, Kansas drawl and would end up in ranting fashion, telling them all that things would be different when he and the rest of 'new' Hollywood were running things, and they would all be clapped in irons, which was hardly the brightest way to inspire confidence at a time when you were seeking film money.

His most bitter disappointment came when the music entrepreneur Phil Spector pulled back from financing a screenplay Hopper had written called *The Last Movie* (it was eventually produced in 1970) about Hollywood's exploitation and destruction of South American Indians. Everyone he had shown it to had described it as brilliant, and by all accounts it was; rejection hurt. It destroyed him and for a time he was engulfed by a deep chasm of despair, drinking heavily, taking amphetamines and LSD – and he was in his sixteenth year of smoking marijuana. *Easy Rider* was like an ambulance arriving to perform an emergency resuscitation on his ego.

Added to the volatile, almost certifiable, personality of Hopper was the ambition of Peter Fonda, who would never admit it but was wanting – at that point in his life – to really show his father and sister, not to mention a whole legion of critics, that he could act – a considerable undertaking in itself. He had made money from his movie *The Wild Angels* and now he wanted to prove he could do something worthwhile. Alongside Hopper, Fonda was a very stable character, loved his wife and wanted for little, except self-fulfilment, which gnawed away at his mind and caused him to drink and trip occasionally on LSD.

The third element that made *Easy Rider* the runaway, roaraway success that it became in the counter-culture movement was Jack Nicholson, angry and surely envious – though he denied it – at seeing some of his flash contemporaries and some younger actors making it very big indeed in the legitimacy of more sumptuous surroundings of Warners, Paramount, MGM and the rest. The disappointment of not being selected for *Rosemary's Baby* had merely made him more determined to change his life. In a way, the three of them were like moles, digging their way to the surface looking for freedom, coincidentally at the same time that counter-culture was doing the same and searching for heroes. It was purely by chance that Nicholson was cast for the film. At quite an early stage, there were reports of trouble from the location work in New Orleans. Rip Torn, who was first choice for the part that Nicholson eventually played had finally rejected the pleadings of Fonda and Hopper and pulled out of the project. He wanted $4500 for the job – once he had seen what it entailed – whereas because of the limited budget everyone else was on scale, amounting to a few hundred dollars. There were rows between him and Dennis, who could become exceedingly tired and emotional and was already shooting in New Orleans without a script.

BBS seriously considered firing Hopper; the pressure of moving a production team of twenty-three people from state to state, writing the script on the run and persuading innocent citizens of the United States of America who just happened to be passing at the time to appear in the movie, was a heavy burden for all. Hopper will probably agree that he – and the movie – were saved by Nicholson who was sent down by Rafelson as a trouble-shooter in the role of executive producer and ended up playing the third man, the part reserved for Rip Torn.

Nicholson brought instant stability to the production and introduced some of the rigid controls he had learned from the Corman *modus operandi*. He was also responsible for bringing in Lazlo Kovaks, the cinematographer whose filming of the American landscape brought untold dimensions to the movie itself; he also joined later in the selection of another of the film's major plus-points – the magnificent scoring and numbers performed by Steppenwolf, the Byrds, the Jimi Hendrix Experience, the Electric Prunes, Electric Flag, the Band, the Holy Mondal Rounders, Fraternity of Man, Little Eva and Roger McGuin.

Easy Rider was the motivation for a lot of things and for those not familiar with the story, it is one of free love and excessive drugs and of American society as perceived by Hopper in 1968, with some moralistic warnings about drug use and undertones about the consequences of such a lifestyle – but only if you were actually looking for them. Otherwise, any tendency towards moralizing was overshadowed by the exciting, humorous, tragic and horrifically violent elements. The two central characters played by Hopper and Fonda are Wyatt, nicknamed Captain America, and Billy – Billy the Kid – who embark on a drugs deal, selling cocaine in California, to provide the finance to purchase a pair of magnificent Harley Davidsons for a journey across America and to the Mardi Gras at New Orleans. It was the ultimate biker-drug-sex film, which also owed a lot to Kerouac's *On The Road*. Unfortunately, Jack Kerouac never lived to see the success of it, ironically passing on to that great hippie gathering in the sky on 21 October 1969. They see all America and its split personality; the American Dream and the American small-mindedness, which are typified by the two bikers' confrontations with hippies on the one hand and red-neck American bigots on the other. As Hopper said, 'Don't be scared. Go try and change America, but if you're gonna wear a badge, whether it's long hair or black skin, you'd better learn to protect yourself.'

The New Orleans sequences were filmed first, even before Fonda, Hopper and screenwriter Terry Southern had finished writing. They moved back to California, on to Arizona, New Mexico, Texas and Louisiana. Then, they stopped for two months to write and prepare the rest before taking to the road again. Nicholson, Fonda and Hopper had become the best of friends.

As he watched Hopper work, Nicholson came to the conclusion that he was working with a genius, flawed perhaps, but a man whose artistry was, and still is, quite awesome. Hopper's direction of *Easy Rider* had much to do with his own appreciation of historical art and his painting skills. Nor can the quality of his writing be denied, though it often needed the expertise of Terry Southern to translate the confusion of Hopper and Fonda's joint (no pun intended) efforts into filmable dialogue. The script they came up with was trendy and repetitive, rather naïve but tuned directly to the youth of the moment. There was a Dylan Thomas in Hopper, not just in his abilities but in his self-destruct mechanism and it was a great pity in many ways that he spent so many years in James Dean's gloomy black shadow, because he is talented and perhaps even more diverse. He did not realize it in the Sixties, nor the Seventies. Perhaps in the Eighties, it began to dawn on him and he cleaned up his act but by then some of the early potential had passed.

There was a moment in the shooting of *Easy Rider* that typified Hopper's abilities. It had to do with his insistence on using 'real' people, which was seen as a daunting prospect by many of the crew. However, when they arrived in a town called Morganza, Louisiana, looking for locations, they came across a little café with a sign outside which read 'Homemade Pies and Coca-Cola'. Dennis spotted the place and fell in love with it. When they returned with cameramen, the advance production team had picked up some local teenagers for the film. When Hopper and Fonda arrived – Hopper looking rough and hippyish with his long hair and wild beard and stetson hat – some other youths who did not know what he was about began crowding in on him, saying, 'I can smell him. Can you smell him?'

Another said, 'Yeah, I smell him. It's his hair. Have you ever seen hair as long as that?'

Hopper insisted that he wanted these lads in the film, not the one the production people had selected. He and Fonda retired to their trailer, smoked some marijuana and then came out and told the crowd of local youths that they should imagine that the two of them had just arrived in town, and, on the way, they had picked up a local girl of fifteen, and raped and left her in the bushes.

'They began growling, man,' said Hopper. 'Straightaway they got the mood of what we wanted.' He used other personal experiences in the script. Once in Montrose, Colorado, when he was on location for a small role in John Wayne's *True Grit*, he was standing in a bar, scruffy and long-haired, and for no reason at all, one of the locals took a swing at him. 'He was screaming at me, "Get outta here, my son's in Vietnam" and then the local sheriff came in and he shouted that his son was in Vietnam and why wasn't I in Vietnam?

It got real heavy, man. So I put that kind of experience in the play.'

Nicholson entered the scheme of things when Captain America and Billy the Kid are put into jail when a police force regards them as mere undesirables. There, they meet a naïve, alcoholic young lawyer named George Hanson – played by Jack – a once good-intentioned liberal who is now equally at odds with the heartland of American society. He awakes from a bender, slow and bleary, and introduces a sardonic charm that jolts the film to a sudden halt and he is a star, instantly. He decides to join them as he springs them from jail and they continue their journey. That night, they filmed the most memorable and supposedly dramatic scene in the picture, the one in which Nicholson does his monologue on what is wrong with American society, for which he became famous. If only the great wide world of cinema audiences knew exactly what happened. ...

It was the campfire scene where the three of them were sitting around talking, discussing the problems of the world and they introduce Hanson to marijuana. It started well, but Hopper, who was acting, directing, and smoking, could not get the take he required. Did anyone out there, when they saw the movie, realize that they were smoking for real? And could anyone imagine that in order to get those few minutes of screen imagery in the can, the three of them inhaled 105 real joints of excellent quality Mexican grass?

Each time they did a take, or reshot to get an angle, it was necessary to smoke almost an entire joint. This in itself created a double problem because the action of this scene moves from a point where Nicholson is talking normally right through to the point where he is stoned and slurred through smoking marijuana. There were so many takes and retakes for angles that the reverse situation was occurring for Nicholson, the actor. Because by then he was stoned before the scene began, and instead of having to play normal and act stoned, he was having to act normal and play stoned. There was an added difficulty that the three of them would break into convulsions of laughter, verging on hysterics, with Hopper some-where off-camera rolling around in the bushes and, according to Nicholson, 'totally freaked out' while Jack was forcing himself to be relatively straight, do his serious acting and hold the whole thing together: 'This used to be a helluva good country ...'

The trio of actors became close off set, though with Fonda a committed monogamist, Hopper and Nicholson often went off into the night; on one occasion they shared a memorable experience with LSD, so memorable, in fact, that both men have chosen, separately, to recall it in detail, as best they could. In Nicholson's case, the description came with the ever-present prefix that on the occasions he has tried acid, it was used properly to avoid bad trips; thus, he had 'come to terms with things that you perceive would be otherwise impossible – things that help you understand yourself ... plus, if used properly, it can means quite a lot of kicks.' On this particular day, they had been shooting at Taos and at the end of it they dropped some acid and took off with two other friends to visit the nearby tomb of D.H. Lawrence.

The descriptions of their hallucinatory images as they lay at the foot of Lawrence's grave are too visual and complicated to do justice to and are no longer relevant, anyway. Later, as dusk began to fall, they got sentimental about each other and began to cry. Jack said, 'We're geniuses. You know that? Isn't it great to be a genius?' Dennis agreed that it was. Somehow, and from somewhere, a beautiful young woman appeared – this was no imagined vision – and she took them to some hot springs where they all ended up naked. Dennis eventually went off with her on his own, leaving Nicholson to return alone to their hotel where he acted out some kind of ritual guarding of their rooms, ready to forewarn of an attack he was expecting at any moment from some non-existent Red Indians. None came and still under the drug's influence at dawn, he found himself looking out from the top of a forty-foot tree – he had no memory of climbing it – and looking down on a vast meadow, flecked with patterns of multi-coloured light and rocks which turned into horses, all of which filled him with 'tremendous emotions'.

That was a real-life experience, not acted for a film. Meanwhile, *Easy Rider*, itself, began to take on more menacing tones as it neared its climax.

Nicholson had completed his scenes, having been kicked to death by two marauding red-necks, leaving Captain America and Billy the Kid to continue their journey to New Orleans for the Mardi Gras, their adventures in a brothel and the LSD scene which took a week to shoot because no one could focus on what they were supposed to be doing. As they finally leave the city and head out for the open road, Billy the Kid says, 'We made it, didn't we?' Captain America is pensive and is about to deliver the film's conscience, the message to the counter-culture, the moral of the story: 'You know, Billy, we blew it.'

Now there was no explanation for that in the film. Hopper wrote the line and Fonda could not understand it.

'Why did they blow it? . . . '

'Well, they were criminals,' said Hopper. 'They smuggled drugs and used criminal ways to buy their dreams and get out of the system.'

Fonda began to get Hopper's point. 'So they gained their freedom from an illicit source.'

'Correct,' said Hopper. 'That's why they blew it.'

Fonda examined the premise and eventually saw that they were making a much broader statement about the American Dream and the state of the nation itself at that precise moment in time. It was not just about hippy society, it was about society at large. Captain America and Billy the Kid had blown it when they believed they could make a lot of money and retire, but life was not simply about economics; they had, according to Fonda, found their freedom but their liberty was like the statue in New York harbour, surrounded by polluted waters. That's why Nicholson's character had to die; he was the innocent and the only reason he was killed was because he was with two undesirable characters. If he had not been with them, he would have gone through that town quite safely. The wider issues were to show that politicians had blown it, for dragging America into Vietnam, germ warfare, ABM and all those other starting points of peace protesters. Worldwide governments had blown it for different reasons. These were the discussion points.

And now, the film turns on the two escapists and finally delivers its punishment. Out on the road, they become involved in an argument with a trucker who shoots Billy and then Captain America. The film ends with the two Harley Davidsons going up in flames. . . .

Few people paid much attention to *Easy Rider* until the previews, and slowly word got around that Fonda and Hopper had produced a very good film. The establishment magazines began by deprecating the film's free and easy attitude to drugs and sex, and especially to violence. It promoted the use of marijuana, they said, although it started with an anti-drugs message. The underground and radical publications more readily saw some of the intentions of the script and the overall concept. In fact, *Easy Rider* was rather slow to catch on but when it finally caught the attention of the counter-culture, even the establishment newspapers and magazines began to offer up praise. Nicholson especially won some excellent notices although Fonda reckoned that Dennis Hopper's performance had been the best of the three. Fonda himself once again suffered the attribution of the word 'wooden'. His father had other comments. Henry Fonda was apparently heard to say of his son, 'That little bastard . . . he and some other punks have produced a movie out of nothing and have made more money from that piece of crap than I have made in a whole lifetime in Hollywood.'

There was praise in that statement somewhere but more for his son than the film. Hollywood did not especially like it. It was one of those pictures that went totally against the grain of everything that the movie industry believed it stood for. To generalize and say that it stood for anything at all was self-delusion and deceit. The truth was that they were just jealous they had not thought of it before and made all of that money. That was the key – the final arbiter of success or failure. *Easy Rider* took $45 million worldwide for an outlay of less than $400,000 and there are few comparable profit-to-cost examples in the history of Hollywood.

For once, when Hopper said 'Wow!' it was an understatement.

The stardom sort of crept up on Nicholson over a period of weeks. He knew he had performed well and he was able to present himself in the best possible aura, that of self-satisfaction, because Hopper gave him *carte blanche* to edit his own part on film. The result was that in spite of some misgivings about the script and the incessantly repetitive dialogue about them doing their own thing, reviewers spoke glowingly of 'an actor named Jack Nicholson . . . is magnificent' and 'he gave a brilliantly witty performance'. It was an odd fact that they spoke of him in terms of discovering a new talent – a new star who had emerged quite suddenly – and apparently unaware that he was a veteran of a string of past films. The *New York Times* demonstrated how he had made little impact on the movie world, until that point in time, with the observation that the lawyer Hanson was '. . . played by Jack Nicholson whose sharp, regular features may be vaguely familiar to kids who go and watch drive-in movies.'

Easy Rider also gave a new edge and meaning to the phrase 'anti-hero'. There were plenty of examples of performances which fall into this category in cinematographic history, most notably those of James Cagney and Humphrey Bogart dating back to the Thirties, and the more lovably roguish role, in Bogart's case, in *The African Queen*.

Hollywood's modern-day anti-heroes appeared that year in the shape of John Voight and his smelly companion Dustin Hoffman in the 1969 Oscar-winning film, *Midnight Cowboy*. While that was a brilliant evocation of living by your wits in or near a New York gutter, which pushed out several boundaries – largely sexual – in relation to the old Hollywood code of conduct, there was a degree of tameness in comparison to the anti-heroes created in *Easy Rider*; Fonda, Hopper and especially Nicholson were used as role models for many future films, and thus it broke new ground. The very fact that Nicholson should be nominated for an Oscar as Best Supporting Actor spoke for itself.

With hindsight, of course, it is now possible to question the glamorizing of drug-taking in such films as *Easy Rider*, *Psych-Out* and *The Trip* and others; the in-built health warnings were seldom noticed and there was a certain drugs bandwagon rolling, anyway, largely created in the pop industry where drug usage was not only referred to, even poetically eulogized in song, but physically demonstrated by some of its more tragic exponents like Brian Jones, Jimi Hendrix and Janice Joplin, to name but three in a long line of fallen idols and heroes. Nicholson was always quite adamant in his own mind that his films did not encourage drug taking. If anyone was to blame, it was the anti-drugs policy of successive governments, and especially President Richard Nixon's, but that's another talking point on which he would hold forth at the drop of a hat.

What *Easy Rider* and Nicholson did capture was the mood in America and elsewhere at that time. It was not a 'brilliant' movie; the script was flawed and the premise was suspect, but the underlying presence that Fonda, Hopper and Nicholson caught, perhaps without even realizing it, was an air of tension that prevailed among youth right across the world in 1969. Headlines of that period will recall some of the concerns: the assassinations of Bobby Kennedy

and Dr Martin Luther King (the previous year); Black Power and
the police shoot-outs with Black Panthers; the continuing Vietnam
War, claiming its 40,000th American victim; fever-pitch anti-war
demonstrations and the symbolic burning of draft cards; draft-
dodgers escaping to Canada; massive public demonstrations for
peace in every major western city; and two million acres defoliated
in South Vietnam by the beginning of 1969.

Then there were the Paris student riots, the Biafran conflict and
scenes of devastating suffering and starvation; Yasser Arafat became
head of the PLO and enlisted thousands of young people into his
army; Muammar Gaddafi threw out the Libyan monarchy and
installed himself as his nation's leader and hero of terrorist factions
everywhere; the streets of Ulster became a battle zone with troops,
fire bombs and unbelievable scenes of street-fighting; Jan Palach, a
twenty-one-year-old Czech student set fire to himself in Wenceslas
Square to protest at the Soviet invasion of Prague. And, soon, in
this great new age of student protest, the National Guard – in a
repetition of the horrific violence ordered by Chicago's Mayor
Richard Daley only a few months before – used bayonets and tear
gas to disperse anti-war demonstrators at Kent County University,
Ohio (in May 1970). Two nights later, in the grounds of the same
university, four students – two of them girls – lay dead, shot by the
bullets of fellow Americans in the National Guard.

It hardly seemed credible, whichever side you were on, that such
events could occur. More incredible was that all of this violence, all
of this blood and gore, all of this inhumanity and human sacrifice
was being conducted in the corner of our living rooms, because
suddenly it was also the nightly fodder of the television stations,
who were only just realizing the potential of on-the-spot coverage
of such despicable yet compelling viewing matter. In that respect,
Hollywood had a lot to beat.

Some of the lighter moments around the time of the release of
Easy Rider and Nicholson's coming-out party, provided contrasting
and bizarre elements which were all relevant to the age in which he
would become established as their hero. For example, in London,
stage censorship ended the previous December, and the all-nude
musical *Hair* was enjoying packed houses. *Myra Breckenridge*, the
sizzling exposure of sex in Hollywood by Gore Vidal had just made
its appearance in London, along with Norman Mailer's *The Armies*

of the Night, about the invasion of the White House the previous October of pacifists and hippies protesting at the war. John Lennon and Yoko allowed the world's media into their hotel suite in Amsterdam for their bed-in, a honeymoon to epitomize the institution of love not war. Mick Jagger put on a charming little Greek skirt and gave a free performance to thousands in London's Hyde Park, while Bob Dylan headed down to the Isle of Wight for a three-day festival of dope, sex and rock 'n' roll attended by 150,000 fans. It was the wildest party Britain had seen, and the media had a field day with a revelling of nude and painted bodies, cavorting to fine music under a dense cloud of cannabis smoke and punctuated by the occasional screams of an acid drop gone wrong.

For those in the middle of these events, there was in addition to the tension and the menace, a certain air of unreality; this raises the part played by drugs, not merely in the emergence of a forceful counter-culture, but in the attitudes of plain straightforward young people to whom any kind of illicit substance a couple of years earlier would have been a complete mystery. Drugs provided the wherewithal for the actual suspension of reality – a route so desperately sought, for instance, by those young men wearing American uniforms in that far-off land of Vietnam. As young people were being encouraged, if not forced, to raise the stakes of involvement, by the pressures of the wars, brutal police, terrorist causes and other assorted hostilities, violence suddenly became an integral part of the youth movement as the feeling of the impending apocalypse heightened.

Is this all too serious a scenario to attach to one simple biker movie called *Easy Rider* and a biography of one supporting actor in it? Of course; the film was just one minuscule component of a particularly significant period of the last half-century, at a time when many millions of people still viewed film and pop stars as providers of some kind of visionary lead. What happened next in Hollywood shocked it to the core and brought Nicholson and Hopper to the heart of one of the great tragedies of this drug-infested era. . . .

6

Brave New World

Charles Manson was not merely a symptom of the drug age; he was
the epitome of a certain sickness that gripped some sections of
society, by whom he was exalted as the inspiration for the killing
of so-called pigs, the word daubed in blood on the living-room
walls of director Roman Polanski's home, after the so-called Sharon
Tate murders, for which the bearded prophet of the drug age is still
serving life. Polanski, on the other hand, was, in Jack Nicholson's
view, the recipient of Western justice: 'His situation is a very
interesting case of what notoriety can do to you. I always felt that
Roman was exiled because his wife had the bad taste to be murdered
in the newspapers.'

Irony seldom works in print and this blunt appraisal of the
troubles that had beset his friend was made to Nancy Collins and
published in *Rolling Stone* some fifteen years after the Tate murders
at Polanski's rented home in Beverly Hills in August 1969. It barely
represented the true drama of the moment, though Nicholson was
better informed than most on the subject because apart from being
a friend of Polanski, he gleaned first-hand accounts by attending the
trial of Manson and his disciples, whose story proved to be more
gruesome than even Hollywood could either manufacture or exploit
in a movie. Five innocent people lay mutilated and dead in Beverly
Hills. Real bodies; real blood – and with 115 very real bayonet
wounds and six gunshot wounds between them. What the murders
did reflect in an odd way was the convulsing extremism – at both
ends of a polarized spectrum – that existed between right and left,
counter-culture and establishment, in 1969, when *Easy Rider* was
released. It was demonstrated by the fact that even after her death

Sharon Tate was listed among the enemies of one extreme group, along with Lyndon Johnson, Richard Nixon, Mayor Richard Daley of Chicago and the Governor of California, Ronald Reagan who had just instructed his forces of law and order to 'take whatever action necessary' to quell campus riots.

The killing of Polanski's wife – who was in her last month of pregnancy and carrying a 'perfectly formed' baby son, also murdered – along with three friends and a totally unconnected young man of eighteen who had been visiting a caretaker living in the grounds, naturally caused Polanski extreme mental torture, made worse by the knowledge that he had promised to return to the house himself and had not made it in time. It was the start of a series of events that led finally to his fast exit from America, never to return, and many close to him believe to this day he was eventually ostracized by powerful Hollywood money for bringing the film industry into such disrepute.

Thus, a few years later, when Polanski was accused of drugging and raping a thirteen-year-old girl in Jack Nicholson's home, it was – some said – time for him to go, and he has been exiled in Paris ever since. Nicholson has remained a devoted defender of his rights for – at the very least – a fair trial, which, it appeared, was going to be rather difficult to achieve.

In 1969, Polanski and Nicholson were party acquaintances, friends of friends who shared common interests; it was Polanski who claims to have introduced Nicholson to one of his passions, skiing. Their friendship developed soon afterwards, to the point that they shared each other's homes and became very close chums. They were also both to become heroes of the counter-culture movement. Counter-culture, it might be said, was no loose term applied to a bunch of idle west coast hippies, whose philosophies were being trendily copied the world over. It was a strong and diverse movement which originally had its roots in the hippie communes and the pop lyrics of the earlier Sixties, but had, by the end of the decade, encompassed so many political and social causes – particularly in America – that governments had a full-time spy network, through the likes of the FBI, the CIA and Scotland Yard's Special Branch, keeping tabs on its leaders.

In the summer of that year, Jack and Roman had a common interest in the talk in Hollywood, which was, as Polanski recalled in his autobiography, largely about the drugs and sex culture, a topic fanned through their own recent and separate films, and then by the tragic events in the Polanski house. The topic was pretty universal, in fact. Britain had its own discussions, spurred on by the Wootton Report on Drug Dependency, published in July 1969, which recommended substantially reduced penalties for pot-smoking. In Los Angeles, discussions centred not merely on drug usage as a topical exploitation subject for movies but also on the widespread and varied substances which were readily available, being increasingly used and largely blamed for the incredible recent upsurge in violence within the protest movement.

Very quickly, Polanski and Nicholson became darlings of the west coast film and rock-music communities, who were also selecting the new heroes of the screen – anti-heroes in fact – because it was old values that had kept those handsome, pristine hulks of the last generation at the top and old values were now strictly taboo amongst the young and trendy. The likes of Polanski, Nicholson and Hopper all talked freedom – even if it was at the movies – and that was music to the ears of those who followed the anti-war, hippie-inspired trend of throwing off inhibitions, of which there were plenty of public demonstrations when the beautiful people gathered, be it Los Angeles, New York, London or Paris.

Nicholson, at this point, was in the news through the acclaim being bestowed upon him for *Easy Rider*, and his first taste of stardom was received with some apprehension; his on-screen con-nections with marijuana and LSD also attracted a great deal of media coverage; serious press interviews, with him personally as the focus and centre of attention, were also unfamiliar territory into which he ventured nervously, almost unsure of what he was going to say and how he was going to express his feelings and opinions; he had plenty, and serious ones at that. No one had ever asked his opinion before for the specific purpose of putting it into print in a newspaper article that might be read by millions of people.

It was happening in the summer and autumn of that year, and having now established who he was, people in the movie business were asking if this was going to be his big break, while out there in the communes and on the streets, the rebels were electing him and Hopper, and, to a lesser degree, Fonda, their champions. The sudden success and appeal of *Easy Rider* was not without its critics;

indeed, there were some heavy broadsides launched against the film in the media. An example was written even before the Sharon Tate murders by Stephen Farber for the winter issue of the respected journal, *Film Quarterly*, in which he examined the reasons why young audiences responded so passionately to *Easy Rider*.

It was almost prophetic in its wisdom: 'There is really something morbid about the film as a whole – a fascination, almost a wallowing in death and suffering that represents one of the least appealing tendencies in the audience as well as the film-makers. The people who conceived this film and the people who applaud it take certain masochistic fascination in casting themselves as the martyrs, poor innocents slaughtered by barbarians.' Polanski had received notices of similar disquiet over his films. *Rosemary's Baby* had done well, financially and critically but the American Catholic Office for Motion Pictures, the former Legion of Decency, gave it a 'C' rating, meaning condemned, for its explicit sexual content and its perverted use and distortion of fundamental Christian beliefs. In London, the British Board of Film Censors insisted that the rape scene should be cut because it contained elements of 'kinky sex associated with black magic'. Sharon Tate's own artistic contribution to this current genre was in her starring role in the film adaptation of Jacqueline Susann's true-life novel, *Valley of the Dolls*, about pill-popping, sex-crazed Los Angeles womenfolk, and that was an exploitation movie if ever there was one. When that was done, she and Polanski flew to London to be married in high profile, with the London Playboy boss, Victor Lownes, having arranged everything.

And so, the media was not kind after Sharon's slaughter by the Manson disciples, hence Nicholson's remark about Sharon having been murdered in the newspapers. Hollywood was scared, not simply because of the threat to personal life and limb, but by the implications being meted out in the press which followed two distinct inferences: first that Polanski through his and his dead friends' involvement with drugs had brought this tragedy upon his own house, and, second, that the 'new' Hollywood in general must accept some guilt through its current fascination with violence, drugs, sex and the lifestyle of what appeared – in the eyes of the establishment – to be a mortally sick section of society. Though the moguls had gone, there were still plenty of people left from the old school to lay down some pretty awful accusations.

Time magazine, as always reflecting the indoctrines of the Luce family and assuming the mantle of the responsible voice of America, recorded that: 'it was a scene as grisly as anything depicted in Polanski's film explorations of the dark and melancholy corners of human character ... and the most likely theory is that the slayings were related to narcotics.' *Newsweek* went further: 'Almost as enchanting as the mystery [over the deaths] was the glimpse the murders yielded into the surprising Hollywood sub-culture, in which the cast of characters played. All week long, the Hollywood gossip about this case was of drugs, mysticism and off-beat sex, and for once there may be more truth than fantasy in the flashy talk of the town.'

These were the milder forms of speculation. The wilder ones were rampant about black magic, the gruesome style of the mutilations, of kinky sex videos starring Polanski and his wife found at the house, and of the deep drug involvements of three of the victims. Once again, the fiction of Hollywood merged with fact; scenes of fantasy portrayed on celluloid for entertainment – like those in *Easy Rider* – had become, it was said, the acted-out realities of a group of people whose minds had been expanded to breaking point, until they performed deeds so indescribably vile that it barely seemed possible that one human being could inflict such wounds upon another for no apparent reason. Did Hollywood and the underground film-makers, in particular, hold any responsibility for such behaviour? Nicholson has always strongly denied the view that his films could have influenced anyone in their decision whether or not to indulge in drugs.

Easy Rider happened to become the film of the moment because it reflected the mood of the moment. It also was perhaps a trifle ironic that when Charles Manson wanted to have his life story told on film, he instructed his lawyers to get the *Easy Rider* team. Nicholson himself had been attending the Manson trial, taking copious notes, and was especially keen to observe the machinations of a non-sequestered jury. 'I just wanted to see for myself,' said Nicholson. Dennis Hopper went to the meeting with Manson and sat face to face with him for two hours in a room on the eighth floor of the Hall of Justice. Hopper listened, and was clearly taken by some kind of presence while in Manson's company because when he recalled the meetings, he made some frank comments about the murders. He said, 'The people at the Tate house were killed because they were into some bad shit. *What goes around comes around.* The people in the Tate house were victims of themselves because they had all fallen into sadism and masochism and recorded it on video-tape. The LA police told me this. I know that three days before they were killed, twenty-five people were invited to that house for the mass whipping of a dealer from Sunset Strip who'd given them some bad dope. And Jay Sebring, one of those killed, was an old friend of mine. ...'

Easy Rider made its name in the middle of this melée and specific-ally at a time when the whole counter-culture movement had taken on an explosive, manic air. Some treated Charles Manson as a hero, and the underground newspaper, the *Los Angeles Free Press* allowed Manson to write a column for them while he was in jail; another, called *Tuesday's Child* depicted him on a cross. *Life* magazine put him on the cover and that single photograph of Manson, with his evil, hypnotic stare, became for the hysterical mass media, the face of a violent, drug-crazed substrata of society: the monster hidden in the heart of every hippie and longhaired supporter of a culture which seemed certain to encompass an increasing section of youth and bandwagonners.

Sixties author Todd Gitlin, appalled, wrote a piece called 'The end of the age of Aquarius', in which he asked: 'If there is so much bad acid around why doesn't this contaminated culture, many of whose claims are based on the virtues of drugs, help its own brothers and sisters? Why do the underground papers leave it to the media narcoticizers to deplore the damaging possibilities of drugs. ...'

Nicholson remained as philosophic as ever. He was and is extremely honest about his feelings towards the use of drugs, and he did not hold back when questioned on this highly emotive topic. His answers would return to haunt him. A couple of years later, when he did the *Playboy* interview, he fuelled the controversy by saying exactly what he thought. He could have side-stepped the issue completely, but he chose to give a frank response, dismissing as 'garbage' a Federal Bureau of Narcotics' pamphlet which described marijuana as 'a powerful narcotic in which lurks murder, insanity and death', words that might well have been taken as a reference to events in Hollywood, because they were almost identical to words used by the mass media in descriptions of Manson. He reaffirmed the belief he held then, that the use of soft drugs did not necessarily lead to a progression to hard drugs, although he conceded that he would never have encountered any other drug if he had not become involved with smoking marijuana. 'I started smoking grass around 1957. I'm a social smoker but I can go for months at a time without even thinking about it. But, I think it's insane making criminals out of a huge percentage of our population, particularly when it is something that involves morality.'

He said his was perhaps an 'old-fashioned' view – that he did not want to see the entire world addicted to drugs, like the synthetic existence described in *Brave New World* – but it was an enormous leap, he thought, from 'smoking a little grass to that grim picture'. He admitted having tried cocaine but said it did not seem to do much for him; cocaine was in 'because the chicks dig it sexually'. He referred unashamedly to certain usages, as recommended by Errol Flynn: 'The property of the drug is that it inflames the mucous membranes, such as those in a lady's genital regions. That's the real attraction of it. In his book, *My Wicked, Wicked Ways*, Errol Flynn talks about putting a little on his dick as an aphrodisiac. But his conclusion is that there isn't such a thing as an aphrodisiac. I sort of agree with him, though if you do put a numbing tip of cocaine on your cock because you're quick in the trigger, I guess it is considered a sexual aid.'

Later, he made some corrective statements pointing out that although he had made these observations, he was certainly not advocating the use of any drugs, although he continued to ridicule some of the US government's attempts to stem the tide as being the wrong way to deal with the problem.

Although by his own admission, Nicholson had 'done all the drugs' he did not become addicted to any. Twenty years later, he was still, in his own words, an 'old pot head', smoking marijuana occasionally. Unastounding today, his openness shocked and per-plexed the establishment and anti-drug abuse authorities at the time, especially in the panic-stricken aftermath of Sharon Tate and other horrendous drug-related deaths of that time, including Brian Jones, Jimi Hendrix, Janis Joplin and Jim Morrison. Purely for his admitted views on drug abuse, the FBI had him watched but the authorities never found cause to have him arrested.

Despite the fact that he was personally on only the periphery of the Polanski affair, he was caught up in the backwash, in the resultant discussion of the wider issues of the counter-culture, and it was in this category that the critics had firmly placed their new star as the analysis of his role in *Easy Rider* continued through the run-up to the Oscar presentations and beyond. Each critic and each interview discovered and reported the uncanny fact of what had happened in the production of the film, that it was one of those once-in-a-generation happenings, bringing together the right story, the right people and the right tone at exactly the right time.

Two years previously it would have been just another biker film, and two years on it would have been dated in terms of attitudes. Importantly for Nicholson, this quirk in the social order was all that was needed to give him the kick-start he required, and it also provided him with more money than he had ever earned before.

Even though he was on salary for the film, and not a huge one at that, when it began to take off and the weekly gross takings at the box office began mounting in millions rather than thousands, Hopper arranged for Jack to get a percentage. As Nicholson pointed out, he need not have done that, since most percentage deals are struck at the time of pre-production contracts. Nicholson was obviously very grateful and benefited from the continuing rewards as the film made its way to Europe, where Dennis was voted the best new director of the year at Cannes.

When Jack was given the accolade of Best Actor by the New York Critics' Award for his performance, he responded by sending them all a polite thank-you letter; those critics who had mentioned him in the past had not been especially kind. Those who were kind now would remember him in future – if for nothing else than the thank-you letters. It was an inspired piece of public relations, though more motivated by sheer pride and genuine gratification than any other motive. Nicholson and Hopper suddenly became the flavour of the month. Nicholson made the mistake of telling someone, 'My phone number's in the book. Anybody in the world can get me', and very soon they were all trying.

Dennis Hopper, meanwhile, was resurrecting his own very personal project, *The Last Movie*, which again had as its theme an attack on the great American Dream. As the box-office grosses mounted, establishment Hollywood was beginning to talk in less insulting terms about him, and, one day out of the blue, he called Nicholson. *The Last Movie* was finally going into production. Hopper was showing all the emotions possible in his delight.

'I got the money,' he squealed. 'Universal are putting up. How much? I'll tell you how much. $850,000 – that's half a mill more than we got to do *Easy Rider*. Gee whiz, man. You know how much this means to me; that's four years of my fucking life. And, wow man, I've gotta show them that I can produce. If I foul up now, they'll all laugh and say *Easy Rider* was a fluke.'

Jack said was he really sorry, but he couldn't do it. He had already committed himself to more work than he could handle because he was inexperienced at making deals and having to turn down work.

'And anyway,' said Nicholson, 'You know you want to play the lead yourself.'

'True,' said Hopper, 'but I thought I'd give you the chance of testing for it. . . . '

They laughed and called each other foul names, and Hopper cleared off to Peru to begin filming *The Last Movie*, with an assembled group of friends who included Peter Fonda, Jim Mitchum and Michelle Phillips, of the pop group Mamas & Papas, whose former husband John Phillips had been involved in some bitter activity to gain custody of their child.

As it turned out, this rejection of Hopper's advances was the wisest career move Nicholson ever made. Quite apart from the fact that Hopper's movie was eventually virtually sabotaged by the studio (or himself, depending on which side you were on), director Bob Rafelson had a good script which would without question consolidate Nicholson as the finest exponent of counter-culture appeal available anywhere in America in that year.

Before that, however, there was a postscript to *Easy Rider*. In March 1970, he flew to New York, with his girlfriend Mimi Machu for company, to receive his New York Critics' Award. The relationship with Mimi had survived its stormy months, though it was not destined to last much longer. She wanted, still, a career of her own to match her partner's and, unlike Jack, the break eluded her. They checked into the St Regis Hotel and when some people discovered who he was, they called at his hotel room and asked for autographs. It had never happened before. Mimi did not appreciate what this meant to him and sent them away, but Jack went downstairs looking for them and signed.

Someone, and not just one, asking for his autograph.

Wow!

And then, later on in the evening, he began to get agitated as the presentation neared. He was pacing about the room, pulling at his collar, and eventually he asked Mimi, 'Do they let you into Sardi's without a tie?'

Mimi didn't know.

'Well, they'll have to,' said Nicholson pulling the necktie from his shirt and flinging it across the back of a chair. It was perhaps one slight rejection of the conformity that was expected of him that night.

7

Divided Loyalties

'Restraint,' Nicholson in the aftermath of *Easy Rider*, 'is my favourite characteristic in art. It has taken me a while to be successful and I've had a good time in arriving. But a character [in one of his films] states that clawing your way to the top is very bad for the fingernails ... and, basically, I am very laid-back person, anyway.' His next film was very laid back and one, he admitted, which was the clearest-cut job of acting for the money he had ever done ... and he vowed he would never do that again. 'I needed the money then, and I spent it on whatever I needed it for. I can't even remember what it was; I should have known better.' It also presented him with an interesting little self-discussion about his future prospects because it came when he was on the cusp between low-key acting roles and moderate fame.

Vincente Minnelli, a director of the old school and greatly renowned and respected for such classics as *The Band Wagon* and *An American in Paris*, was looking for a touch of modernism to attract a young audience to a rather old-fashioned film called *On a Clear Day You Can See Forever*. On paper, it seemed a very bankable prospect, based as it was on a successful stage musical by Alan J. Lerner and Burton Lane. *Easy Rider* had not yet burgeoned when he cast Nicholson to co-star alongside Barbra Streisand. Minnelli had seen Jack while studying the film *Psych-Out* for some lighting effects at about the time he was in the pre-production stage. He decided to write an additional part into his movie especially for Nicholson. This surprise offer of a legitimate job with a very famous star, a very famous director and a lot of money caught Jack on the hop. It came out of the blue, before he knew he was famous. 'It was not an uninteresting character,' said Nicholson, 'but it was a sort of aside from the film itself because the part wasn't in the original script. They added it, I should have known, to try and get a younger audience and it wasn't well understood by the people who wrote it.'

The role was that of a sitar-playing hippie-type character. He also had a singing part – he had to sing 'Don't Blame Me' – which was eventually left on the cutting room floor, along with about twenty minutes of Nicholson's spoken dialogue. He had not done any singing – apart from in the bath – since Marty Landau's acting classes when he did those 'Three Blind Mice' exercises; he wasn't much of a crooner then and he had not improved with age.

So much of his part was cut there seemed hardly any point in leaving him in at all. Nicholson was in awe of Minnelli; this was, after all, his first experience of a mainstream director of Minnelli's vintage, and he began to worry after the first day when it was suggested he might get his hair cut. Whoever heard of a hippie with short hair? His nervousness about working with Minnelli was also tinged with optimism and, for a moment, it looked as though he was going to cross the bridge into the establishment camp. Rex Reed, a writer for the *New York Times* saw Nicholson when he had just finished making *On A Clear Day* and thought that Jack was starting to make establishment noises, cleaning up his image, shaving his stubble and ditching the sandals and hippie clothes. It seemed that he had a foot planted firmly on both sides of the generation gap. A few weeks later, when the film was released, Nicholson's nervous optimism was shattered by the severe cuts made in his role on film. Rex Reed said that Nicholson was 'wasted so criminally, that he should have stayed in bed.'

More disappointment followed when he did not receive an Oscar for his 'best supporting' role in *Easy Rider*. He hoped for one, earnestly, and looked forward to these accolades and people telling him he was good. If he had won, he would certainly not have snubbed the Oscar-night celebrations as did that year's recipient of the Best Actor Award, George C. Scott, for *Patton*.

★ ★ ★ ★ ★

The lure of big money was on the way and director Bob Rafelson had fortunately obtained Jack's signature for another BBS film before the price went up and put him back on track as a counter-culture player, a route which Nicholson analysed in terms of the way he wanted his career to go. There were plenty of promises of big money, fame, glamour, fast cars and all the trappings that any actor might lust towards. It was all on offer as scripts began arriving almost daily. Nicholson simply turned away from the great open doors that lay before him. There was no question that he could have gone into some major productions and worked with some of the more notable directors; he refused point blank, especially after seeing *On a Clear Day*.

He seemed to want to try to remain in the underworld while still reaching out for life's little comforts and luxuries. He felt it was possible and he opted to at least try to stay out of the glitterama; and, as the movie industry would soon learn, this cool-headed assessment of the way he hoped his career would pan out would soon include his rejection of many scripts including *The Godfather*, *The Sting* and *The Great Gatsby*. Any one of them would have promoted him instantly into mainstream Hollywood and even some of his friends thought he was mad. He insisted that he did not believe that any of them was right for him, in spite of the huge money that would be on offer. He was not a mercenary actor. He had made that mistake already, by accepting Vincente Minnelli's offer and he knew, at the end of the day, it was not right; that Sixties way of thinking that rejected anything that had the stamp of establishment on it was also his philosophy. Nor did he agree with the tag that the media had given him, that of anti-hero. 'If there's a constant in my work, it is the principle of affirmation. It's the little guy, and sometimes he may be moved back, squeezed down by the system, but he tries to creep back up, move forward, affirm his life. That's where the vitality and sense of adventure has to come from, that affirmation of basic human values. It's not anti-anything; it's pro, it's positive.'

With quotes like that, Nicholson also became tagged as a 'thinking' actor, and, in 1970, as some of the stronger influences of the Sixties began to fall away with remarkable speed, was another influence that could be troubling any actor: the state of Hollywood itself. During the past decade, cinema audiences had evaporated like snow on a hotplate.

The old Hollywood was in trouble, almost bankrupt of money and ideas and in disarray; they were closing down the back lots, demolishing the massive stages and selling off the vacant land for shopping malls and car parks. There was still enough money and enough going on for a 'hot' property like Nicholson to walk in and begin making fortunes immediately. He calmly turned away their offers and chose to remain with BBS, where all his friends were working.

As with most projects in Hollywood, there was always an overlap between one and another, sometimes of a year or two simply because of the time it takes to get an idea, or a script or a novel, written, financed, budgeted and into production. Bob Rafelson had been toiling with Nicholson's friend and associate Carol Eastman on a script for a new film and as it came towards completion, they began to see it as a perfect vehicle for BBS to capitalize on its success with *Easy Rider*.

Nicholson went down to Rafelson's office where he had a room made permanently available to him. The company had acquired the trappings of one which was doing very nicely. Rafelson, Bert Schneider and Steve Blauner had smart quarters and were seeing very substantial returns on *Easy Rider* and other films, and BBS was growing with it. Their well-equipped offices in Los Angeles came complete with a fifty-seat private theatre, and producers, writers, editors and directors walked determinedly around the corridors, calling each other 'babe' and 'doll'. The mood of the place, and an indication of what they were about, could be gleaned instantly from the huge posters around the reception office walls of blow-ups of the 1968 French student riots. It was as if they had read F. Scott Fitzgerald and were acting out *Crazy Sunday*.

More than that, BBS was populated with his pals. 'Bob and Carol are among my friends whom I had very familial feelings for; it's like we grew up together,' said Nicholson. He had read the script of *Five Easy Pieces*, whose title, it did not need a genius to work out, was designed to link back to *Easy Rider* (though there were no physical connections whatsoever, apart from Nicholson himself, and the thematic stance of *Easy Rider*). Also challenging American values as the new decade turned, the themes of *Easy Rider* were repeated with considerable success, and mercifully *Five Easy Pieces* was devoid of drugs, which were becoming a bore. Carol had written it specially for Nicholson; he could read some of the special nuances that would mean something to him and no one else, nuances that could only come from a friendship and working relationship spanning fifteen years. This is another reason why he likes working with people he knows, because they also know him and his quirks, and Carol knew what to write for him. At this stage in his life, this was as important to Nicholson as searching for the character he was playing. In *Five Easy Pieces*, the biographical elements were there to be discovered, slightly falsified, perhaps, and for those who did not notice them, Nicholson made a point of mentioning them in interviews. It made good copy and helped with the film's publicity; they also gave an insight into what others thought of Nicholson and the way he saw himself, then.

He played Bobby Dupea with explosive sensitivity, as a promising musician who rejects a career to become an oil-rigger; a rebel who, like Nicholson himself, had the chance of taking a particular course in life which would have provided him with comfort and stability, but chose a different route to that which might have been expected of him. His own description was, 'Dupea was an extraordinary person posing as a common man'. So it is another road movie, with a Kerouac-style character, depicting a man who had 'auspicious beginnings' – a line he wrote himself – searching for fulfilment and running into some harsh realities of life. There were other similarities in character which could be applied then and later in that Dupea was to be portrayed, in many ways, as the bastard who walks out of his family and a pregnant girlfriend, refuses to tell the girl he lives with that he loves her or to play the role of a caring son. Dupea did not want to be tied down by anything or anyone – which seemed Nicholson's own philosophy – and he wanted above all to keep on the move. Deep down, however, and reading his own comments about always having to fight for employment and never being superbly successful, one can't help feeling he actually yearned for the stability that steady and better paid work would bring.

Carol Eastman had also written in some other characteristics of Nicholson himself, such as his directness, his honesty and his ability to cut through hypocritical jargon. It was also in this film, when he had a long and exacting monologue at the end, that he finally saw it as what he termed an allegory to his own career: he had the chance of taking a university scholarship but instead chose to take to the road and share his life with some interesting characters, though by this stage of the story in the film itself, Dupea's liberation is being challenged. He is unable to stick to stable relationships and finally he breaks down in front of his father and admits to disappointment with the life he has chosen. It all seemed important at the time, but notwithstanding the subterranean implications, *Five Easy Pieces* established Nicholson beyond doubt as the most effective actor of his kind around, and he was immediately rewarded with a second nomination for an Oscar; he did not win it but his very inclusion meant two in a row for a relative unknown, a situation unheard of in recent Hollywood history.

Critical acclaim also had a pleasant ring to it, with phrases extolling his virtues such as 'one of the few gifted movie actors we have' and 'a superb performance'. *Time* magazine still regarded him as a bit of an upstart, stating that his attempts at humour made him look like a third Smothers Brothers, and his laconic manner appeared to be a handy substitute for acting. His audiences were clearly defined, perhaps more so than any actor around, and they appeared to be generally under thirty, longhaired, with bearded males in the predominance, and 'intelligent' – what a silly description that was – females, usually blonde.

They were quite different in perspective to the followers and reaction of the more conventional actors like Newman and Redford, as the romantic anti-heroes of *Butch Cassidy and The Sundance Kid*, also released in 1969 and which turned Redford into what was termed as a 'bona fide' box-office star. Karen Black, herself blonde and Nicholson's co-star in *Five Easy Pieces* fell in love with him, but they never managed to get together. She was, however, able to describe and explain the scenario that would be repeated in most of Nicholson's most spectacular films – where he personally falls in love with his co-star.

'I was going with someone and he was going with someone so we never made it,' said Karen. 'I think working with someone like Jack, an actor of that quality, turns you on. A lot of leading ladies end up marrying their leading men, simply because they mock-up that guy as their husband while they are working with him. The next thing you know they are getting married. That doesn't happen when someone works with you as a director, and Jack was like a director, too. So we had gotten to be friends and it stayed like that.'

Jack's 'going with someone', as Karen Black put it, was still Mimi, a relationship which which had survived all predictions; and, though it may have stopped a few magic moments between him and Black, it did not prevent an entanglement with another of his co-stars, Susan Anspach. She fell momentarily under his spell and into his bed. Some time later, she said Nicholson had left her with a permanent reminder of their relationship during the making of *Five Easy Pieces* – a son. She gave birth in 1970 to a boy whom she named Caleb James, but it was not until five years later that she said Nicholson was the father. He said he wanted to be pleased at this news, but had been unable to confirm whether it was true or not, since Susan had not requested assistance in the boy's upbringing, nor did she intend to call on him for support.

Nicholson remained fairly ambivalent about the thought of having a son, mainly, he explained, because of Anspach's attitude. He said she was an avant-garde feminist who – when he first met her – was proud of the fact that she already had a child whose father no one knew. 'It took her six years to mention the second child to me, and because of the way she's been towards me, I've never had an avenue to find out whether he was my son or not.'

Susan said that she had no intention of letting him into her life; she did not trust him or his relationships with women, 'from what I observed of him, and I don't think he felt very secure with me because of my straightforwardness'. If they had been on an island, in a one-to-one situation, they would have fallen deeply in love, said Anspach. But they weren't on an island; he had other relationships and she did not wish to complicate her life with his inadequacies and hang-ups. That was why she did not tell him about her pregnancy.

Soon after *Five Easy Pieces* and his affair with Anspach, his own personal life fell into disarray. Mimi found out, of course, that there were other women. There was now the added problem of his huge work schedule, and she was being viewed as the girlfriend of a very successful actor – when time allowed. So Mimi walked out, and suddenly he faced a kind of emotional turmoil he had never before experienced. Now, it was his turn to be hurt. Mimi Machu, who had been in his life for longer than any other woman, apart from Sandra Knight, left him quite suddenly for pastures new, which some said was due to his own attitude to their relationship. Whereas his parting from Sandra had been 'sensibly negotiated', this time Nicholson was left with what was, for him, an odd feeling of what he termed being 'dumped on'. He said, 'I had been with her for three years, in love. After she left I couldn't even hear her name mentioned without breaking out into a cold sweat.' It played on his mind for a time and eventually he had to work out a kind of therapy to get her out of his brain. At thirty-three, he was like a lovesick teenager, which was a strange way for a man of so many experiences to be struck.

$\star$ $\star$ $\star$ $\star$ $\star$

Nicholson was also preparing another project from which he hoped he would emerge as a recognized director, and again it was in part an overhang from that period in 1968 when he seriously considered giving up acting, and moving into writing and directing. It was a story close to his heart and dated back to 1964, before the Vietnam War was being viewed with quite the same violent passions it was arousing in the late Sixties. He had read a novel by Jeremy Larner called *Drive* and there was talk of the book being made into a film, with himself in one of the leading roles. Nothing came of it until 1968, by which time Larner had achieved additional fame as speechwriter for the anti-war Democrat Senator Eugene McCarthy, as he made his challenge against Lyndon Johnson for the Democratic presidential nomination.

In the furore that followed in its wake, Larner targeted McCarthy's speeches towards the campuses and the young of America. He wrote lines like: ' ... whether they came with beards to shave or not, these are kids who react against the violent anti-Americanism of the New Left whom they far outnumber. Though they hate the war and they hate the draft, they still believe America can be beautiful if it lives up to its own principles.' And he got Peter Paul and Mary to sing 'This is Your Land' at McCarthy rallies. The speed at which McCarthy gathered support stunned America and had the campuses screaming with delight, especially when, on 31 March, their arch-enemy Lyndon B. Johnson announced he would not stand for re-election.

This also placed Robert Kennedy in a dilemma. Though he was, like McCarthy, anti-war, he believed Johnson to be invincible; now he too entered the race, much to the chagrin of the McCarthy camp who accused him of muscling in on their act. The months that followed were, of course, some of the most emotional, turbulent, violent and traumatic in recent American history. At the end of it, Robert Kennedy was dead and McCarthy was defeated in the nervousness that engulfed American politics, leaving Hubert Humphrey to battle for the White House with Richard Nixon.

By then, Jack Nicholson had, after a lot of heart-searching, agreed he was going to make a movie out of Larner's book for BBS, with Larner himself as joint scriptwriter. Nicholson could not now appear in the film because he was too old for the original role which had been designated for him, and anyway he wanted to give it his fullest attention as director. He chose two untried actors for leading roles and recruited some of the BBS 'family' for other parts, including Karen Black, Robert Towne and Bruce Dern. It was to be entitled *Drive, He Said* which was taken from the Robert Creely poem:

> *Drive, he sd, for*
> *christ's sake, look*
> *out where yr going*

The basic story is the conflict between two college students: Hector, the basketball star who starts out with no political convictions, and Gabriel, a radical anti-war activist. Underneath some fairly violent anti-war protest, the interaction of the two students' lives are played against each other and include some explicit sex. Hector was having an affair with a professor's wife, whose demands begin to affect his basketball. Gabriel, meanwhile, received his draft papers and begins to take large quantities of drugs to make himself medically unfit, until he verges on insanity. In this state, he attacks the professor's wife and tries to rape her, while she, in turn, has discovered that her former lover had venereal disease and has also made her pregnant!

Apart from the political overtones and undertones, Nicholson knew he was breaking new ground with one specific sex scene in which he showed full-frontal nudity and a fairly complete filming of the sex act itself, still unheard of in the movies, in spite of the musical *Hair*.

The sexual content would not, Nicholson always believed,

guarantee that the film would become a major commercial success; nonetheless he thought it was a film worth making, one which would make a statement and provide BBS with a good return. When he screened it privately for the director of the Cannes Film Festival, he was delighted with the reaction and was duly invited to exhibit *Drive, He Said* at the next festival in May 1971. He eventually flew to Europe, nervous and not knowing what to expect. The lights went down and he sat at the back, trying to gauge the reaction of a packed audience. Word had already gone around about the sex sequence, and there was also some interest in the political content, coming as it did shortly after the attempts at peace in Vietnam and Nixon's pledge to end the war.

As the film ended and the lights went up, Nicholson got a surprising reaction. First there was cheering, then jeering. Blows were exchanged between members of the audience somewhere at the front and the whole scene developed into a riot, with others not wishing to get involved in a fight scrambling for the exit. Nicholson said that the level and violence of the response at Cannes surprised him, then flattered him. Then, when he thought seriously about the reaction, it left him puzzled, because he did not see it as being especially controversial. It was only later when he saw that the comment seemed to centre around the sexual scene that he realized the riot would hurt the picture. He reflected, 'It was a disaster, this movie, and I knew then it was going to set me back.'

The publicity the film attracted in Cannes followed Nicholson back to America where it was due for New York opening in July which, as Karen Black told me later, was an odd time: 'It was a college film and so it goes on release at exactly the same time as the colleges are closing down for the summer and everyone is going home.' This technicality was a minor one. Jack now discovered that the Motion Picture Association of America had given it an 'X' rating and Columbia – who were to release the movie for general distribution – had a policy at that time that they would never release an X-rated picture. That, complained Nicholson, was because of the full-frontal nudity, and the fact that it had someone who 'was fucking and having an audible orgasm. The rating system was corrupt; they said they were protecting the family unit and thus you got "X" if you suck a tit and "GP" if you cut it off with a sword.'

Columbia fought the rating by hiring a major law firm and produced several hundred affidavits from psychiatrists, social experts and church men to support their view that the film should be seen by audiences under eighteen, because it was a realistic look at social behaviour. 'We were seriously examining an event of social consequence,' Nicholson still maintains, 'and it was in no way meant to be exploitive.' Eventually, the rating was revised in America, but Nicholson still faced problems in Canada and Europe. The British censors refused to allow it to be shown unless he removed the sex scene in the back of a car – or, as Nicholson put it, 'they didn't mind the fucking so much, it was the coming they objected to. You could have someone saying 'Screw me' but not 'I'm coming' which was a fascinating reaction.'

The Canadian authorities, in the meantime, asked for forty-five cuts to be made, which Nicholson refused to do, and so by the end of 1971 the film had been shown only in selected cinemas in America and even there, the reaction had been mixed. Even the highly cosmopolitan and very trendy audiences of New York City did not know quite what to say about it; a typical reaction was from May Okon, of the *New York Sunday News* who wrote: 'Jack Nicholson's *Drive, He Said* is how it read on the marquee of the Third Avenue movie house. The audience was predominantly under thirty, dungareed and apparently predisposed to like the film, despite the controversial reviews. The single explicit sex scene elicited deep silence, the full-frontal nude scenes, mostly of males, were greeted by raucous/embarrassed laughter. When it was over, and the house lights went up, there was a sort of bemused smile on the collective face of the audience. I felt it on my own . . . '

The sex scene apart, there was another more fundamental reason why the film was a commercial disaster. The extremes of the anti-war protest movement, which was very central to the film itself, had had their day. When the script was being written, when the film was being filmed, the violence was still very much in vogue; suddenly it had disappeared. The Beatles sang: '*Let it be . . .*' and had switched allegiance from the Maharishi to Mother Mary and then shocked the world by their final break-up, with John Lennon denouncing and renouncing all the Sixties had stood for, from Kennedy to the Beatles themselves. Simon and Art sang 'Bridge Over Troubled Waters', and the fads that had been the preserve of

y 1980, Nicholson had become one of Hollywood's most sought-after actors, scaring the living daylights out of audiences all over the world with his underhand menace in *The Shining* (*Warner Brothers*).

Jack Nicholson's Bizarre Family Secret

For 37 Years, He Never Knew His 'Sister' Was Really His Mother

By RICHARD BAKER

Superstar Jack Nicholson was an illegitmate child — the son of a woman he grew up thinking was his older sister.

And Nicholson himself only learned the bizarre secret in recent years.

"It's true — my sister June was Jack's mother," admitted Lorraine Smith, a New Jersey housewife who pretended to be Nicholson's sister when she knew all along she was really his aunt.

JACK NICHOLSON

"Jack didn't know any of this until he was 37. My mother, father and sister preferred to die with what they thought was their secret."

June Nicholson gave birth to Jack in 1937, when she was 17, but her parents raised the child as their own. He grew up thinking his grandparents were his mother and father.

Then Nicholson received a mysterious letter from the wife of a man named Don Rose in Toms River, N.J. The letter said Rose was Nicholson's biological father.

But even after learning of the 37-year deception, Mrs. Smith said, Nicholson still considers himself her brother.

"What's he supposed to do? Call me Aunt Lorraine?" she said. "He's Uncle Jack to my children and he's Uncle Jack to the daughter June had after she married an airline pilot.

"So, Jack is illegitimate. Who cares? Jack is famous, successful, a superstar and a millionaire."

Nicholson, 43, is still reluctant to talk about his tangled family tree. In interviews he refers to his grandparents as his mother and father, and to Mrs. Smith as his sister.

And recently, he confessed to a reporter, "I have an unusual family background. I'm an illegitimate child."

He wouldn't comment any further, saying, "I want to write about it myself."

One person who insists

JACK'S MOTHER June as a young woman.

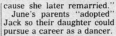

FAMILY PHOTO shows Nicholson's real mother June, left, grand mother Ethel May, Nicholson when he was 4 years old, an uniden tified family friend, and Lorraine Nicholson, on far right.

Nicholson is legitimate is his self-proclaimed father, Don Rose, 70, a semiretired businessman.

Rose says he fell in love with 16-year-old June when he was 26 and a singer with a band.

When they discovered that June was pregnant, Rose claims, he and June were married in Elkton, Md.

However, an ENQUIRER check of marriage records for late 1936 and early 1937 failed to turn up any such license in Elkton.

According to Rose, the couple never told June's mother they had been married, and June returned to live with her parents.

"For months, June disappeared," Rose said.

"I was told that she had gone to New York City to have the baby under another name.

"I guess she got one of those quickie Mexican divorces, be-cause she later remarried."

June's parents "adopted" Jack so their daughter could pursue a career as a dancer.

"But I always kept track of my son," Rose said. "I couldn't contact him because June had sworn me to secre-cy. I didn't say anything."

But eventually Rose's new wife did. Two years after she wrote the fateful letter, Rose said, Nicholson called.

"He asked if I needed any financial help," Rose said. "I said 'No.' We talked for a while, and he was excep-tionally nice."

Mrs. Smith said she doesn't know who Nicholson's fath is but admitted her sister d date Rose.

"Jack lived here in Ne Jersey for the first 17 years his life," she said. "No o was hiding him.

"Where was Don Ro then?"

DON ROSE, who says he's Nicholson's real father, a mires a magazine bearing the star's photo.

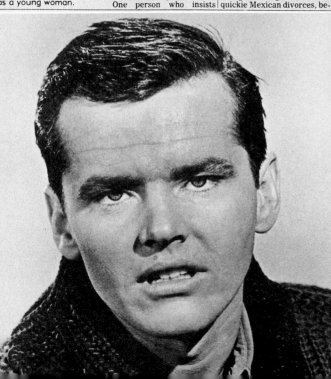

Above: In 1980, the *National Enquirer* ran the story of Nicholson's alleged father, Don Rose, whom Nicholson had never met. Only recently had he discovered that his 'sister' June was in fact his mother (*National Enquirer*). *Left*: In 1960 Nicholson was a struggling young actor, searching, like hundreds of other Hollywood hopefuls, for that elusive break. He thought his chance had come with *Studs Lonigan*, but he was disappointed (*Academy of Motion Picture and Library Arts*).

Above: By 1963, Roger Corman's horrors had become the mainstay of Nicholson's career. In *The Raven*, he appeared with Olive Sturgess. His co-stars were Peter Lorre and Vincent Price (*Kobal*). *Left*: In 1971, after his amiable divorce from Sandra Knight, and his split with Mimi Machu, Nicholson began a relationship with the lovely Michelle Phillips, of Mamas & Papas fame (*Rex Features*). *Below*: Jack Nicholson and his former wife, Sandra Knight, in *The Terror*. One of the few surviving photographs of their joint screen performances (*Private Collection*).

The age of Aquarius was upon them and Nicholson joined in a wave of exploitation films that explored the increasing use of drugs among the youth of the Western world. In *Psych Out* (*above*), based on the LSD craze, he played the character Stoney (*Kobal*). *Easy Rider* made Nicholson an overnight star after fourteen years in the business. While filming the famous campfire scene (*below*), he and Peter Fonda smoked well over 100 real marijuana joints (*Kobal*).

Above: Nicholson, Fonda and Dennis Hopper hit the road in *Easy Rider*, a picture of the moment, of the era, and of its age (*Kobal*). *Below*: Nicholson soon acquired a certain reputation with the ladies. None helped better (or worse, in the case of irate women's libbers) than his appearance with Art Garfunkel in *Carnal Knowledge*, for which he was heavily criticized (*Kobal*).

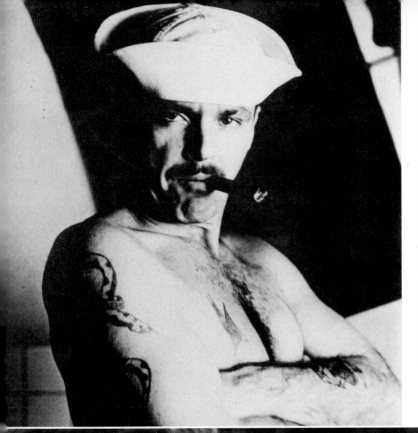

Opposite page (clockwise from top left): In 1984, Anjelica Huston came into Nicholson's life for the first time (Daily Mirror). A classic performance in the highly acclaimed The King of Marvin Gardens (Columbia Pictures). In Five Easy Piecés, he starred with Karen Black, in the role of a drifter, which he said was semi-autobiographical (Ronald Grant). When she gave birth to a son, after Five Easy Pieces (1970), actress Susan Anspach alleged that Jack Nicholson was the father (Daily Mirror). This page (left): Nicholson as the foul-mouthed tough guy with a heart of gold, Billy 'Bad Ass' Buddusky, a performance which won him an Oscar nomination (Columbia). Below: Nicholson's début as director in Drive, He Said (Columbia).

Above: Many critics have listed *Chinatown* as the film of the Seventies, the one which was, in a way, seen as a reflection of the Watergate scandal. It saw a new kind of Nicholson – cool, urbane, like a cleaned-up Bogart (*Kobal*). *Right*: The role for which he became famous, as Randall Patrick McMurphy in *One Flew over the Cuckoo's Nest*, in 1975. It won him his first Oscar (*United Artists*).

counter-culture spread into the young middle classes of America and Europe. The reasons for violence were disappearing and with them went the appeal of films like *Drive, He Said*. Quite simply, the movie had been overtaken by events.

*   *   *   *   *

Dennis Hopper fared no better with his masterpiece, *The Last Movie*, and the outcome, especially in his personal life, would hold some interesting developments for Nicholson. Hopper's film, which he first began writing four years earlier, had now also become a touch dated but that was not the major problem. Universal, who had advanced him the $850,000 were even prepared for the fact that it challenged the American Dream and attacked American society for 'destroying itself', told through its hero – played by Dennis – who is a Hollywood stunt man devoured by his quest for big cars, swimming pools and gorgeous girls.

It is set in Peru where the stunt man has been making a movie. When the film is complete and the company has pulled out, he stays behind and watches with awe as the local Peruvian Indians – who had been watching the film being made – begin to re-enact it. Into this somewhat bizarre plot, Hopper built in his odd interjections designed to remind the cinema audience that it was only a movie they were watching, that nothing was real. 'Every time I got them involved with the story,' Hopper explained, 'I'd come back at them and say, "Ha, ha, it's only a movie. ..."'

The usual kind of mayhem followed Hopper, as was expected in Hollywood, who noted that his cast included some of the most conspicuous individualists in the business. On the first day the film was already assuming some real-life events which were remarkably similar to those which the script itself called for, as some 10,000 local residents turned out to watch. They were fascinated by the arrivals: Peter Fonda turned up in a huge sheepskin coat and carrying an ivory-handled .44–40, which had once belonged to Tom Mix. Sylvia Miles, fresh from her role as the bleach-blonde prostitute in *Midnight Cowboy*, flashed in wearing a dazzling chrome catsuit. Russ Tamblyn appeared in cowboy boots and a fully grown Afro hair-do, and actor Severn Darden, who had just learned his next job was to play the lead in a revival of *Dracula*, was going around practising vampire attacks on every female member of the cast.

Writer Brad Darrach, who had flown down for an interview with Hopper, described the scene that developed: 'By mid-afternoon, the games became serious. Somebody made a cocaine connection and a number of actors laid in a large supply at bargain prices – seven dollars for a packet that cost seventy dollars in the States. By ten p.m. certain members of the company were sniffing coke or had been turned on by acid or speed or grass. By midnight, much of the cast had drifted off to bed in twos and threes. At two a.m., I was awakened by screams. A young actress who had taken LSD was having a bummer. At three a.m. I heard rapping at the window beside my bed and another young woman whom I hadn't met was standing on the window ledge of the hotel. It was raining and her nightgown was drenched. "Do you mind if I come in?" she asked vaguely. . . . '

It got worse. One actor took so many drugs in quick succession he almost died. Then, during a scene involving horses, a beautiful chestnut stallion was scared by gunfire, bolted, fell off a twenty-five-foot wall and broke its back. One of the crew pulled out a Colt .45 and shot the beast through the head to put it out of its misery and a group of local Indians gleefully pulled out their knives and instantly began butchering the stallion for its meat. Two of the cast fainted and most of the rest repaired to the nearest bar. Hopper pressed on. Having had the bloody debris removed, he called the cast to order and began work. He appeared calm and cool-headed. That night to Michelle Phillips he broke down and cried like a baby. To the cast, he gave no outward clue to his inner feelings and on the final day when he completed a particularly difficult scene in two takes and called 'Cut and print', everyone on the set cheered.

Those who had been watching him work believed that in spite of the traumas, Hopper the actor was a star, and Hopper the director had completed an extraordinarily good film which, according to one description, included some 'hauntingly beautiful footage'. He spent weeks editing and was personally convinced it was a work of art; he made gross statements that he had the movie that would end all movies. The reality represented the truth about movie-making itself, and a final shattering of all the illusions that had ever been presented to a cinema audience, for, seemingly, he had not realized that he had built into his masterpiece a piece of self-destruct mechanism. He returned to Los Angeles and then caught a plane to Europe where he had been invited to show the finished article at the Venice Film Festival at which *The Last Movie* was voted the best picture on exhibition.

He came back to Hollywood glowing, and totally unprepared for the reaction he received from Universal. 'They wanted me to change the ending, of course,' said Hopper. 'They wanted a dramatic ending where I kill off the central character and they also didn't like me making fun of the audience. They didn't care how I did it, but just kill him off.' He refused and Universal countered that they would merely give it a limited showing.

Hopper went on television to denounce Universal for suppressing his film and *The Last Movie* became his last for a long, long time. He upset Lew Wasserman, head of Universal, and one of Hollywood's heavyweights, which did not augur well for his future as a director. Nicholson sympathized but was not entirely supportive. 'You don't take someone's bread,' he said, 'and then walk across the street and say "Fuck you". There has got to be some kind of responsibility to deliver what they think they are buying.'

Hopper was in deep depression again – his personal life had once again foundered, and it worked to the benefit of Nicholson. In October, Hopper married Michelle Phillips who had been living with him for some months. She and Hopper were convinced they were in love, but between engagement and marriage her passion for him began to cool. Nevertheless, the wedding went ahead with two hundred or more of their Hollywood friends attending.

At the same time, Michelle also wanted to return to singing and Dennis found her a job, backing Leonard Cohen. She flew up to Nashville for two weeks' work and called Dennis from her hotel room exactly eight days after their wedding.

'I'm not coming back,' she said.

Dennis was distraught. He had not for one minute, he said, imagined this could happen and they had even planned to move to Mexico where he was in the process of renovating a house for them; the bedrooms were complete and he had made a nursery for Michelle's daughter, China, never to be occupied. He was proud of that house, a sprawling ranch in Taos. It was, after all, the place where D.H. Lawrence spent his final days in the company of Mabel Dodge Luhan – the heiress whose home in Greenwich Village had been the spawning ground of some of America's most famous pre-World War I radical and literary figures – and, thus, provided an oddly suitable setting for the desolate position in which Hopper found himself.

'I just can't live with you any longer,' said Michelle, who could not handle his swings of temperament and, coupled with her own desire to find a career in films, she had resolutely determined not to return to Dennis.

The marriage was over and so, for the moment, was Hopper's career. He had burned his bridges in Hollywood and took off for the seclusion of Taos to hide away, his life having come to another dead end, cursed by his own self-destructiveness and sheer bad luck.

Michelle moved on and soon was to be seen around Los Angeles with Nicholson, who had been a friend for years. She was depressed and Nicholson, who had similar feelings himself offered her a shoulder. It developed. One day not long afterwards, Hopper got a call from Nicholson; he was telephoning, he said, out of politeness to tell him he and Michelle were together.

Dennis said, 'Best of luck, man . . . it's over between her and me anyhow.'

Although he was made exceedingly wealthy by the proceeds of *Easy Rider*, Hopper was still brooding and bitter, but life had taken several new turns for Nicholson. Michelle, in many ways, was like Sandra and Mimi in terms of their sophisticated looks. She, too, was a determined character with a personality to match. What she wanted more than anything was the relaunching of her career, which had flagged since the Mamas & the Papas split up. Mama Cass had done better than any of them with her solo career, but then tragically died so soon afterwards. Michelle wanted to break into films and was prepared to accept Jack's help. They talked about a project together with director Hal Ashby, who was trying to raise finance for a film based upon a remake of *The Postman Always Rings Twice* (which Nicholson later made with Jessica Lange), but MGM pulled out because they did not think Michelle Phillips was a big enough name, not apparently appreciating that she was once a starring member of a world-famous singing quartet. Ashby was keen because of the sparking relationship that existed between Nicholson and Michelle – but eventually the script was put on the back burner.

Nicholson's close friend Bruce Dern saw this as one of the developing problems with what seemed to be heading towards a husband and wife relationship; with two people in the same business – as had been the case with Sandra and Mimi – the pressures on their life together were aggravated by the success of one member of the partnership, while the other was still struggling. It was a rather one-sided affair. With the income from the three films he had completed in eighteen months, he had stretched himself to buy a house in Beverly Hills. It was located on the twisting Mulholland Drive, on top of Hollywood's highest hill in a compound of properties, one of which was owned and occupied by his idol, Marlon Brando, with whom he shared the security gate. Charlton Heston lived on the other side and Warren Beatty was also a near neighbour. The stunning two-storey villa of stucco construction was carved into a cliff overlooking not merely Beverly Hills but all of greater Los Angeles. From a vantage point directly across the road, there was a spectacular night-time vision of a 100-mile carpet of lights in the San Fernando valley.

He cherishes the house to this day, and it would become the scene of some of the most private and exclusive Hollywood parties. He installed his ornamental collections of symbolic pigs, and began his art collection and, of course, his library. Reading was and is one of his absorbing pleasures and on the bookshelves in the winter of 1971 and 1972 were: *The Complete Works of Marcel Duchamp*, Shakespeare, Jules Feiffer's *Harry the Rat with Women*, *The Primal Scream*, a selection of Hermann Hesse, *Edgar Cayce on Reincarnation* and *The Group Sex Tapes*. His substantial album collection contained a varied selection, including the Rolling Stones, Dylan, Cat Stevens, George Harrison's *All Things Must Pass*, Strauss waltzes recorded by Fritz Reiner, and *Rimsky-Korsakov's Greatest Hits*. He parked a Mercedes 600 on the driveway, although the battered VW was not discarded, merely put away for occasional use for fear of being accused of reverse affectation. Michelle Phillips moved in; according to Bruce Dern, Jack seemed to want to believe that they were *the* couple, made for each other; he saw them as having it all, on his own terms.

Jack Nicholson, movie star, had at last arrived.

8

A Certain Reputation

There is in every successful actor's life a moment when he acquires a certain aura with which he may be tagged for the rest of his career, and now was the time for Nicholson. His standing as a spokesman for counter-culture, by then rampant among the middle classes at large, was already established. Next, he became a symbol of male chauvinism, the label which was being bandied about with the corresponding rise in women's liberation, and Nicholson discovered an interesting phenomenon 'that occasionally you play a character that creates such an impression with the audience that suddenly you are affected by the feedback and it can change your life.' The role that did it for him was that of Jonathan, the mindless sexual malcontent in *Carnal Knowledge*, which was another kind of anti-hero. He kept saying he did not like the title of anti-hero, but it wouldn't go away.

Anti-heroes were in vogue and they were appearing in varying degrees of regression from the romantic heroes of the silver screen whom they replaced. His attitudes to women and sex were to be examined and pigeon-holed largely, as he said, because of his interpretation of Jonathan in the very commercially and intriguingly titled *Carnal Knowledge,* which delivered all the sexual promise that the title suggests, with a cacophony of adventures in lust and love, sufficient for some to consider it worthy of being banned altogether. It was one of a number of sexually explicit films which appeared in the wake of the abolishment of the Hollywood Production code in 1969 – the one that had enforced the unwritten rule that bedroom scenes must be performed with one foot on the floor.

Apart from putting his own sexuality under the microscope, it also put him in line for considerable abuse, appearing as it did at a time when the feminist movement and the liberation of women was emerging as a vital force in the social scene of London and New York, followed and copied rapidly elsewhere in the western world. In fact, he faced a double-edged attack because *Drive, He Said* and *Carnal Knowledge* came on the circuits at virtually the same time and he was being judged in both quarters – as Nicholson, the director of a film whose sex scenes had caused a riot in Cannes, and as Nicholson, the actor in a film in which, said one critic, 'the obscenity and abuse of women continued through scene after scene.' It must also be said that for all the controversy, the complaints, the indifferent reviews and its lack of quality, *Carnal Knowledge* became one of the big box-office successes of the Seventies, rating among *Variety's* list of 'all-time rental champs' in May 1977.

How much Nicholson deliberately fed to the media for the purposes of publicizing the two films is difficult to assess. It was around this time that he made his eminently quotable quote to *Newsweek*, 'I've balled all the women, I've done all the drugs, I've drunk every drink' which he later corrected as being a slight exaggeration. By then, there was sufficient evidence from his own testimony for the headline writers in the tabloids to begin suggesting that their new-found star had secretly been one of wildest men of Hollywood, without realizing that the secrecy was not entirely intentional; it was merely that since no one knew who he was until a couple of years ago, they had not taken the slightest bit of notice of his private life. Additionally, it was noticed that he had just become friendly with that other Great Seducer, Warren Beatty, whom he met while filming *Carnal Knowledge* in Canada, and with whom he struck up an instant and enduring friendship; it needed no help from Beatty for his own reputation to be catalogued.

However, unlike many before him, for whom the studio publicity machines swung into creative activity with inventions about a particular star's personal attributes and shielding the bad ones, Jack was totally honest with preliminary seekers of 'The Truth about Jack Nicholson'. He made no attempt to glamorize himself – even to the point of refusing to wear make-up for his films – and wanted no truck with artificial, publicity-inspired biographies that the studios were used to pumping out.

At the time, he did not even have a publicist, which in itself was virtually unheard of for a up and coming star of his stature. He preferred to tell it straight, the way it was, the way he saw it at that precise moment in time, and, in doing so, and by refusing to play the Hollywood game, he left himself somewhat exposed. That very point arose in January 1972, when he agreed to do The *Playboy* Interview – well known for the incisive questioning of its subject – and the interviewer himself put a very valid question, 'Why are you spilling your guts in this interview?' Why, indeed. Not once but several times in the Seventies. His reply was this: 'At this moment I'm wishing I wasn't. Maybe because I know when the interview is read it will add as much confusion as to who I am as it will reveal the truth.'

The magic appeal of Nicholson the actor, became as it usually does with new found stars, bound up with his personal and private life. In later years, of course, he began to react to this kind of media attention, treating less kindly nosey reporters and rejecting questions of a personal nature to the point where he would only talk generally about his work. In this early stage, he did not hold back. He told one interviewer who asked if there were any areas which were out of bounds for questions: 'Nothing is out of bounds. You take your chance and I'll take mine' and the writer recalled that the smile was flashing cynically by the time the aroma of marijuana had disappeared. Perhaps it might well be said that if he was to take his place in the higher echelons of his chosen profession, alongside his hero Brando, and to be compared with other Hollywood actors past and present, it was almost a necessary evil that he should lay himself bare and allow his fans and the media, and subsequently biographers, to take a look behind a few closed doors and peer inside his mind. He opened many doors, displayed a few skeletons. At the time, he seemed more willing to do so than some of his contemporaries and, as a result, assumed a much more colourful and controversial hue which merely served as an additional fillip to his rebel image.

*　＊　＊　＊　＊　＊*

Carnal Knowledge was the type of film which even a cursory glance at the script would warn its reader that it was stuffed with very prickly thorns that would, as likely as not, get up the noses of a varied cross-section of the community, ranging from the censors to women's-libbers. In 1971, when it was released, the battle for women's rights was surging forward; on 6 March of that year 4 000 people marched on Number 10 Downing Street to present a petition for equality. The Pill had provided sexual freedom, abortion had become available virtually on demand in England, women were at last being made generals in the US Army, and organized groups of female campaigners brought their fight out into the open.

Fresh from their involvement with the male-dominated anti–war movements, women activists – unkindly dubbed political lesbians in Washington – used that experience as a base to launch their own power-base, urged on by such strangely inspiring publications such as *The Myth of the Vaginal Orgasm* and *The Politics of Housework*, until the call was taken up the popular women's magazines. Certain groups named their enemies. The likes of Hugh Hefner and Norman Mailer were popular targets. Nicholson joined them on the strength of his performance in *Carnal Knowledge* which he went to some lengths to point out was a performance, played to the script. 'I didn't editorialize,' he responded angrily when challenged about his views. 'I was just doing my job and anyway, it was a legitimate representation of male attitudes at the time. I myself try to duck conversations about feminism; it is all so dehumanizing.' A lot of women thought he was making excuses for himself and for his contribution to sexism through the film role. The whole business just blew up in his face and twenty years later, he had still not lived it down.

Carnal Knowledge was written by Jules Fieffer, then famed for his satirical cartoons and commentaries on modern America in the *Village Voice* and as a playwright of note and notoriety. It was based upon a series of so-called cartoon plays, which found popularity off Broadway in the Sixties for the way in which they lampooned current trendy people who were really up to their ears in self-indulgence, be it in sex, material possession or political causes. The film was produced and directed by Mike Nichols, the former comedian acclaimed for revitalizing the careers of Elizabeth Taylor (who won an Oscar for her performance) and Richard Burton with his direction of them both in *Who's Afraid of Virginia Woolf?*. Mr Nichols had already done much to extend the boundaries of artistic licence in the use of sex – obscenity, even – as a selling point. The rating 'SMA' – Suitable for Mature Audiences – was introduced in America especially for the blitz of four-lettered words in *Who's Afraid of Virginia Woolf?*. His most recent success was *The Graduate*, for which he gained the further distinction of putting Hoffman in bed with his best friend's mother, though his underpants were clearly visible. He had provided other sexual milestones, like the full frontal of Paula Prentiss in *Catch-22* and there seemed few other avenues of sexual shock that he could possibly explore, until he and Fieffer got together for *Carnal Knowledge*.

He chose Nicholson for lead primarily because he thought he possessed the on-screen presence that was needed to bring the main protagonist in this film, the part of Jonathan, alive with the very necessary degree of devious sexuality. To that he added for the second male character Art Garfunkel – one of the world's most popular singers – and two of the most attractive female stars around at the time, Candice Bergen and Ann-Margret, whom Nicholson, as Jonathan, brings to the very brink of suicide in the film which spanned a period through the Forties and Seventies.

Bergen – the one who made that oft-quoted description of Nicholson's cobra-like eyes – played the soft and sensitive Susan who, in the film, married Jonathan's best friend, Sandy (Art Garfunkel), although by then she had already fallen victim to Jonathan's bedroom technique. His own description of her was that she was 'a good piece of ass' and with lines like that, the burgeoning women activists could be well inspired to protest. Jonathan himself married Bobbie, the Ann-Margret character whom he eventually discarded with callous disregard for her feelings, which had survived his endless string of affairs and which he recorded on colour slides, entitled 'Ball Busters on Parade', showing himself in various stages of intercourse with his women. It was while watching the slide show that Sandy discovered the betrayal of his wife and his former best friend.

The film is about betrayal, and, as one unhappy reviewer submitted, 'the impotence of the American male'. There was a sufficiently mixed bag of reviews and reactions to *Carnal Knowledge* to send audiences rushing to see it, an aspect which might or might not have been affected by the revelation that Ann-Margret, who had at that point been enjoying a reputation of being a 'sex kitten', as the tabloids said in the Sixties, was appearing nude for the first time on screen. Again, it is worth reminding ourselves that this divesting of clothes before a cinema audience was still a rare event, except in private cinema clubs for underground movies or porno houses, and it was another year or more before *Last Tango in Paris* burst on to the screens – and off again in some protesting parts – with its first public display of male-female buggery, assisted by a half pound of best butter. Still, *Carnal Knowledge* provided sufficient offensive matter for the American judiciary to become involved. The film had been banned within the state of Georgia and the producers fought the ruling all the way to the Supreme Court, where the decision was overturned.

Ann–Margret received an Oscar nomination as Best Supporting Actress for this film and was bitterly disappointed not to get the award. She blamed the controversiality of the subject matter, plus a great deal of 'jealousy ... which was to me incredible. I was shocked. I think it was horrendous to overlook the work that was done and I wish people could get rid of all their prejudices and jealousies and just see it as a piece of work.' She praised Nichols to the hilt, and was similarly enthusiastic about Nicholson; both knew she was extremely nervous about doing the part in the first place, and 'Jack just went out of his way to be helpful.' There was one scene that stuck in Ann–Margret's mind and she has been reminded of it since in two or three later movies of Nicholson. It was a moment where she was dealing with a difficult shot, while lying on the bed, and she had to psyche herself up to get the correct emotions. Nicholson solved the whole thing by bouncing violently on the bed, throwing pillows at her and yelling at the top of his voice.

'I actually got frightened of him. I thought he was going out of his mind,' she said. 'It was just so unselfish of him to help me like that. ...' Furthermore, he needed no personal psyching of his own emotions to get to that state, Ann–Margret recalled. He could just go straight into that kind of scene and come out of it looking relaxed and laid back, which he achieved by complete concentration. Nicholson was assured of trouble with women's rights in the very last scene where he was in the company of a prostitute played by Rita Moreno, having put his women through various forms of sexual and emotional humiliation. The words Moreno had to speak as she indulged his fantasies to achieve an erection were tantalizingly provocative: 'You are a real man ... [with] an inner power so strong that every act no matter what is more proof of that power. That's what all women resent. That's why they try to cut you down. It takes a true woman to understand that the purest form of love is to love a man who denies himself to her . . . a man who inspires worship because he has no need for any woman because he has himself. And who is better? More beautiful, more powerful, more perfect – you're getting hard – more strong, more masculine, extraordinary, more robust – it's rising, it's rising – more virile, domineering, more irresistible. It's up in the air. . . .'

The film ended with the camera close-up on Jonathan's smiling, leering face, complete in his fantasy world in which he had expected his women to join him throughout his life. It was only a movie, as Hopper would say, but the aftermath contained elements of realism for Nicholson, who suddenly found himself being allied with the character to such a degree that he was being questioned deeply about his own sexuality and relationships with women. However, much he tried he would never quite live it down, and periodically his mercurial private life in the ensuing twenty years merely added to the image.

Carnal Knowledge provided him with the makings of that certain reputation; Nicholson's own subsequent actions merely served to consolidate it through his most revealing interview with *Playboy*, the frankness of which seemed to surprise even the highly experienced interviewer himself, contributing editor Richard Warren Lewis, who made that telling comment/question 'Why are you spilling your guts out? . . .'

For instance, when Lewis made a fairly innocuous reference to the theme of *Drive, He Said*, Nicholson's explanations turned into an admission of certain sexual problems he had experienced in the past: 'Some critics think that I oversimplified by reducing everything to sex but if you look at the real facts of your life, you'll find if you're not releasing your sexual energy you're in trouble. If you take a trip and you're away for three days and you don't relate to a chick then pretty soon that's all you're thinking about; within three days in a new town you are thinking 'Why can't I find a beaver in a bar? . . .' It's not that sex is the primary element of the universe but when it's unfulfilled, it will affect you.'

Nicholson gave as an example his own recent experiences prompted by the collapse of his long-standing relationship with Mimi

Machu. 'It ended before I was ready to be out of it. She felt that it wasn't worth her time; she'd had it. It was all very sudden, very abrupt and I was unprepared. I couldn't cope with all that emotion that was released as a result of being cashiered.'

In the weeks that followed and in spite of his workload, Nicholson subjected himself to sexual therapy to get over the broken relationship. The therapy was based upon the very positive theme of Austrian psychologist Wilhelm Reich that was structured to eliminate sexual hang-ups: 'to soften and relieve the holding areas of what Reich described as body armour which comes from pleasure denial or pleasure fear'. Nicholson explained: 'When you dam up energy, sexual or otherwise, you begin to devour yourself. Our society is unhealthy, according to Reich, because we tend to fragment and separate sexuality. We talk about it in terms of scoring; we have ass men, tit men, cunt men and lip men. These are partialisms.'

This brought the conversation nicely to the subject of *Carnal Knowledge* because wasn't that exactly the subject matter of the film? It was, Nicholson agreed, and Jules Fieffer, whose *Playboy* interview had appeared in a previous issue, mentioned that he had written the line for Jonathan that 'Guys don't really like girls.' It was something Nicholson took issue with because it was only true of some men. 'I have an equal number of male and female friends,' he said, 'and I have many non-sexual relationships with women. I am not trying to get into the pants of every women I'm interested in . . . Jonathan in *Carnal Knowledge* is exactly the opposite. I don't think he knows how to communicate with women beyond screwing them.'

Nicholson agreed that he had gone through the same stage himself, and had experienced a lot of infantilism sexually. 'When I began sexual activity in earnest, my point of view was simply to try to seduce everyone I could. At that time, I had trouble with *ejaculatio praecox*. A lot of men have this problem. I had it almost exclusively until I was twenty-six or so. You find yourself making it with a chick and, like, you poke her eight times and right away you're coming. It's a chore trying to go through to the second orgasm and not lose your erection. In desperation you find yourself getting the chicks off without balling them through manipulation of some kind, or you find yourself getting with another chick to share the load with you and to keep yourself from saying, "I've got a major problem here, man. I'm not fucking for shit."'

'I would never tell you this story now if I was still in that situation. I didn't know the story when I was there. I'd say to myself, 'Well I haven't balled anybody for three days and I'm filled up', and then I'd have a premature ejaculation, which is really a form of impotence. The root of it all was some kind of pleasure denial; it was pretty unsatisfactory for the women involved. Somehow, in the sexual experience I was making the woman into a sort of a mom – an authoritarian female figure; that made me feel inadequate to the situation, small and childish. I indulged myself in a lot of masturbatory behaviour. I solved none of these problems in therapy. I worked them out for myself but any of them might reappear. . . .'

And so it was true. The women he came together with in longer relationships were chosen, if that is the right word, for their strengths. It seemed that Nicholson's search for female company had much to do with the domination that women had in his early life when, devoid of a father, he was brought up by three fairly strong women. He sought their imagery in his women, though not uncommonly his less serious affairs and one-night stands tended to be with more attractive women whose sexuality was instantly obvious; it was if he was on the one hand seeking a dominant mother-figure to attach himself to, while having secret liaisons with others, like a boy stealing a kiss behind the cycle-shed at school, only it wasn't a kiss he was stealing.

*   *   *   *   *

The sexual scene in general, as it was viewed in London or New York or Paris, was one which had by 1972 taken on new liberalistic tones; swingers and swoppers, singles bars and one-night stands were the norm rather than the exception. Nicholson admitted that there were people around – especially outside of Hollywood and the upper middle-class set of New York who were not part of the pervasive sexual environment. Nichols and Fieffer, he reckoned, had assumed they were writing about very social people, working New Yorkers, professional men meeting women and having cock-tails, having affairs, and constantly judging and rejudging their own sexuality, trying to find some substance in it, trying to make conquests within it. There were millions of men like that in New York and cities all over the world. 'But excluding the non-sexual person, I think we must assume that the characters played by Artie Garfunkel and myself are probably far more representative than most people care to admit. Obviously they don't represent people who live in a rural area; a man couldn't be as openly promiscuous as Jonathan in a small-town environment. He would be branded a social outcast and considered predatory.'

Once again, fact merged with fiction. True life superseded and became interspersed with fictional characters just it has done so often in the past in Hollywood with life imitating art imitating life – and vice versa – and though occasionally unintentionally, directors have themselves blatantly, sometimes cruelly, chosen certain actors for certain roles because of their personal affiliation to the character to be portrayed.

Given Nicholson's insistence that he did not editorialize, and simply spoke the lines, it was a strange blurring of realities that shook him in the reaction to the film, where women activists – and men who saw him as some kind of a hero – clearly believed that this was a definition of the true Jack Nicholson. Nicholson was stuck with it thereafter, being cast in the magazines and newspapers in the mode of a leery rebel, with two basic aims in life – to fight the establishment and have lots of women. It was a picture of his past in many ways; his life had now – at the age of thirty-five – become a touch more settled.

The desire was still present, though Michelle Phillips had been something of a settling – but not restrictive – influence. She had been a positive influence on his life since soon after she split with Dennis Hopper. But Michelle was not a slippers-by-the-fireside soul, waiting by the kitchen sink for her man to come home from work. She was still a free spirit and a model of the age; a woman on the move and who needed a career of her own so that she need not be the slightest bit reliant on others, especially men. She entered her relationship with Nicholson on 'agreed terms' in that neither wanted to be completely tied down and that they would not live together as such. 'I told her up front "Look, I don't want to constantly define the progress of this relationship. Let's keep it instantaneous." It was working beautifully,' said Nicholson. 'I had spent a certain amount of time completely unattached and I found that being with someone makes me enjoy my achievements more. I liked sharing things ... and I discovered that expanding sexuality was not most satisfied through promiscuity but through continuously communicating with someone specifically.'

Marriage was discussed but it was not a proposition either especially contemplated, and perhaps especially not Michelle, who had been rather troubled of late by relationships which had become more demanding than she wanted. Nicholson had long used the phrase when asked by reporters about his matrimonial intentions that 'I don't have a marriage policy'. His view was that since nothing was a certainty at that stage in a relationship between one person and another, there seemed little point in pre-supposing matrimony until it finally became a natural course. The perception was correct in Michelle's case and they never would come to the point where marriage seemed the right thing to do. Like his previous 'communications' with Mimi Machu, it had its tempestuous moments, often through Jack's inability to stay totally faithful, and they were able to slam respective doors in each other's faces because Nicholson had an adjoining property, the smaller house in the Mulholland Drive compound, into which Michelle could go to find peace during trying times. 'He bought it to try to save their relationship,' his friend Robert Towne remembers. 'She seemed to be wanting to get out of the affair. A few of us had seen it coming – so he thought that by having her own place she could retain her independence. He was trying hard to keep her but I could see it wasn't going to work.' Michelle was with Nicholson during her own emotional difficulties, when her daughter, China, had to go into hospital to have a tumour removed. They were spasmodically close but there were also intermissions of coolness between them, though Nicholson was sufficiently fond of both Michelle and her daughter to have photographs of both handy to show friends and interviewers, and remind them who she was.

Two years after he and Michelle got together they had, in her view, drifted apart, and Nicholson's workload had not helped. The affair ended without bitterness or malice, even though Michelle was about to move in with one of Nicholson's best friends and near neighbours, Warren Beatty, in a repeat performance of what happened when Michelle left Hopper and found companionship with Nicholson. Both Michelle and Beatty both felt guilt when they decided to take up together but they need not have worried on Nicholson's account. He said that they both did exactly the right thing in the way they broke the news. He reckoned Beatty's 'school-principal parents' would have been proud of the way he handled the situation. And Michelle, 'being the lady that she is, took the trouble to call and ask if I had any feelings about them going together which I did have – I thought it was fabulous because I am fond of them both. Michelle is a real stand-up lady, incapable of anything dishonourable.' Anyway, it all worked out for the best because Anjelica Huston was about to come into his life and if at that moment Nicholson seemed less inclined towards the rakish behaviour of past years, there were still some high profile events waiting in the wings. ...

★ ★ ★ ★ ★

Professionally, the year of *Carnal Knowledge* continued with much the same frenetic work schedule as the previous twelve months and he made two more films in quick succession, both of which were with former Cormanites in the rebel alliance at BBS, his professional family circle of friends, and it remains even now something of a mystery why he continued in this area of film-making when mainstream possibilities – and upwards of $250,000 a film – were clearly available. It can only be that he wanted to remain in the relatively unglamorous 'new wave' of Hollywood, of which there had been much talk and of which he could certainly be classed a member. It might also be said that one or two people in that group had made, or were about to make, very substantial fortunes for their efforts. It was around 1971 and 1972 that this group of men of similar ages and similar backgrounds – several from the Corman school of movie-making – came to the fore with a variety of projects, some of which were in some kind of trouble, either with scripts, money, production or distribution. Others were doing very nicely; either way, there was always someone around when needed. Martin Scorsese says that they all helped each other out in their misery, advised each other and influenced each other. He tells the story that one day, much later, he was editing *New York, New York* and one of the gang came in and looked at it and said, 'Marty, if the man and the woman walk away together at the end of the film it will add ten million dollars at the box office.' Scorsese replied, 'Yes, I know but it just doesn't work for this story.'

Some were doing better than others and Francis Ford Coppola was the catalyst, creating a piece of cinematographic history with *The Godfather*. Coppola had won an Academy Award for his script of *Patton* in 1969, but since then his star had waned. He had directed two more pictures, *Finian's Rainbow* and *The Rain People* for Paramount, which the studio's production chief, Robert Evans said did not make enough money to pay for the advertising on one of them, and, more so than ever now, success was judged by the money the film made – not by its artistic acclaim. Evans, however, chose Coppola to direct *The Godfather* purely because he was of Italian origin. Thus, according to one pundit, the film became the Trojan horse of the new wave; it broke into the closed, closeted and cosy Hollywood society and once inside, Coppola unlocked the gates for the rest of them. He also, incidentally, earned $8 million as his cut from *The Godfather*.

The Schneider-Blauner-Rafelson alliance which had already astonished Hollywood with its trio of Nicholson films, *Easy Rider*, *Five Easy Pieces* and *Drive, He Said* – even though the latter was not a box-office success – also financed another ex-Cormanite, Peter Bogdanovich for his creation, *The Last Picture Show*. Unkind factions in Hollywood made the obvious comparison between his and Dennis Hopper's *The Last Movie*, which had still not achieved a commercial release. However, *The Last Picture Show* was not about the movies (it was a story about a small town in Texas), and as Nicholson correctly perceived, their tune would change when Bogdanovich put his film out on the pre-release Bel Air circuit of private screening rooms where much excitement was created.

Overnight, he became the hottest director in town – just as Nicholson had become the hottest actor a couple of years earlier. *The Last Picture Show* attracted eight Oscar nominations and, by then, Bogdanovich was already making his next, *What's Up Doc?* starring Barbra Streisand and Ryan O'Neal; this was quickly followed by *Paper Moon* and thus he achieved his third major success in a row. Very soon, Mr Bogdanovich was, like Nicholson, also able to move in with the elite. In 1972, he purchased a substantial $366,000 house opposite Hugh Hefner's ridiculously flamboyant Playboy Mansion to which he and others in the new wave became regular visitors. He met and fell in love with centrefold model

Dorothy Stratten, and there began another tragic sequence of events that has gone into the annals of Hollywood history. . . .

★   ★   ★   ★   ★

The establishment was both annoyed and fascinated by these upstarts from independent studios who were trying to break the mould of ultimately disastrous family-audience pictures, for which demand had ended long, long ago. In the end, the establishment won because the upstarts were eventually carried off by fame and fortune towards their own individual destinies to the point where they would eventually become the establishment by the sheer weight of their bank balances and their only recognition of their rebellious past lay in their public unorthodoxy – such as wearing sneakers with their evening suits.

For the time being, Nicholson remained with them in the back-waters of the rebellion and subversion, loyal to his BBS comrades, having rejected a role in *The Great Gatsby*, which once again went to Robert Redford, similarly turning down an offer from Fred Zinnemann for the lead in the film of Freddie Forsyth's novel, *The Day of the Jackal*, seemingly because he did not think the characterization of the Jackal was suitable for his style. He still talking about concentrating his efforts towards directing – the same road taken by Coppola and Bogdanovich with very profitable results. He certainly confounded the pundits by his next appearance on celluloid, especially with the knowledge of the type of films he had turned down. He agreed to the lead in *A Safe Place*, produced by Bert Schneider and directed by his old friend Henry Jaglom who had appeared in *Drive, He Said*. This was Jaglom's own first attempt at directing and he persuaded one of Nicholson's idols, Orson Welles to co-star. The film was about the generation gap, a phrase in such common usage then that it could be applied as a reason for anything – except perhaps this particular film which Derek Sylvester described as 'an indigestible mound of yesterday's lukewarm whimsy'. Enough said.

Jack had been charitable enough to do this for an old friend just as he did the following month for another one, Bob Rafelson, who brought him an intriguing script called *The King of Marvin Gardens*, which Nicholson saw instantly was another in typical Rafelson

123

style, that of an enigmatic drama, a one-off picture, unlike anything that had gone before and which, given a touch of luck and a fair wind, might just capture the audiences' imagination and take off, just as *Five Easy Pieces* had done. At best, it required courage for an actor at such a vital stage of his career to take it on. Nicholson did not need to be asked twice. Another of his compatriots, Bruce Dern, joined him and the result was another movie which received 'cult status', i.e., lots of intellectual analysis but very little reaction at the commercial box office. Nicholson and Dern were highly commended as players providing a 'superb metaphor for the American Dream, the dream of getting rich quick with a minimum of effort and a maximum of manipulation'.

Even before those two movies were released, Nicholson jerked himself back on course with his agreement to take a leading role in *The Last Detail*, written by Robert Towne from Darryl Poniscan's best-selling novel. Towne sent him a proof of the book before it was printed, with an outline for the script. It was a powerful book with strong characters. He knew immediately that audiences would like him in it. It was an intuitive piece of judgement. The audiences loved him as Billy 'Bad Ass' Buddusky, one of two career sailors given the task of transporting a seventeen-year-old recruit from their base in Norfolk, Virginia, to Portsmouth, New Haven, to begin an eight-year jail sentence for theft. Out of sheer disgust at naval officialdom, Billy decides to give the young man one last look at life, on the five-day journey.

The journey develops into a long party of whoring and drinking and swearing that he would never forget during his ensuing years of confinement, and, largely due to Nicholson's riveting performance, the film achieved a near-perfect balance between tragedy and comedy. It also earned him another Academy Award nomination but not the Oscar itself – which turned out to be one of the few acting accolades available in America at the time that he did not get for his treatment of this part. Billy Buddusky ran up against the establishment again, because of the foul language. Columbia, who were financing and releasing it on to the national circuit, even postponed production because they were nervous over the amount of cursing; they wanted the number of swear words trimmed. Robert Towne refused. Servicemen swore. There was no getting away from that; for some men every sentence contained an expletive and he could not see the reasoning, anyway, to cut the number of 'motherfuckers' from forty to twenty. If the word 'motherfucker' caused offence, it would cause it whether it was used once or forty times, and the script called for it to be used forty times. Director Hal Ashby and Nicholson both agreed, and eventually the film went ahead without any major surgery to the script.

The lack of cooperation elsewhere, however, did cause further delays. Columbia sought permission to film Nicholson in a drunk scene on the steps of the Supreme Court in Washington. Chief Justice Warren Burger refused, apparently because he had heard Nicholson had signed a petition for the impeachment of President Nixon. The film crew was barred from two other locations and the Navy did not provide a great deal of help, either, since they viewed the subject matter with some considerable disdain. The film itself, while bringing new praise for Nicholson, also established his pattern of not allowing himself to be typecast; the characters he had played in every movie since *Easy Rider* had been vastly different to the last, though oddly roles over which his own casual style could be overlaid. As Mike Nichols had already observed, 'He is so good because he brings part of his own life into virtually every scene.'

He refused to become a Hollywood commodity in spite of the financial rewards such films offered. Clint Eastwood had started his own genre with movies like *Dirty Harry* and never strayed far from what he perceived audiences expected of him. Directors Terence Young and Michael Winner had just re-discovered one of Hollywood's finest, Charles Bronson, who also stuck to what he did best. These were unashamed examples of typecasting and there was nothing wrong in that; but equally it was not unusual for the new breed of actor to be non-fiscal when weighing up future prospects. James Caan, for example, turned down the prospect of $4 million by refusing to do *Superman*. Brando telephoned and asked, 'What's the matter? Isn't the money enough?' Caan replied, 'The money's incredible . . . but *you* don't have to wear the suit.'

Nicholson was of like mind. Money was secondary to the type of role he would accept. And after *The Last Detail*, Robert Evans, who was unsuccessful in getting him for *The Godfather*, was about to make him an offer he could not refuse – and for which he would take a ninety-degree turn for another enigmatic characterization in *Chinatown*.

9

An Incestuous Little Tale

Chinatown was the quintessential 1970s movie, embodying some of the major themes of that decade, such as corruption and conspiracy, and commenting metaphorically on Watergate. There were also some secret ingredients to the film's other theme of a tangled sexual relationship that helped make it the success it became. Off-stage, there was a kind of triangular situation that was occurring during its making. Nicholson explained, 'I had just started going with John Huston's daughter, which the world might not been aware of but it could actually feed the moment-to-moment reality of my scene with him,' referring to the specific line where the Huston character said to the Nicholson character, 'Are you sleeping with her?'

There was another secret behind the Nicholson characterization in the film *Chinatown* – which most agree finally secured for him the stardom he enjoys today – in that he modelled it sartorially as a sort of memorial to the man whom he thought was his father, John Nicholson, but who he was about to discover was not. But, perhaps the most significant of all the relationships which happened for the making of *Chinatown* was the coming together at last of Nicholson and Roman Polanski in a professional capacity because there is a belief that the mercurial little man brought to the film a moodiness that turned it from something confusingly average to classic proportions. Nicholson and Polanski had been spending a good deal of time together the previous winter, skiing at Gstaad. Polanski had retreated to a rented villa there, licking his wounds from his latest venture, which had unfortunately turned into something of a financial fiasco and a public slinging match with their old friends, Victor Lownes, head of the London Playboy Club and the

Playboy supremo, Hugh Hefner. It was in the farcical aftermath that the Polanski-Nicholson collaboration on the much-heralded and much-praised *Chinatown* had its beginnings, if for nothing else than the fact that during it, Nicholson had been a regular house guest of Polanski, who was teaching him some of the finer points on the piste and, since they were both unattached, introducing him to some of the finer points of the *après* scene, too.

Polanski joked about Nicholson's early skiing prowess; like his early sexual problems, he improved with age. A word about Hefner and Lownes is also necessary, because it explains why Polanski was suddenly available when Nicholson pushed *Chinatown* his way. His professional association with Hefner, Lownes and the Playboy organization had mystified and amused Hollywood onlookers, not so much over the fact of their business arrangement, but in the choice of subject matter. It was to be, and almost not to be, 'Playboy Productions Inc. presents ... William Shakespeare's *Macbeth*' (or *MacBeth* as two famed American columnists insisted upon calling it). Polanski had been working on the project for months with Kenneth Tynan and the involvement of Playboy was not as daft as it sounded. In sympathy with the current trendiness of nudity on stage and film – much propagated by Tynan himself – Polanski and Tynan had both agreed that Lady Macbeth should appear naked in the sleepwalk scene; there were other additives to jack up popular interest such as 'realistic' death and more, much more violence.

With the screenplay completed, Polanski touted his idea around, looking for finance without success until one day he mentioned it, almost as a last resort, to his friend Victor Lownes who told Hefner and spoke of the prestige value to the Playboy organization. Disregarding the advice of his film people, who were against it, Hefner flew to Europe in 'Bunny', his jet-black jet, a DC-9 full of girls and travelling retinue. His international Playboy business was reaching the height of the post-Sixties sex boom; he could certainly afford the gamble and agreed to put up $1.5 million. On the strength of that, Columbia, who were to distribute the film, followed suit with a guarantee of $1 million. To cut short an exceedingly long story – involving production delays, overspending and a Royal Command performance – *Macbeth* was treated with a mixture of mirth and disgust in America where there were complaints about Polanski's over-realistic violence, in spite of a fairly enthusiastic response in

London. *New York Daily Mirror* recorded that the only noticeable audience reaction was the laughter that greeted the line 'A Playboy Production'.

Apart from his anger about the film being over budget Victor Lownes was furious when told of Polanski's remark to a journalist who asked why he had taken Playboy cash to finance a Shakespearian production, and replied, '*Pecunia non olet*' – money doesn't smell. Lownes took this as a personal insult and immediately returned a gift he had received from Polanski and Sharon some years earlier, which was a statue cast in pure gold in the shape of an erect penis, commonly known amongst them as 'The Golden Prick'. With it, Lownes attached a note stating that he could no longer bear to have this 'life-sized portrait' of Polanski around the house and he was sure that he would have no difficulty in finding another 'friend' to shove it up. Polanski donated the statue to Release, the drug rehabilitation charity, who auctioned it off amid some embarrassing publicity suggesting it was actually a cast of Polanski's own organ. Lownes reached for his pen again, saying he had not seen a retraction and could only assume that Polanski relished this totally erroneous implication.

Nicholson arrived in Gstaad as this episode was ending and almost stepped into another of Polanski's ventures, which seemed to have the hallmarks of an equally interesting aura. Roman explained that he had been 'kicking a few ideas around' and was writing a part especially for Jack in a film provisionally entitled *The Magic Finger*. Did Nicholson laugh or break into a cold sweat? He chuckled. The plot was about a film producer modelled on one of Nicholson's heroes, Sam Spiegel, casting for a film which in some way involved the hopeful actresses sucking the man's little finger. Polanski was serious. Nicholson said kindly that it wasn't quite him and he would look out for something else for them to work on when he returned to the States. Meanwhile, Polanski flew to Rome, talked Carlo Ponti into parting with $1 million and set about making his film, except that the title changed to *What?* and its central character was now based on Gulbenkian, the oil magnate. It flopped.

It was fortuitous that with the public battle with Playboy out in the open and Polanski hardly the flavour of the month that Nicholson came on the telephone and suggested he should get his 'ass over to Los Angeles pronto' to direct a new Robert Evans movie for Paramount, called *Chinatown*. It was his for the asking.

There was already a history. Robert Towne, during moments of depression on the making of *The Last Detail*, when it seemed that Columbia might scrap the whole thing because of the foul language, had dreamed of becoming a director. Bob Rafelson told him he should stick to writing. He was good at that. Anyway, he had conceived a detective story which he decided he would write and direct, on the basis that a simple detective story should not present a hugely difficult problem for a fledgeling director and it ought to keep the punters interested, whether he made a good job or it or not. The idea for the story was inspired by his casually reading a west-coast magazine called *Chandler's LA*, in which there was a story recalling the troubles between farmers and land speculators earlier in the century. The name Chandler – as in Raymond Chandler – also struck a chord and out of it came an intriguing detective story, with sufficient detail for him to approach his old friend Robert Evans, still the boss at Paramount. They went to lunch, naturally, because as it happened Evans was also looking for a writer to sort out some problems on *The Great Gatsby* which was proving to be rather difficult to get on to film. But, having dealt with his own troubles, he listened to Towne's idea for a new screenplay, liked it instantly and gave him some money to proceed with an outline. Evans was, incidentally, also seeking a starring role to amuse his new wife, Ali McGraw.

There was a proviso to the deal, however. Towne could not direct. Evans said, 'This ain't no Roger Corman outfit, you know. This film will cost big bucks. I will want a name director.' Towne was in no financial position to bargain. One thing they were both agreed upon was that they should offer the leading role, that of the detective, to Jack Nicholson, who was brought in almost from the beginning and was able to offer his thoughts to Towne as they went along.

Another year passed.

The Last Detail was a success and so was *The Godfather*, which Evans had produced and for which Marlon Brando was up for an Oscar. Evans, Towne and Nicholson were flushed with pride for different reasons and great expectations now rode on the bulky script Towne had produced for *Chinatown*, whose title was as enigmatic as the film itself because it was largely devoid of any oriental characters or settings. Enter Polanski after the Nicholson telephone call, which was followed up by a firm proposal from Robert Evans who, it will be recalled, was also the backer of *Rosemary's Baby* and an old friend. Polanski's return to Hollywood was greeted by a rather mixed reception, ranging from welcoming handshakes to sidelong glances which said, 'What in hell's name is he doing back into town?' The Sharon Tate murderers had barely commenced their prison sentence; memories were fresh and Nicholson was still of the view that the 'moral majority was out to punish him because his wife was murdered'. That apart, Polanski hated the Hollywood syndrome and was paranoid about the attacks he had suffered from across the board, having been branded a megalomaniac by some he had previously worked with.

He was a difficult person to assess and even more difficult as a working partner, especially now that he was depressed about two failures, his row with the Playboy set and his uncomfortable re-emergence in Los Angeles. He discovered that few of his old friends were still around which made him even more miserable. He noted also that the Manson trial had virtually put an end to hippiedom and LSD, and the lifestyle which abounded when he left; cocaine and Quaaludes were now the favoured substances.

Nicholson believed that all Polanski ever wanted was to make brilliant movies; he dreamed of art on film. And Nicholson never would be swayed in his support for this side of the man, though he admitted that he did find him a trifle wearing at times. Robert Towne disliked him and his 'I-know-better-than-you' attitude, not so much as a person but for the abruptness of Polanski's decision to make substantial changes to the script Towne had been working on for almost two years, and which he felt was the best work he had ever done. Polanski conceded patronizingly that it was a masterful play, brimming with ideas and packed with some sensational dialogue; hidden away in the 200 pages was, he thought, a powerful movie.

'But it's too long and complicated. There are too many people in it. It wants stripping down to more manageable levels,' Polanski told Towne over lunch at Nate 'n' Al's, the Beverly Hills eatery. 'It cannot be filmed as it stands. I am going to take it over and rewrite it from start to finish,' Polanski pronounced.

'No you're not,' said Towne.

'Yes, he is,' said Evans.

'It should be trimmed,' agreed Nicholson.

Towne insisted on making the changes himself and Polanski went back to Rome while the cuts were made. He returned to discover that the script was still almost as long and he remained unmoved in his opinion about a confusion of characters who were graphically painted but added nothing to the action. Polanski still wanted to do the film; for one thing, he needed the money and Evans had promised him plenty. He agreed to spend two months with Towne on a rewriting effort and they worked long hours for eight weeks until a new draft was finally complete. For moments of relaxation, and to get away from Towne's procrastinations and his infuriating habit of finding things to do other than write, like taking his sheepdog for a stroll, Polanski began taking flying lessons at Santa Monica airport. Evans was getting slightly worried and Nicholson was getting it from everyone, especially Polanski, who had moved temporarily into his home in Mulholland Drive until Evans rented a small house for him on Sierra Mar with a soothing waterfall and swimming pool where eventually he was able to put the finishing touches to the completed script.

Polanski had altered the thematic base of the story so that it had a very definite Chandleresque quality with shades of *The Maltese Falcon* and *The Big Sleep*. Nicholson's character, the private detective J.J. Gittes, was in the mould of a smartened up Humphrey Bogart, smoother and less inclined to talk from the side of his mouth, though still rather monosyllabic. It was a brave Thirties piece, relating to a period of time when Jack could utilize the image of photographs and descriptions of his own father/grandfather, John Nicholson, dapper and smart in his flash clothes that won him the Best Dressed Man prize in the Easter parade before the drink took hold. The story was still complicated. Gittes was a cool and cynical former police detective who once worked the Chinatown district, and was now out on his own, as a private eye largely in divorce actions. He was hired ostensibly by a woman client who produced evidence to show that her husband was involved with another woman. But then the story fragmented along several different, and eventually converging paths as Gittes realized he had stumbled into something big, bringing in sub-plots and undercurrents by the score; corruption reaching into high places, violence, sex, incest and death. The action and corruption was centred around a huge reservoir and for those who studied scripts and analysed the spoken word in films, *Chinatown* provided not merely a feast of nuance, symbolic and real, but also a model for future documentary-dramas based on true-life situations. The original story that inspired Towne was actually set in the early 1900s when corrupt officials of Southern California made themselves millionaires in what became known as the Owne River Valley scandal. He added to that and blurred the facts with a fictional scandal of a woman who carries a secret that her daughter is the result of her being raped by her father, the character played by John Huston, original director of the classic Bogart film, *The Maltese Falcon*.

The actors who were to join Nicholson in the venture were the subject of almost as much pre-production discussion as the script itself. Ali McGraw, whom Robert Evans had wanted for the lead, had since decamped with Steve McQueen, her co-star in *The Getaway*. Evans then wanted Jane Fonda, but she turned it down without discussion – 'I'm fed up with people telling me how good Jack Nicholson is' – and Polanski suggested Faye Dunaway. Evans was uncertain because he thought she could be difficult. Certainly, she had had her moments in the past, and there were more in reserve for the future. Polanski got his way, and he found a surprising measure of agreement over his choice of Huston for another strong character. Huston, gruff and great and a better, more pernickety director than Polanski could ever be, was also set in his ways. Thus, with Polanski's own genius temperament which earned him a permanent nickname of the Little Bastard (which was also the name James Dean painted on the front of the Porsche in which he was killed), the scenario was set for the sparks, as they say, to fly.

They did.

One example was recounted by Polanski himself. It concerned a scene involving Faye Dunaway as the central character, and loose strands of her hair kept catching the light. The hairdresser made several attempts to flatten it, until Polanski went over to her and distracted her in conversation while grasping the offending strands between his fingers and pulling the hair out, hoping she wouldn't notice.

Dunaway, not unknown for her ample adjectival vocabulary, burst forth: 'I just don't believe it. He's just pulled my hair out.'

She stormed off the set, with Evans running behind trying to persuade her to return.

Polanski complained that she was hesitant and nervous in her delivery, which, he claimed, was borne of her insecurities; she would explode in a hysterical, expletive anger every time he altered or cut one of her lines, because she was convinced that he was attempting to massacre her role.

But there are two sides to every story. Dunaway complained, 'That little shit wouldn't talk to me about the part. He would explain nothing and give me no clue as to the motivation of the character. What was I supposed to do ... read his mind?'

When she repeated her question to him about the motivation for the part, he screamed: 'Motivation. I'll tell you motivation. All the money you're being paid to do it. That's motivation.'

Freddie Fields, Faye's agent, demanded an apology from Polanski, who gave one, half-heartedly and then ruined it by adding, 'She's nuts anyway.' Faye was not pleased and the Little Bastard was lambasted with some more well-known phrases and sayings before work resumed.

Nicholson remained cool. He arrived late a few mornings because early calls were never his forte; old habits die hard and he was still a night owl, sometimes on the prowl. Occasionally, his eyes were bloodshot but by and large he generally refused attention. Life's like that, he would say. People have late nights even in the movies; sometimes their eyes get bloodshot and sometimes they get baggy. So what? He never cared much how he looked, and in *Chinatown* he must have become the first male lead to spend half the picture with half his face covered by plaster and bandages to the slit in his nose, affected by Polanski himself who was doing a Hitchcock and playing a bit part as the knife-wielding punk. It looked so effective, audiences actually thought it was a real wound.

Peace remained between leading male and director until the very last day, when there was a basketball game on television that Nicholson particularly wanted to see; his favourite team, the Lakers, were playing the New York Knicks. Polanski was retaking a shot and could not get it right, because of some complex lighting; between takes Nicholson kept running back and forth to his dressing room to find out the Lakers score until finally the Little Bastard screamed for him to return.

'I told you we wouldn't finish this scene,' Nicholson shouted.

Polanski came back, 'OK, if that's your attitude . . .' and then he called 'It's a wrap', hoping that Jack would realize the scene had not been shot correctly and stay until it had been. On this occasion, however, he did not. The Lakers game had gone into overtime and he shuffled back to watch it. Polanski stormed after him, barged into Jack's dressing room and smashed the television which exploded with glass shattering everywhere.

'You are an asshole,' he fumed at Nicholson, grabbing what was left of the television set and hurling it forward out of the door; Nicholson also delivered a few choice lines.

Later, as they were driving home, they pulled up together at some lights. Jack was in his old VW. They turned and looked at each other. Nicholson mouthed the words, 'Fucking Polack.'

Polanski grinned. Nicholson grinned and the fight was over.

Chinatown was made and Nicholson knew instinctively that he had done a good job. This was confirmed when Robert Evans called him to view a rough cut.

'Mogul,' said Nicholson, 'we've got a hot one. Get those cheques ready.'

Then he called his friend Bruce Dern, with whom he swopped some needle now and again. He used to say that Dern and 'the man on the hill' (Brando, now his next-door neighbour) were his only competition.

'Hey, Dernsie,' Nicholson jibed. 'I think you'd better retire. I got it all covered babe – know what I mean?'

The critics were not entirely at one in supporting this opinion. Though they raved about Nicholson's acting, *Chinatown* received a patchwork of reviews which indicated that several were stumped for appropriate words, not knowing quite what to make of the undercurrents. There were those who still could not resist drawing their readers' attention to the 'lurid violence' which suggested, they said, that Polanski was still possessed by the Manson family massacre in his home and his exploration of depravity. The film took off. It was a box office success and received eleven Academy Award nominations for everything from technical merit to acting, with both Nicholson and Dunaway nominated for best actor and actress. Robert Towne converted his nomination into an Oscar for his outstanding script. For the moment, an Oscar still eluded Nicholson.

He was happy and cheerful. The mood was brilliant and not entirely because of his new acclaim, which undoubtedly settled his future; that of actor first and director occasionally. He could now name his own price and the figure he had in mind was $750,000 a picture plus a piece of the action.

Gee whiz!

He was happy about his life and because Anjelica Huston had just walked into it. For all his philandering and prowling around town with Warren Beatty skunk-spotting, he was a romantic at heart. He needed to be with someone on a semi-permanent basis although his serious love affairs, ending tempestuously on the last occasions, had also been punctuated by a burst of sheer one-off pleasure; he boasted to one friend in early 1973 about a highly paid fashion model who was arriving that weekend for a secret assignation. 'Jesus,' he said proudly, 'she's flying 10,000 miles just for a weekend with me.'

Anjelica was also a model, having rejected the acting career mapped out by her father. She was slender and willowy, taller than Nicholson; her silky black hair fell neatly around a classically oval face and her eyes seemed to have a natural outline, even without make-up. They met at a party at Nicholson's house during the filming of *Chinatown* and she stayed, on and off, for the next seventeen years.

She was taken by his eyes. 'And who isn't?' she said. 'They were kind, his whole face lit up when he smiled.' He was taken by her natural sophistication, which was very similar to her father's in that, as Lauren Bacall said, they could look equally at home and at ease somewhere in the wilds of Africa or in formal clothes at a hunt ball in Galway, where Huston had his castle. She has got class-*s-s-s* said Nicholson, emphasizing the word.

Nicholson's reputation had preceded him; she was fascinated by this older man who was as enigmatic as her father, and just as big a womanizer by all accounts. Eyes met, they circled each other like gladiators and became engulfed almost simultaneously by each other's presence so that if there was ever a moment to believe in love at first sight, it was then and if that sounds like the description in a corny love story, it was probably because it was related by a writer who happened to be in close proximity at the time. Suffice to say, it was that kind of memorable meeting which they would both remember for several, many, years to come, until, in fact, they did not care to remember it any longer.

Jack was also in awe of her father, and his late father Walter Huston who were two more of his old-time heroes. This great titan figure of the movie industry, whom Bogart nicknamed the Monster while they were filming *The Maltese Falcon*, dominated a room by his being there and, of course, commanded such huge respect from true film-makers and film buffs like Nicholson who especially admired him for the way he waved dismissiveness at false and sycophantic nondescripts of the type who seemed to surround Roman Polanski. Those actors who worked with him or for him are always ready to pass on a horror story about their experiences with Huston. Some, for instance, still blamed him for Clark Gable's death, for pushing the star into his own stunts for *The Misfits* which contributed to his heart attack at the end of the film, although Marilyn Monroe was also a cause. Some blamed him for finally pushing Monty Clift over the top in his search for perfection during the making of *Freud*, which turned the actor into a shambling, sweating wreck as the director insisted he deliver a long *Freud* lecture in one take, ruining Monty's confidence and hastening his decline into the drug-haze that killed him.

He was undoubtedly a psychologically cruel man but many also testified to his lovableness and generosity. Anjelica Huston loved and hated her father for many of the same reasons given by those who worked for him – and who, incidentally, saw more of him than she. One supposes that she was also affected by the years of domestic suffering by her mother, Ricki, who witnessed some of his most boisterous womanizing and gambling years before and after they became legally separated in 1959. In many respects, there were curious parallels in the coming together of Nicholson and Anjelica, and her mother and father and some friends both new and old were moved to comment, 'It's happening again.'

John Huston was still married to his third wife, Evelyn Keyes, when Anjelica's mother, Ricki Soma, became pregnant – not with Anjelica, but her brother Tony. A quickie divorce in Mexico enabled him to marry Ricki before the baby was born in 1950. Ricki was then nineteen years old; Huston was forty-four. They first met when she was a child of thirteen, daughter of his friend Tony, who had a restaurant on West 52nd Street in New York. When they met again at David Selznick's home, Ricki was eighteen, with stunning classical beauty and had already made the front cover of *Life*, who classified her as the modern Mona Lisa. They began seeing a lot of each other and in the summer of 1949, Ricki announced that she was pregnant.

It took Huston another five months before he divorced Evelyn, in what was a financial catastrophe, and he married Ricki on 11 February. Anthony was born in April and Anjelica arrived just over a year later, in July 1951. At the time, Huston himself was mosquito-swatting in the heart of the Belgian Congo with Bogart and Katharine Hepburn on location for *The African Queen*. Shooting was momentarily interrupted by the arrival of a runner from Butiaba. There was no other form of communication and it had taken him three days to get to the film crew, bearing a telegram from Ricki's mother announcing that the baby had arrived and that mother and daughter were fine. Huston read it silently and stuffed it in his pocket and then carried on filming the scene.

'For heaven's sake, John,' cried an exasperated Hepburn. 'Tell us the news. Is it a girl or a boy?'

'It's a girl,' said Huston. Thereafter, life was very much like that for Anjelica, who had long periods of separation from him, especially immediately after her mother's departure from the marriage. Her early years were spent on Huston's estate in Ireland; Ricki chose to live in a cottage in the grounds and Anjelica was taught by local nuns. When the marriage ended, Ricki took Anjelica to London where she continued her life with her mother, and a difficult adolescence of always being on the move. Furthermore, her father virtually forced her into acting, casting her for a role in *A Walk with Love and Death* and announcing that decision to the press before he even told his daughter.

This, Jack Nicholson surmised years later, was just a man clumsily dealing with events in a difficult father-child relationship. Anjelica tackled it courageously and her father said that in spite of her fears, she had great talent; she did not agree. She was petrified and for years to come constantly rejected any further thoughts – and plenty of opportunities – of becoming an actress. She saw even less of her father, nor did she want to, until tragedy moved them closer together in 1969 when her mother was killed in a car accident in France. She had no one but Huston himself at that moment, other than two brothers and a sister: Tony born to Ricki and Huston; Danny, born of Huston and actress Zoë Sallis during their liaison in 1962, and Allegra, born to Ricki in London in 1964 and who took the Huston name. But as Huston admitted to Hal Boyle of Associated Press, a few months later, 'Anjelica was frantic after Ricki died. I just didn't know how to reach her.' As the grief subsided, Anjelica went off on her own, to try a career in modelling.

In 1973, she was lonely again. A relationship with photographer Bob Richardson, who had captured her as a model for *Vogue*, had just ended. She was more at peace with her father than she had ever been, though it was still a tenuous sort of tranquillity, and accompanied him to the party in Mulholland Drive, where she stood, absent-mindedly gazing into Nicholson's eyes in which she saw kindness and warmth, hence the special meaning to the line in *Chinatown*, in which Huston had to say to Nicholson, 'Are you sleeping with her yet?' He was, and continued to do so through many ensuing years of a chequered relationship which was conducted, in true Hollywood style, with the keyhole attention of the world's media.

They saw a great deal of each other during those months of filming *Chinatown* and it was apparent to Nicholson's closest friends that he was falling in love with the stylish, sophisticated lady who actually appeared his exact opposite in the way she dressed – compared to his favourite mode of crumpled slacks and sweatshirt – and in her aloofness, which could be taken for snobbishness by those who did not know her. Before the year was out, Mulholland Drive had become the focal point of her life. She had no other, as it happened, because she did not seem madly keen on pursuing her modelling career and she had come into Jack's life at exactly the moment he was seeking that superior female figure which seemed, still, ever necessary to his psyche. And, soon, she would rarely be away from his side.

10

Shooting the Cuckoo

'I guess,' said Nicholson towards the end of 1973, 'I'm a man in transition.' He was, as someone said, like a college student who had just taken some major exams and was waiting for the results. The labours of the past twelve months had not been placed on public view and though success was well signposted, he was taking no chances. He talked about being pliable and obviously spent a lot of time considering his next move, as if he were in the middle of a championship game of chess. Redford, Pacino, Beatty, Newman and Hoffman were pliable, he said. McQueen, Hackman, Bronson and Eastwood were not. His career needed variety and movement, and the reluctance he had displayed earlier about being categorized as a rebel remained, except that now he realized he had to exert much greater control over what he did, for fear of seeing his advantage coming to nought.

It also went much deeper than merely the selection of roles and weighing up his audience appeal. Whereas he had been carried along by events of the age when he made his breakthrough, sex, drugs and rock 'n' roll as a collective was as dead as yesterday's news. There was still plenty of mileage left in each subject individually, but as Hollywood had long ago discovered to its cost, changes in society can move on at such a fast pace that trendsetters can actually be overtaken by events. That was already beginning to happen in swinging London, where some of the high priests and priestesses of that movement were falling into receivership.

Nicholson tried to shake off the tag of anti-hero which he disliked so much, but he could not discharge it that easily. The characters that had made him famous so far were nothing short of a gallery of flawed men, insecure, drop-out, sexually delinquent and cynical, all attached to that departing era of protest. Something heroic could be found in each one of them for those who were looking. Only J.J. Gittes, though cynical, broke the mould but with that characterization Nicholson was being dubbed the 'second Bogart' and he still did not want to be the second anyone, not even Bogie!

When he was asked about his future prospects, he distracted people by holding forth on his hopes of spending more time directing, although almost everyone who spoke to him with a job offer wanted him as an actor. Robert Evans, realizing his dilemma, gave him some pertinent advice, 'Grab the million dollar deals while you can. You can be a director when you're an old man.' There was no greater truth than that at the time, because when *The Last Detail* and *Chinatown* finally secured his unquestionable place in movie history, he could ask $1 million, plus a profit share, as an actor, and a mere $75,000 and percentage points as a director, simply because he wasn't in the Coppola league in terms of proven success.

Activity was nothing less than frenetic in these months during the overlap between filming *Chinatown*, seeing *The Last Detail* come to its New York première in January 1974, and holding never-ending talks with a small queue of other directors and producers knocking at his front door. The telephone never stopped ringing, as anyone who called at the house would verify, and there were often many at the house who could, because the doors were always open to his select but not small band of friends for whom, in his spare moments, he liked to arrange things.

He was a great organizer of junkets to first nights in Las Vegas – Sinatra, Torme, Midler – or concerts in New York, or ringside seats at major sporting events, or skiing at Aspen or Gstaad. Opportunities, social and workwise were there for the taking and he was making the most of everything. He was incapable of saying 'No' with conviction; he would shake hands with anyone who showed tentative signs of recognition and seldom refused an autograph signing. One of his friends in that set observed candidly that it was as if he was afraid he would wake up the following day and find everything back just the way it was in 1967. And, as is often the case with new money, he swung violently through the gamut of extreme generosity and high spending to nothing less than meanness. The house, the Mercedes, the skiing trips and shopping excursions with Anjelica set him back thousands; he dug deep to help out friends who were less fortunate, yet according to Polanski he was stingier than W.C. Fields, usually on inconsequentials. He kept the Mercedes in the garage and used the battered yellow VW, except when going out with his pals – 'I couldn't shove my friends in the back of the VW.' They received VIP treatment, with his tapes of the Rolling Stones, Ellington or Ray Charles blaring away while they indulged in an ever-present selection of booze and food in the backseat bar, which always contained a correctly chilled bottle of his favourite champagne. Actress Helena Kallianiotes, who had small roles in a couple of his early films – she was the talkative hitchhiker in *Five Easy Pieces* – came seeking refuge from her marriage and stayed on as his 'totally platonic companion', personal assistant, house cleaner or nagger. Helena saw his friends and women come and go.

He retained possessions and memories from his past – he threw every single review he could find about any of his films into a huge drawer – and the people stayed in his life, too. 'There were always lots of friends around,' said Helena, who'd moved into the house in the grounds that he'd bought for Michelle Phillips, 'not hangers on or bloodsuckers, just genuine people. If he liked something, he'd bring it home whether it was a lampshade or a person. Two or three house guests were around in any single month.' Around this busy period he hired Anne Marshall, daughter of actor Herbert, as his secretary, and they enjoyed a tempestuous but friendly working relationship. She would get mad because he was always losing things, and he would get mad as well over minor events, while remaining laid back if the world was falling in around him. He lost seven wallets in the space of a year, and 'it drives him out of his mind when he can't locate something.' Once, in Rome, he telephoned Anjelica who was in London to ask if she had packed his comb, because he couldn't find it and did not want to go out and buy a new one if it was there.

The years of shuffling were paying off, notwithstanding a slight dip in his fortunes with *Drive, He Said*, and the autumn of 1973 marked his final departure from that protective familial environment that had virtually maintained him throughout his career, first with Roger Corman and then with BBS. Beckonings from other quarters laid before him some diverse situations and for once he was able to ally his directorial interests with the work he accepted. European directors had always fascinated him and contracts were on the horizon which would present the opportunity of working with three of the most discussed and controversial, Michelangelo Antonioni, Ken Russell and Milos Forman. They figured in three of his next four movies.

The first was Antonioni, who called Nicholson to talk about his top-secret new film, *The Passenger*, even before he began filming *Chinatown*. It seemed a prestige approach from the man who had recorded such a bizarre commercial success with *Blow-Up!* after his string of artistically praised exercises in his humourless world of sentimental dismay. It was more in the director's interest to get Nicholson than for the actor himself to become involved, because Antonioni badly needed a bankable modernist to raise the finance for his new project. The disastrous flop of his last, *Zabriskie Point*, pretentiously described as a quiet contemplation of emptiness, had put him at a low ebb. It took him months to raise the cash and only succeeded with Nicholson's name on a contract. His producer Carlo Ponti, who had taken note of Polanski's enthusiasm for Jack during talks about *What!* was also keen to secure the financial viability of *The Passenger* to help keep at bay the line of creditors who gathered philosophically and daily at his offices over the Piazza Aracoeli in Rome, clutching their unpaid bills. He had also noted a new trend emerging in Hollywood, loosely termed packaging, which meant putting together at least two big names who would appeal to nervous distributors and lure the fans back into audience-depleted cinemas. Such efforts were badly needed.

In 1973, *Variety* reported that between 1969 and 1972, the major studios had lost $600 million between them. Annual attendances had fallen from 4060 million in 1946 to 820 million in 1972. Packaging big names in highly hyped films was taken to quite extraordinary lengths and by the mid-Seventies the major distributors were loathe to back a film without a star partnership. It was not necessarily the answer. One of the most expensive was the packaging of Burt Reynolds, Gene Hackman and Liza Minnelli in *Lucky Lady*, for which the studio had to wait a year until they were all available; it was not a success. However, for the actors like Nicholson themselves, it meant fatter pay cheques on offer and the promise of joint billings with the biggest of names.

Ponti and Antonioni wanted to team Nicholson with the awesome, liberated sex princess, Maria Schneider, fresh from her nude entanglement with Brando which made Bernardo Bertolucci's controversial essay in male sexuality, *Last Tango in Paris*, the smash hit that it became. Ponti said she and he were two of the hottest actors around, which was true; even rumours of them appearing together brought the gossip columnists out in force, though after the several miles of column inches she endured in the aftermath of *Last Tango*, Maria refused to speak to any journalist, much to the chagrin of the MGM publicity department, who were putting up most of the money. An off-the-record briefing by the MGM people at the time highlighted just how much they relied on pre-production stories, any stories, to help get the film on its way.

'The trouble is,' they said jaundicedly, 'that people who have overnight success get carried away by the glory of it all and their ego feeds on being able to say 'No' to everybody. One way or another, it seems nobody will know our film is being made.' But there are more ways than one of skinning a cat. Jack and Maria could be placed together in a past liaison, which is always good for business, and there was nothing like a good romance story to stir up interest. Two was even better. Jack had, according to the newspapers, also fallen in love with his *Chinatown* co-star Faye Dunaway, and she did turn up in Munich while he was filming *The Passenger*. In spite of Anjelica, people were prepared to believe that with Nicholson anything was possible.

Jack and Maria Schneider were indeed old friends. He admired her for her company, her body and her ability: 'I always thought of her as a female James Dean, a great natural. Tony Richardson [the director] once told me he asked Maria what she thought of me and she said, "Jack is a professional. He likes to know what he is doing. I do not." She started trying to be a success when she was fifteen, hustling her ass, and she achieved it. She did not like the public image bit, being photographed in restaurants, and it was only her work that stopped her going a little wacky.' With a nod here and a wink there, MGM was getting some coverage at last. Anjelica needed to be an understanding companion. She too had joined Nicholson for part of his European location work, which took him to London, Germany, Spain and back to New York. She had seen it all before, with a lifetime of stories about her father. Legend is not always what it appears; sometimes, when it is exactly that, there can be tears. She knew that even then.

As for the film itself, which Antonioni had co-written, it featured Nicholson as a TV reporter who was fed up with his own life and switched identities with another man who had died. It had the dramatic potential of *Day of the Jackal*, but the drama became secondary in a typically obscure Antonioni piece. Even Nicholson admitted that some of the gripping melodramatic sequences were underplayed because of Antonioni's insistence on achieving visual effect, or affectation, and so it was clearly not going to appeal to mass audiences; the director's well-known habit of using actors as items on his cinematographic landscape, or furniture in a room, speaking lines and not acting them, was perhaps becoming *déjà vu*. Nicholson did not mind that too much. He also put up with the director's tantrums, two or three a week. 'That's why he's good,' said Nicholson. 'He drives you crazy when you're working for him but he's been one of the greatest influences of film-making in the past three decades. They told me I was the first actor who got along with him in twenty-five years, probably because I gave him the performance he wanted, the one you see is exactly what he wanted.'

Unfortunately, by 1975 Antonioni's film artistry did not command the instant applause that it once had, when he was the darling of the avant-garde, although success with him could never be judged in financial terms. Carlo Ponti's creditors did not agree. It was received with relaxed enthusiasm; it was a film to look back on and reflect, guess at the meanings and work out what inspired Antonioni to make a script less compelling on film than it was on paper. Jack liked it and defensively upheld his comment that 'I know people who have managed to live out double lives. . . .'

★ ★ ★ ★ ★

The Passenger was the first of four Nicholson films which would be released during 1975, which meant that he was working virtually non-stop almost to the end of 1974, although his next date was hardly taxing. British director Ken Russell signed him for a cameo appearance in Pete Townshend's rock opera, *Tommy*. He was the singing Harley Street specialist, and this second attempt at musical rendition remained in the picture, unlike his last for Vincente Minnelli. Nicholson's appearance amid this selection of the best available rock music including Elton John's 'Pinball Wizard', was brief but it paid $50,000 for two days' work. He saw old friends and met lasting new ones – the film had the likes of Tina Turner as the Acid Queen, Oliver Reed, Keith Moon, Roger Daltrey, Eric Clapton and, of course, Nicholson's former co-star in *Carnal Knowledge*, Ann-Margret, which brought back memories for him and her, too.

Anjelica was with him in London when he heard he had been nominated as best actor at the Cannes Film Festival for his portrayal of Billy Buddusky in *The Last Detail*. They hopped on a plane to be there and do some unashamed politicking and glad-handing. He'd still shake anyone's hand, and give any woman a continental kiss, left, right, left, and then smile innocently when they handed him the award.

Back in Hollywood, another package deal was in the making, the one to set the stalls alight, it was alleged: Nicholson and Beatty together for a film being directed by Mike Nichols. Jack's old friend from *Five Easy Pieces*, Carol Eastman, had written the script and with that kind of line-up, funding their project was no problem. It had the makings of a minor blockbuster during that age of depressing box office returns and a script designed to cheer up the audiences. It was again a Thirties setting, a 'screwball comedy' in which the two real-life friends plot to marry the overweight daughter of an extremely rich aristocrat, and thus get their hands on his fortune. It was not one of his best. He and Beatty were compared to a cad and a weasel, romping through a story with little of the hilarity that it had promised. He even looked different. His hair was frizzed daily so that it had an Art Garfunkel look to it. Comedy for Nicholson needs to have an edge to it, not necessarily black but certainly with a touch of the weird so that he can get the brilliance of drawl and facial expressions into play.

At the end of the day, he and Beatty had to do some personal hyping after initial low returns at the box office. And so he held court in the lobby of a New York hotel, looking lightly dishevelled in a Hawaiian shirt and designer stubble, before designer stubble was even thought of, and proceeded to talk to reporters and interviewers about his life, but more specifically about *The Fortune*. Helen Dudar of the *New York Post* found him angry over reviewers' claims that no one in the audience laughed. He was incensed that one had reported the movie to be unfunny, yet failed to report that members of the paying audience had laughed. Helen said, 'I told him I also found it unfunny and had watched it in the company of paying movie-goers who had not laughed much either. Nicholson said quietly, firmly, gently, "I don't believe you." Ah Hollywood, the reality factory. . . .'

*   *   *   *   *

These three eccentricities could have seriously damaged a lesser man's life and it might have, except that he was already working on the film that would win him the accolade he so badly wanted, an Oscar. It was *One Flew over the Cuckoo's Nest*, adapted from Ken Kesey's explosive novel, published in 1962 and written long before the counter-culture movement of the Sixties and the anti-heroes of the Seventies. Anti-heroism was one of the keys to the success of the film combined with the very considerable contribution of Nicholson and the talent of Czech director Milos Forman, who turned an enormously difficult project into a movie verging on the classic.

It had been a long time in coming to the screen and the story is filled with uncanny coincidences. Kirk Douglas bought the rights to Kesey's book even before it reached the shops and was convinced it would make a terrific picture with himself playing the leading role of Randall Patrick McMurphy – the one eventually played by Nicholson. Douglas got as far as Broadway with his project where he played McMurphy in a short run; the play of the book flopped badly, leaving Douglas free to accept to an invitation from President John Kennedy to join a goodwill mission to Czechoslovakia – a trip which he had previously turned down because he was expecting to be tied up on Broadway for rather longer than he was. It was while in Prague that he met Milos Forman, then a thirty-one-year-old scriptwriter and director with the Prague Film Faculty of the Academy of Dramatic Arts and whose family had, like Roman Polanski's, been largely wiped out by the Nazis. It was probably his discussion with Kirk Douglas that eventually led him and his young family to America as immigrants five years later.

Douglas himself was so taken with Forman that when he returned home, he sent him a copy of *One Flew over the Cuckoo's Nest* to see if he was interested in joining Kirk in the project. With all hope of Hollywood finance seemingly vanished through disenchantment with the play, there was a vague hope that it could still figure somewhere in the advancement of East–West cultural relations. For some reason, still unknown to this day, Kirk Douglas's package was never delivered to Forman who remained in Prague blissfully unaware that one of Hollywood's once greatest Fifties stars wanted to do business with him. There, it rested without further progress.

One other reason for the delay was that the rights became locked in a protracted legal battle between Douglas and his former partner in the Broadway project, but when it was free, his son Michael Douglas – himself gathering fame after his successful TV series, 'Streets of San Francisco' – became interested in getting it produced. He had a new script written to suit contemporary events and tastes. Naturally, Kirk would still liked to have played McMurphy but appreciated it needed one of the new young stars who would bring more youthful appeal for the audiences and a more bankable prospect for the backers, someone like Burt Reynolds. Like his father, Michael Douglas also found reaction in the major studios lukewarm at best and positively cold at worst.

A few even remembered, 'Look what happened when your dad did it.' Then he introduced it to Saul Zaentz, head of Fantasy Records, who was so enthusiastic he agreed to put up most of the production money, budgeted at $4 million. In seeking a director – 'He has to be exactly the right one,' said Michael Douglas – they turned coincidentally to the new young Czech, Milos Forman, unaware that ten years earlier, Kirk had sent him the book. In the years that had elapsed, Forman had made a name with films like *Blonde in Love* (1965), *Fireman's Ball* (1967) and *Taking Off* (1971) in which he showed a remarkable ability at satirical lampooning of authority – so much so that the Czech fire brigade went on strike in protest at his *Fireman's Ball*. As the play was further discussed, it became apparent that Burt Reynolds – though a major box office attraction at the time – was not right for the part and Mike Douglas instead approached Nicholson. A further coincidence was in store.

'It's funny,' Nicholson told him. 'When the book first came out, I tried to get an option on the rights and was told Kirk Douglas had bought them.'

Forman and Nicholson became instant comrades. Nicholson's

interest in and respect for European directors, and Forman's admiration of some improvisation scenes he had Nicholson perform for him convinced everyone that a certain magic between them was developing. Nicholson kept in touch with pre-production work and marvelled at the fact that Douglas and Forman saw more than 900 actors, from whom they were selecting the relatively small cast of a dozen primary actors.

Forman said, 'We told Nicholson we were going for the best we could get. He agreed. Some actors don't like that because they could be outclassed in a such a movie where the actor is one of a group, but he said straightaway that good actors would enhance his own performance rather than detract from it.' As an example of the perfectionist search for the right people, they looked long and hard for an actor to play the large Indian Chief who was supposed to be deaf and dumb until McMurphy got him to talk. They found him in Mount Rainer National Park, where plain and ordinary Mr Will Sampson was working as an assistant warden. 'Suddenly, two men appeared on horses, and offered me a career in the movies,' said Sampson later. 'I thought they were kidding.' They weren't and he thus became a minor celebrity, appearing later in such movies as *The Outlaw Josey Wales*.

The story of *One Flew over the Cuckoo's Nest* was said to be based on Kesey's own experiences. It was the type of film that crossed all social barriers, largely through the way it was conceived and handled, and because it was so good in so many parts. It dealt with the then very topical and vexed question of 'curing' mental patients with electric shock treatment. Audiences were given the most realistic view of life in a mental institution than anything that had gone before, but it needed the humour of Nicholson to lift the story from becoming an abject, depressive tale of woe. He kept it bouncing with his sympathetic humour almost to the dramatic end, when he is himself immobilized by the shock treatment.

The film was a dramatic observation of a convicted rapist, R.P. McMurphy, who had convinced the authorities that he was mentally disturbed in order to extract himself from heavy prison duties. At the same time, Nicholson had to tell the audience he was feigning insanity, and then show them that he had a very definite mental disorder of which he was unaware. He arrived at the institution as the epitome of a man who has spent a lifetime baiting the establishment. Once inside the ward, where a controlled calm prevailed, he pitted himself against the hospital bureaucracy in the person of Nurse Ratched who daily supervised the administration of tran-quillizing medication.

Naturally, McMurphy – and Nicholson – resisted and began his own one-man rebellion, leading his fellow inmates into riot, escape and a party with imported drink and prostitutes. McMurphy's personality was magnetic and destructive, both of himself and fellow inmates. There was one other difficulty to be overcome. The film had to be told without alienating the American mental health administrators and it was a wise move to obtain their cooperation. There was also a measure of concern among certain actors who were approached, that the film might upset a lot of people – or was it just that the subject matter might not have improved their own image? Among those who turned down the part of the domineering Nurse Ratched, for example, were Anne Bancroft, Jane Fonda – 'I'm still fed up with people telling me how good Jack Nicholson is' – and Faye Dunaway.

Nicholson had not the slightest concern about image; this was not a film to promote him as a romantic idol. He attacked it with his usual methodical tenacity, analysing the implications, dissecting the character, measuring its demands and psychological tones. As he read the script, he underlined key phrases in his lines and assigned numbers to certain words to signify beats and phrases. Before memorizing his lines, he flew up to a mental institution in Oregon, which was going to be used a setting for the movie. There were 582 inmates, most of them classed as criminally insane. He had talks with the chief of staff, with nurses and inmates. He was shown all around the hospital and personally persuaded the hospital's medical chief to let him watch patients undergoing shock treatment.

Then he went into the maximum security ward and was already sitting in the hallway when the patients were brought out of their cells. There were a number of especially violent cases, including several murderers. They all thought he was a new patient, and most were anxious to engage him in conversation. One was a handsome blond man who had killed a prison guard three weeks earlier with twenty-eight stab wounds. Nicholson went to lunch with them and continued his conversations, with hospital staff never too far away. When time came for filming, the hospital's superintendent, Dean

Brook, readily gave permission for some inmates to appear in background scenes; Brook himself even appeared in the film and although he later ticked off the producers over certain inaccuracies, he felt it 'a great honour to do a scene with Jack Nicholson who is an absolute genius in getting across the character of McMurphy, a sociopath of whom there are plenty around. Jack's performance typified them.'

Filming in Oregon was to cover a period of eleven weeks and Nicholson arranged some accommodation nearby for himself and Anjelica. Within a few weeks, however, he had so immersed himself in the role that Anjelica found him becoming increasingly difficult to live with. Nicholson explained, 'Usually I don't have much trouble slipping in and out of a film role but in Oregon, I didn't go home from a movie studio, I went home from a mental institution and there's a certain amount of the character left in you that you can't get rid of; you are in a mental ward and that's it. It became harder and harder to create a separation between reality and make-believe because some of the people in there look and talk so normal. You would never know they were murderers.'

In fact, he became so engulfed by the institutionalized life he was acting out that Anjelica started to get worried. His behaviour towards her when he came home at night after a day under the cameras, was distinctly odd and getting worse as the days went by.

Eventually, she challenged him, 'Can't you snap out of this? You're acting crazy.'

He could not and so Anjelica packed her bags and flew back to Los Angeles, complaining 'I'm no longer certain whether you are sane or not. I'll see you when you come back into the real world.'

Michael Douglas took the trouble to apologize to her for the difficulties she was experiencing with her lover.

'If it's any consolation,' he said, 'this movie is going to be a smash. I've never been more impressed with any actor in my life.' Saul Zaentz, whose $4 million was riding on the *Cuckoo*, added his praise. 'I can think of only one other actor to compare him too, Paul Muni.'

Nicholson's peers agreed and the following April, they awarded him his first Oscar, an Academy Award for best actor, which he accepted with joy, his talents now – he believed – fully recognized and he was glad to participate in the system which bestowed this honour. The film picked up nine Academy nominations in all and took five Oscars: Jack for best actor, Louise Fletcher for best actress, plus best film, best director and best adapted screenplay. The widespread reaction to the film was, however, far more interesting, and displayed two crucial and slightly disturbing elements about society and how Nicholson himself was seen by it, in his anti-something-or-other perception. Actors, film buffs, producers and reviewers alike were all completely stunned by the tumultuous audience reaction to *One Flew over the Cuckoo's Nest* when it opened in America, and these scenes were repeated across the land. It was not merely the light-hearted moments that brought such stirring participation; even the most soberingly dramatic moments when McMurphy was trying to strangle Nurse Ratched to death were received with cheers and applause. For that reason alone, while praising Nicholson and Forman's direction, reviewers sounded many notes of caution. Stanley Kauffmann, in the *New Republic*, noted quite adamantly that the film was warped, sentimental and possibly dangerous. Pulitzer prize-winner Roger Ebert, one of the most influential critics in America, is still of the view that Nicholson and Forman milked the film so that it became a simple-minded anti-establishment parable. 'I think there are long stretches of a very good film,' he says, 'and I hope they don't get drowned in the applause for the bad stuff that plays to the galleries.'

And so, spitting in everybody's eye, another important notch was added to the Nicholson reputation.

11

Brando on Cue

Though he had been his neighbour in their lofty commune, gazing down on Los Angeles from a high point in the hills on Mulholland Drive for two years, Nicholson was not what you would call 'close' to Marlon Brando, who was often away for long spells on his South Sea island retreat to which he escaped from the cruel world and all its problems. Even when he was at home in Beverly Hills, Brando did not go out of his way to socialize, although between the two households, the comings and goings at the top of the hill were indicative of the colourful domestic lives of the two star residents. However, behind the scenes, there were moves to bring them together professionally which would inevitably lead to a closer – but never close – friendship; those who remembered the fiasco when Brando turned down his Oscar for *The Godfather* smiled at the irony of the situation, because the new project was a western, and hadn't he been bitterly critical of this type of film?

The opportunity came when Brando needed money for a variety of reasons, including his considerable alimony payments to two ex-wives, a property venture in Tahiti and, embarrassingly, his financial support for his latest pet political cause, the American Indian. This was demonstrated at the end of 1974 when he appeared on television on the steps of a court house in Lincoln, Nebraska, announcing that he was going to give away his house in Mulholland Drive – and other property – to the Indians. He had come to court in support of some Indian activists appearing on a variety of charges. Though a firm supporter of civil rights himself, Nicholson was nonetheless disposed to comment of his self-confessed idol, 'Jeez, what's that sonofabitch doing now? He's crazy.'

Neighbourly interest in the activities of his professional comrade was more than advanced by some of the happenings at the Brando household which, over the past couple of years, had ranged through a variety of domestic incidents, often involving tragic and very public battles between Brando and Anna Kashfi over custody of their thirteen-year-old son Christian, whom Anna had once snatched from Brando's custody and then vice versa. The resultant court action cost Brando dear, financially and emotionally, and hung out a lot of dirty family washing.

Brando's political affiliations had also attracted a lot of media attention at Mulholland Drive where he received visits from his friends of the American Indian Movement in various rank, ranging from chief to squaw. One of them, his friend Sacheen Little Feather went to the last Academy Awards on his behalf when he was nominated for best actor. 'And the winner is ...' said Liv Ullmann, 'Marlon Brando.' He was not present but sat at home in Mulholland Drive watching the live television coverage. Sacheen Little Feather, who had been given a seat next to Jane Fonda, ran up to the podium carrying a long speech Brando had prepared. But, since it would have over-run the allotted time limit, she was not allowed to read it, and thus refused to accept the Oscar from the presenter, Roger Moore, stating this was Marlon's protest at the treatment of American Indians in movies and on television. As Moore politely tried to usher her away, she begged, 'In future, in our hearts and our understanding, we will be met by love and understanding.'

An icy silence was followed by some cynical remarks by other presenters and recipients: Clint Eastwood said, ' ... on behalf of all the cowboys shot in John Ford westerns'. Academy resident Daniel Taradash: 'If Marlon had any class he would have come down here and said it himself ...' Michael Caine, 'I agree with Marlon's principles but he should have done this himself instead of sending some poor little Indian girl.' He added, 'a man who makes $2 million playing a Mafia Godfather should give half of it to the Indians.' Even Chief Dan George, who had given up his Indian life to become a movie star, and who had won a best supporting actor nomination for his role in *Little Big Man*, said Brando's protest was ten years out of date because movies were more accurate now.

Coincidentally, the same director who made *Little Big Man*, the admirable and scholarly Arthur Penn, now wanted Brando for his next film. He had heard on the grapevine that Brando was short of cash and looking for work, which seemed incredible after his recent films like *Last Tango in Paris* and *The Godfather*, but he had invested heavily in a South Seas project that went bust the following year. Having offered to give away his property to the Indians, he also stood costly bail for some activists for the Indian cause, two of whom were later charged and convicted of first degree murder. Amid a ceremony complete with tribal drums he handed over his gift to the local Witch Doctor of forty acres of land west of Los Angeles worth $200,000; it was land which originally belonged to the Chuwala Indians before the settlers forced them off. Then after the publicity of this gesture had died, Brando suffered the humiliation of the fact revealed in the newspapers that the land was heavily mortgaged and the Indians would have huge repayment costs. He promised he would clear the mortgage and did so ten months later, by which time he earned sufficient funds to cover it by signing with Arthur Penn for his movie with Nicholson.

Jack was the junior partner in the alliance, and producer Elliot Kastner had promised him $1.25 million for ten weeks' work plus ten per cent of all gross receipts in excess of $12.5 million. This was a landmark in Nicholson's career – as the first guaranteed salary exceeding one million dollars and the prospect of more to come. Apart from achieving his goal of playing opposite Brando, it also provided him with the opportunity of working with another of the directors he most admired for his string of 'new wave' films, which also included *The Left-Handed Gun*, *Bonnie and Clyde* and *The Chase*, all controversial documentaries on the conflict between the law and that violent age. The new western, *The Missouri Breaks*, contained similar off-beat elements with a script written by novelist Thomas McGuane who lived in Montana. It was based upon his research on the historical significance of the cattle business and the skilled system of rustling, which accompanied the settling of northern Montana; he said it showed that some basically decent people perpetrated some pretty awful things.

Brando made a cursory study of the script and characteristically asked for half a million dollars a week for the duration of filming, with a million to be paid immediately. They haggled and he settled for $1 million for five weeks' work and ten per cent of the gross takings after the first $10 million, thus giving him the potential for three million dollars or more if the film was a success, plus overtime if filming over-ran the five-week limit.

Penn had not seen Brando lately and was shocked when they finally came face to face. Marlon had ballooned to a considerable 250 pounds and hardly looked the man they had in mind for the role of an eccentric leather-clad gunfighter, hired to track and kill a band of cattle thieves led by Jack Nicholson. However, from the point of view of a box-office package, Penn felt he could not have done better: Brando, the greatest draw in the business, and Nicholson, the most talked about new star of the age. And so they all moved down to Billings, Montana, for location shooting and discovered the pre-production crew hot and bothered and sweltering in temperatures of 112 degrees Fahrenheit.

'You'll have fun,' everyone told Nicholson in advance of his first encounter with the man on the hill.

The location village had been set up on a sprawling ranch twelve miles outside of town. Penn had assembled his relatively small cast of extraordinarily good actors who included Nicholson's old chum Harry Dean Stanton, along with a motley crew of 112, dressed in a variety of headgear and heavy footwear that kept the dangerous rays of the sun off their heads and the fatal fangs of the rattlers off their feet and legs.

Brando's huge air-conditioned trailer had 'Executive' painted on the side in silver against the pale blue background; there was also a candy-striped awning to shade the side which took the most sun. In true Hollywood conformity to protocol, Nicholson's was slightly smaller, because he was a slightly lesser star. So much of the discussions about how to play a scene were to go on in the Brando wagon. Tempers were already over par before shooting began because, as per usual, Marlon wanted some changes to the script, nothing substantial he said, as he unfolded his copy covered with a mass of notes and crossed out lines over which he had written new ones. He wanted it at least to include some propaganda for his Indian cause. Tom McGuane was furious, especially because he knew the area well and his research had been meticulous. Penn wasn't too happy either. And neither was Nicholson when he discovered that Brando wanted Jack's part to be played as an Indian.

McGuane refused point blank. Penn said he did not care for the idea and Nicholson, less partisan, calmly proferred the opinion that he did not think it would work. Brando sat back in his chair, pondered for a moment and announced that he was quite unhappy with this lack of cooperation with his suggestions. Nicholson was keen to get started. He turned up bright and early on the first day, ready for his first scene with the great man. He too had put on a touch of weight and he had a straggly beard and greasy hair, and he lounged about in sandals, baggy jeans and an open-necked brown shirt. Brando appeared wearing riding breeches and a battered brown hat looking more like a renegade from the Australian outback.

Brando and Nicholson tried a couple of scenes together and spent some time in Brando's trailer with Arthur Penn. The crew outside were becoming impatient in the broiling heat as the minutes ticked on into half an hour and then an hour.

A muffled voice over someone's walkie-talkie summed up their feelings: 'Has God's gift to the world appeared yet?' He had not.

Nicholson was slightly bemused by it all; everyone was, even those who had worked with Brando before. They held in him in awe. Some were scared of him, especially the producers and the publicity people, to whom his very presence brought on attacks of anxiety. Few argued with him for fear of upsetting him or throwing him off his line of thought, although more often than not he wasn't even thinking of the scene. At that time, the intricacies of wind power were occupying his thoughts because he was designing a wind-driven electricity generating unit for his house in Tahiti, and often sat sketching a new idea. His mind could be a million miles away.

On the first day of serious filming, Nicholson was to discover some of Brando's eccentricities, apart from another of his already noticeable diversions, that of collecting grasshoppers and spending some time studying their curious leg movements, which intrigued him.

'Cue cards?' said Nicholson to Penn, mystified. 'Who are they for?'

'Himself.'

'Marlon?'

'Yes.'

'Why does the greatest actor in the world need cue cards?'

'Because he hasn't learned his lines, that's why.'

The cue cards, with large letters written on them, were held up in strategic positions off camera; some were pinned to the anatomy of other actors, some were on shirt sleeves or in the inside of his hats. But cue cards there would be all through the film and there were moments of humour because of them. Once Brando was doing a scene with John Liam and he asked if he would mind terribly if he stuck his lines to Liam's forehead while they were doing the shots over Liam's shoulder.

Liam replied, 'I don't mind but I would like to see your face.'

'OK,' said Brando, 'then we'll punch two holes in the paper.'

Even then, it did not work and new cue cards were drawn up with four-inch letters, and stuck on a wall behind Liam. The cameras rolled and Brando started speaking, and then interrupted himself.

'Shit,' he said, 'there's an airplane coming into shot over your left ear. . . .'

On another morning, a gale blew up as they were filming in what was supposed to be the garden of a wooden shack. His cue cards got blown into the cabbage patch, neatly planted the day before and Brando couldn't see them properly, although in this particular instance it did not much matter because he was changing the lines almost to the point of ad-libbing and a production assistant was having difficulty in taking down a note of the new words.

The scene was aborted when it became plain it wasn't going to work and Brando rode off into the prairie in disgust.

'Oh well,' said Nicholson, trying not to sound bored, 'another day, another twenty grand . . .'

The Brando aura slipped a little and after a couple of days, Nicholson was giving a cheeky impression of an actor, i.e., Brando, being filmed while reading cue cards.

'Watch the eyes,' said Nicholson, moving his own from side to side. 'That's what happens when you're reading cue cards.' But, in spite of this piece of satire, Nicholson was full of admiration for Brando as an actor, especially for the sparseness of his mannerisms, and the power of his voice; even though it does not sound powerful, it carried across the set once he had decided how he was going to say that line. His walk and his movements were graceful, like a dancer almost, despite his overweight form.

The crew liked him, too, especially when early on in the proceedings Brando protested at the long daily schedules the producers had drawn up, which meant a six a.m. start and often not finishing until late in the evening; he felt it was too long, both for them and himself. It might have been a mistake. They only wasted their extra leisure time drinking and dancing at the War Bonnet motel two miles out of town where the management began to get upset. The night Nicholson hosted a party for the crew resulted in the whole set being given notice to quit by the manager – not simply because of the drinking. By now, the crew had moved in for the summer with their wives, girlfriends, in-laws, children and pets. On the notice outside, someone had added 'Un' to the sign which read 'Welcome Missouri Breaks'. The assistant governor for Montana became involved and a compromise was eventually worked out, whereby half would leave the motel for other accommodation.

Anjelica flew to Montana for the summer and stayed with Nicholson at the house he had rented outside of town. His daughter Jennifer, now twelve, also came for a visit during the school holidays and Nicholson spent half his time trying to dissuade her from playing poker with the crew. This was now a fairly typical summer holiday for Jennifer. Father and daughter had a good relationship; there had never been any animosity or curiosity as to their meeting like this. She was a toddler when her parents parted and so she had never known anything different. With Jennifer verging on teenage, Nicholson had decided upon an open and honest relationship with his daughter, whom he idolized, but not obviously so, and who visited him often. He did not duck her embarrassing questions about his affairs, nor would he necessarily hide other aspects of his lifestyle. Poker with the crew was good fun; she was not over-awed at all by the position of her father who she never seemed to regard as a star.

Meanwhile, back on the set, Brando remained the centre of attraction, if not for his acting then his other activities. He had gone on a diet, eating only raw vegetables, and boasted that in the first two weeks he had lost three inches round the waist, much to the concern of the wardrobe department who had visions of their star vanishing in stature before their very eyes, and having to make up new gear for him.

Nicholson worked hard, though he did have a row with Arthur Penn over the interpretation of one scene, for which the producers publicly accused him of holding up production for five hours, at a cost of $20,000 an hour. Jack rejected their claims. He actually saw little of Brando, who was there for only five weeks of filming while Jack was required for ten weeks. Most of the time, when he wasn't on set, Marlon was either riding on the prairie in search of grass-hoppers or sitting alone in his trailer tapping away on his bongo drums, or phoning his Indian friends. His involvement with the Indian activists had hotted up and proceedings on the set of *The Missouri Breaks* were also enlivened with gossip for a day or two when a carload of FBI agents swung their car into the set and their leader said he wished urgently to speak to Brando privately about two renegade Indians. They were on the run from the police and the FBI had reason to believe they were using a mobile home belonging to Brando. The actor was decidedly uncooperative but later admitted that he had indirectly assisted the two men in their escape.

So that was Nicholson's first and last professional encounter with Brando, on which Brando himself commented, 'Poor old Jack. He was running around cranking the whole thing out while I'm zipping in and out like a firefly.' And he added a note of vitriol about his next-door neighbour, 'I actually don't think he's that bright – not as good as Robert De Niro, for example.' Oh well, it would be a long time before Jack invited him around for a barbeque!

What did the critics make of it all? Brando never reads their opinions and perhaps too much is made of their observations, anyway. They remain nonetheless the only historical guide – apart from box office records – of how a particular film was received at the time. The social aspects which Penn – and Nicholson – sought and fought so hard to get across, even to the point of sitting up half the night talking about how a particular scene should be played, were disappointing in the film. Penn said as far as Nicholson was concerned he had never previously encountered an actor who worked so hard. *Newsweek* went for a populist view, billing it as the great shoot-out between Brando and Nicholson, facing each other not merely as characters but as magic icons; Brando had become a symbol of lost innocence while Nicholson radiated the new kind of beleaguered innocence, 'grinning hedonistically against the moral confusion of our time'.

Opinions varied. Nicholson himself even seemed unsure of the picture's box-office appeal. Although his original deal for making

The Missouri Breaks gave him $1.25 million plus ten per cent of the gross receipts over $12.5 million, he obviously had second thoughts as to how successful it would be, after viewing the final cut version. On 14 May, a week before *The Missouri Breaks* opened in Los Angeles, he sold back to producer Elliot Kastner half of his ten per cent of the movie's eventual receipts for $1 million to be paid within ten days. However, when the money had not been received by the agreed deadline, Nicholson's company, Proteus Films, filed a suit for breach of contract in Los Angeles Superior Court. The case was eventually settled amicably.

*   *   *   *   *

Brando's comparison of Nicholson and Robert De Niro had some bearing at the time because both actors had been possible choices for the lead in *The Last Tycoon*, based loosely on the life of the legendary boy mogul, Irving J. Thalberg, from F. Scott Fitzgerald's unfinished novel. It was being heralded as a new blockbuster from the same team that brought Brando to the screen in *On the Water-front*, producer Sam Spiegel and director Elia Kazan, with the backing at Paramount of Robert Evans – the living legend and positively, some say, the very last tycoon. The added ingredient this time was the famed British playwright, Harold Pinter, who had been commissioned to write the screenplay about the sexual and power struggles of old Hollywood. Nicholson and Spiegel were good friends and Jack's name was being pushed by the producer for the lead. Kazan had other ideas.

'I told Sam to forget Nicholson for the role of Irving Thalberg,' he recalled. 'I wanted Bobby De Niro. I knew very little about him but I was playing a hunch.' Could it be that he had been speaking to Brando? Sam Spiegel gave Kazan his head. His hunches had been good in the past. He chose Brando for *A Streetcar Named Desire* as well at *On the Waterfront* and James Dean for *East of Eden* to name but two stars he had pulled from virtual obscurity.

'It was much the same now,' said Kazan, 'because I had to transform De Niro from a New York Italian kid into Hollywood royalty. That wasn't easy. He was a thin, somewhat sickly Jew with erudition and culture. But we came together on instinct, his and mine.'

Spiegel still wanted Nicholson in the film, and so he was offered a cameo role as the Communistic union leader, thus joining some other good names like Ray Milland, Donald Pleasence, Tony Curtis and Robert Mitchum for which he was paid $150,000. Spiegel, however, used him to batter Kazan all the way through the making of *The Last Tycoon* – and afterwards when it was met with a lukewarm response by the media and the public. Spiegel kept saying that the leading man was a problem and that Nicholson would have done it better. He said De Niro was 'common', once describing the actor as a 'petty punk' which Kazan insisted was grossly unfair. At the end of it, Kazan wrote in his diary, 'The picture hangs together; the performances are good, outstanding in the case of De Niro and Ingrid Boulting and the film has class, beauty, humanity and subtlety.' That, Kazan admitted, was 'the only supremely favourable notice we were to receive'.

★　　★　　★　　★　　★

Nicholson was also talking to Sam Spiegel about the finance for a new film called *Moontrap* which was his own project and which he wanted to direct but not appear in; this ambition was proving difficult to achieve. United Artists who had also released *The Missouri Breaks*, were firstly disappointed at the initial box-office takings and by the time contracts came up for discussion, they were wary of the film's viability. As always in Hollywood when large money is at stake, negotiations went on – and off – for several months until UA said they could only consider it if Nicholson himself took the leading role. 'If the picture goes into millions, then we've got to have Jack in it otherwise it is too much of a gamble,' said UA. Nicholson said he was not prepared to do that; he wanted this picture to be a demonstration of his directing skills and he could not give it full attention if he was also in the starring role. There matters rested and Nicholson took off for Europe in anger, though not especially at the UA attitude, more at recent developments in his personal life.

He and Anjelica had moved apart quite suddenly; only a couple of months earlier the gossip columns had been suggesting that they were considering marriage, though long-time friends of Nicholson like Harry Dean Stanton said they would believe it when they saw it. Stanton was convinced that at that point in time, Nicholson had made up his mind never to marry again. Two deep involvements (with Mimi and Michelle) that might, in other circumstances, have developed into marriage, would by now have meant that he had three failed marriages behind him and that was a statistic he did not want attached to his biography. Later, he did want to marry Anjelica – but it was she, we will see, who refused him for exactly the same reason, that she had seen too many marriages fail, including three of her own father's. Then and there, they were all fairly agreed on one thing, however, that Anjelica had been good for him. On location in Billings, Montana, he had been a model of decorum and cooperation. He had certainly come out of his shell – into which he had retreated after the split with Michelle Phillips – with Anjelica on his arm, and was a frequent attender of some of the more establishment social functions and parties.

They appeared warm and 'frocklicksome' as one observer put it. Anjelica seemed to be devoted to him as was noticed when Jack was doing his important person bit, holding court to a group of people hanging on his every word and she assuming the position of quiet attentiveness, sometimes sitting at his feet like an Oriental Geisha. There appeared to be a strong bond between them, enforced by the fact that Anjelica had no demanding career of her own, although therein lay one of her own deep personal concerns. All too often these days, she was being referred to either as John Huston's daughter or Jack Nicholson's lover – Anjelica Huston, person, did not appear to exist in the eyes of the media; she did not want to become a adjunct to the life of Nicholson just as her father's wives had done with relentless misery and unhappiness.

Anjelica had become important in Nicholson's life but perhaps he did not appreciate just how much she had moved towards being the supportive companion of a firm relationship, nor did he appreciate entirely that there should be two-way traffic and that Anjelica needed something in return – so that she would not brood on being just Jack Nicholson's girl. She was probably also getting a bit sick of his continual assertion that he understood women – a by-product which had lingered from his battles with women's libbers after *Carnal Knowledge*. He was forever in the papers with patronizing quotes like, 'I knew how to be friends with women before I knew how to be sexy with them.'

There was another story he was fond of telling. It went like this: 'I was talking to Bernardo Bertolucci [director of *Last Tango in Paris*] at a Dylan concert the other night. And, when I made some little intimate gesture to Tootie [his nickname for Anjelica], he said "Ah, you really understand women, don't you?" I said, "Of course, just as you do" and then he said something which I find to be so true: you can write a book or a play or almost anything but you cannot make a movie if you do not appreciate women.' To which his old father-figure and brother-in-law Shorty would continue to respond, 'I still think you hate women.' Who knows? Perhaps he did, and anyway, the conversation between a director and an actor who had been involved in some of the most degrading scenes of sexual exploitation of women so far shown in the cinema, could hardly be taken as a recommendation for understanding the psychological finesse of the opposite sex.

Either way, Anjelica was becoming moody, perhaps broody, and certainly less enamoured with the aura of enigma that she once saw around him. She was experiencing what had happened with other long-term relationships in his life, and those looking in at close range could see it coming. Don Devlin, writer and producer friend of Nicholson's from the earliest days on Sunset Strip, recalled, 'The long term ones were very strong, and filled with huge emotional ups and downs and every one falling into the same identical pattern. Jack is such an overwhelming character that girls love him. Then he starts to behave fairly badly, then he starts to lose the girl, then he goes chasing after her again, then the relationship changes and the girl gets the upper hand. Then he becomes like a little boy. . . .'

Anjelica had reached the second phase of the scenario described by Devlin and whispered to a friend, 'What's good for the gander . . .' and took off for London with another of Jack's good buddies, Ryan O'Neal, with whom a certain closeness had been developing for some months. 'He had it coming', seemed to be the general consensus among mutual friends of Anjelica, leaving Jack so devoid of sympathy he took off to Aspen and holed up in one of the two houses he had purchased in the ski resort with the money he made from *Chinatown*. He followed O'Neal and Anjelica to London. They were staying in Kensington while Nicholson checked into the Mayfair Hotel and phoned his old friend, photographer David

Bailey, with whom he shared a taste for good cigarettes and occasionally the same women, like Catherine Deneuve, from whom Bailey was divorced in 1970.

When writer Neil Blincow caught up with him, he discovered Nicholson was still spitting with rage and said all he knew was that Anjelica was in London and she wasn't with him; furthermore, he did not want to be mentioned in the same sentence as Ryan O'Neal. Nicholson hung around for a while and dined with Jerry Hall, but she was Bryan Ferry's girl then and Jack was not going to do to Ferry what one of his best friends had just done to him – at least that's the way he saw it. He mellowed later; when looking back he said, 'If you told me that some women [i.e., Anjelica] could go off and fuck one of my best friends and I'd end up reading about it in the newspapers, and that four years later I wouldn't give a shit, I'd have said, "You're talking to the wrong guy here." That's not the way I am now.' Anjelica's departure hurt him more than he had imagined it might – even if he had ever seriously contemplated it – and certainly it came as a greater blow than the earlier goodbyes of Mimi Machu and Michelle Phillips. In August, he caught a plane to the South of France to join Sam Spiegel on his yacht.

Sam was sympathetic but also the bearer of other sad rumours that United Artists had cancelled their planned financial backing of *Moontrap*. Meanwhile, the paparazzi, who had followed him to the quayside at St Tropez where the Spiegel craft was tethered at the upmarket end, had surrounded the berth on hearing the news that Nicholson had just arrived. Nicholson's response demonstrates his sadness and his anger; he dropped his trousers and mooned at them over the side.

The Nicholson–Huston row rumbled on all summer in the gossip columns. First there was a reunion, and then it was all off again. Jack, in the meantime, was being linked to a variety of other contenders for a room with a view on Mulholland Drive, including Hall and Deneuve, and then Anjelica suddenly rejoined O'Neal who was filming the World War II epic *A Bridge Too Far* in Holland. On 23 September, she received a call from Nicholson 'ordering' her back to America. John Huston had advised him to 'be firm with her'. They met in New York three days later and agreed they would never again separate. In the highly public aftermath of separation, she said she realized when Jack rang how much she had yearned for him and she 'felt so crummy abandoning him – men like Jack you just don't find any more'.

Jack professed his undying love and insisted they would never part again, not even for separate vacations. 'We are side by side now and that's the way it is going to stay,' he said, and added no bitterness towards his friend Ryan O'Neal, left licking his wounds in Holland, and wondering what he did wrong. 'It ended as quickly as it had begun which was a pity. I really loved her – even Tatum liked her.'

12

Goin' South from Polanski

On the evening of 24 March 1977, Princess Anne, president of the British Academy of Film and Television Arts, was attending the annual presentation of the British Oscars and fully expected to meet Jack Nicholson, who had been nominated as best actor of 1976 for his role in *One Flew over the Cuckoo's Nest*. 'And the winner is ...' Esther Rantzen, the presenter of the live television coverage of the awards from Wembley, announced Nicholson's name and the cameras swung around to reveal ... an empty seat where he should have been sitting. Hasty excuses were made and there were rumours that Nicholson, in the mould of other Hollywood rebels like George C. Scott and Brando, had simply refused to honour the London occasion with his presence. Later that evening an embarrassed spokesman for United Artists, the film's distributors, announced apologetically that he had not in fact arrived in Britain as expected, and was still in California 'going about his normal routine'.

Jack's friends in England knew he enjoyed being given prizes, and although he would not go out of his way to get in front of British royalty, he would not be rude to them either. On this occasion, rudeness did not come into it; he stayed out of touch because of the trouble on Mulholland Drive. The reason for his non-arrival was rather more complicated than the bland explanations given by the studio. On the very day he was due in London, Roman Polanski was being arraigned before the Los Angeles Superior Court on six charges, alleging he drugged, raped and committed an act of sodomy on a thirteen-year-old girl in Nicholson's house, and Anjelica Huston was on $1 500 bail after being arrested on the same day as Polanski for alleged possession of cocaine. At the time that Princess Anne should have been presenting Nicholson with his award, he was holed up in Aspen, Colorado, surveying the sensational mass of world press headlines which dragged him into the worst Hollywood scandal since Errol Flynn's infamous rape case.

This complicated and dramatic sequence of events which brought the world's media to set up camp in Mulholland Drive and with it an unpleasant and unpalatable story, had its beginnings fourteen days earlier, on 10 March. Nicholson was already in Aspen. He was spending some time in the company with, among others, Jill St John, whose own recent companions, such as Frank Sinatra and Henry Kissinger had given her almost as much publicity as Nicholson's with Anjelica. Nicholson's love life continued to be conducted on and off in the papers since the public split the previous year with Anjelica. In spite of the pre-Christmas reunion with Anjelica, their relationship had struck another bad patch. Nicholson went off to do some skiing on a separate vacation while Anjelica was preparing to move out of Mulholland Drive, with no other man in mind. Nicholson did not expect her to be there by the time of his planned return in the third week of March, in readiness to fly to London for the British academy awards. In the meantime, Polanski entered stage left with a thirteen-year-old girl whose mind the director filled with dreams of becoming a star.

Polanski, forty-four, had returned to Los Angeles shortly after Christmas following a visit to Poland. He was about to begin research work on a new film. His last, called *The Tenant*, which was another essay in voyeuristic perversion, had been flattened by the critics and Polanski complained once again that they were reviewing him – and his immediate past – rather than the film. He had now signed a development deal with Columbia to write and direct an adaptation of Lawrence Saunders' best-selling novel, *The First Deadly Sin*, which had some Polanski-esque ingredients such as sex and a psychotic killer, whom he immediately decided should be played by Robert De Niro. Polanski had long ago spent the money he received from *Chinatown* and sought an advance from Columbia to begin work.

He also claimed he had been given a commission from the French magazine *Vogue Homme* to do a photographic feature on adolescent girls of America. This offer, he said, followed the success of the Christmas edition of French *Vogue* which devoted numerous pages to a mixture of wistful reminiscences of his life, interspersed with portraits of actresses he had directed, ranging from Sharon Tate to Catherine Deneuve. The feature also included provocative pictures of a teenage girl – namely Nastassia Kinski, the fifteen year old in scenes from a film yet to be made called *Pirates*, for which he was trying to get backing. He was also hoping to persuade Jack Nicholson to co-star with the unknown girl, but, so far, he had shown a distinct lack of interest in the project. Polanski switched temporarily to still photography which would provide him with a small income and the opportunity of pursuing his personal delight in the study of beautiful young women. None was more deserving of the dual descriptions of voyeur and poseur at that time than Polanski himself and the route to his involvement with the thirteen year old whom we shall call Mary was steeped in some intrigue.

Dark rumour suggested that she had been introduced to him by John Huston, while others said that Polanski met her mother in a Hollywood bar a year earlier and came looking for the daughter when he began his photographic quest. Polanski's own story was that a friend had talked about a fabulous-looking teenager who was the sister of a girl he dated, and thus Polanski proceeded to get in touch. The girl's mother, he said, had been warned to expect his call and when he rang, she invited him over to her house. It was she, said Polanski, who reminded him that they had met at a club some months earlier. Mary's mother, an actress who lived with a journalist on the staff of a magazine called *Marijuana Monthly*, was keen for the contact with Polanski to develop because she was also seeking work and thought he might open a few doors. Her resident lover, meanwhile, also sought to use the contact with Polanski to promote the idea of Jack Nicholson giving him an interview for his magazine. And so, with benefits available all round, it was agreed that Polanski should take Mary out on location for his photographic sessions on the afternoon of 10 March. She was to have been accompanied by a friend who, in the event, did not go; however, the girl's mother insisted that Polanski leave telephone numbers of the locations and to call if there were any changes. He drove to Mulholland Drive and went first to the home of Jacqueline Bisset who lived across the road with Victor Drai. On the way, according

No picture better typifies the life and times of Jack Nicholson in the second half of his career than this mischievous shot captured for *Witches of Eastwick* (1987), in which he played the role of the devil himself (*Warner Brothers*).

Above: Another day, another twenty grand, said Nicholson, yawning, during the filming of *The Missouri Breaks* (1976) with his friend and next-door neighbour, Marlon Brando (*Private Collection*). *Right*: In *The Fortune*, Nicholson joined forces with his good friend Warren Beatty. The jokes were good but the box-office tills did not jingle in the hoped-for manner (*Kobal*).

Above: The tough patrolman Charlie in the controversial film *The Border* (1981). It was a fairly downbeat film, in which Nicholson proved an arty flair. *Left*: Later, as middle age set in, so did the extra weight. It was required for this heavy character performance in *Ironweed* (1987), in which he starred with Meryl Streep (*Daily Mirror*).

The ladies that helped create the Nicholson 'reputation'
Above: With Maria Schneider in *The Passenger* (*Private Collection*). *Right*: With Shirley MacLaine in his Oscar-winning role in *Terms of Endearment* (*Kobal*).

Left: With Faye Dunaway in *Chinatown* what some call Nicholson's best role (*Kobal*).

Above: With Jessica Lange in *The Postman Always Rings Twice*. Nicholson reportedly videoed their sex scenes for later use (*Daily Mirror*). *Below*: With Jerry Hall in *Batman*, a role which has made him an estimated $60 million – to date (*Warner Brothers*).

Above: Nicholson gets his second Oscar for *Terms of Endearment*. 'All you rock people . . . rock on,' he enthused, somewhat mysteriously, upon accepting his award (*Universal*). *Right*: Karen Mayo-Chandler, the Kiss-and-Tell sex kitten/actress who sold her story to *Playboy* (*Daily Mirror*). *Below*: There was special significance to the making of *Prizzi's Honour*. It was directed by John Huston (centre), who realized an ambition to co-star with his daughter Anjelica (right). She won an Oscar for her role (*Rank Distributors*).

Above: Nicholson and Anjelica in 1989. Several of his high-profile indiscretions prompted Huston to end their seventeen-year relationship (*London Features International*). *Right*: Nicholson leaving Tramps, the London nightspot, early one morning (*Daily Mail*). *Below*: Jennifer Nicholson, Jack's daughter, by Sandra Knight. Although her parents separated when she was a child, she spent much time with her father who was and is a 'doting dad'. She too is taking up a career in the movies, but on the other side of the camera (*Daily Mail*).

Above: One more look at The Joker in the super-successful *Batman*, a role he will have a job to live down, especially since his pet project, *The Two Jakes*, failed to win great praise from the critics when it was released in 1990 (*Warner Brothers*). *Right*: Finally, a hint of possible future intentions as we see Jack pictured here with his current girlfriend, Rebecca Broussard, who gave birth to their daughter in the spring of 1990. The child was named Lorraine, after Jack's aunt, and, as we go to press, the word was he had proposed marriage (*Daily Mail*).

to Mary's version of events to Los Angeles police, Polanski talked about sex. He asked her if she was still a virgin and if she knew anything about masturbation. Would she like him to show her what masturbation was? Her story was at variance with Polanski's, who claimed she told him how she slept with her boyfriend and that she had first experienced sex at the age of eight.

They arrived at Jacqueline Bisset's house around four p.m.; Bisset had been shopping and arrived home with parcels. Victor Drai and two friends were inside the house while Polanski and Mary went outside by the pool to begin the photographic session. By now, a cold wind had blown up and the sun was going down behind the trees. While they were there, Mary's mother called to check on her daughter and was told by a woman who answered the telephone not to worry. Mary and Polanski were out by the pool and there were other people in the house. Soon afterwards, Polanski decided he had chosen the wrong location for his photographs and suggested to Mary that they should go across the road to Jack Nicholson's house, which they did, he parking his rented Mercedes outside the security gates to the compound which contained Nicholson's two houses and Brando's mansion. Polanski knew that Nicholson was in Aspen so he called Helena Kallianiotes who lived in the smaller of Nicholson's two properties. She still acted as house sitter for Nicholson and Brando while pursuing her own career whenever she could; at that time, she was working on a screenplay. Polanski said he was sure Jack would not mind if he used the house for his photographic sessions; Helena agreed. Polanski had, after all, only recently been a house guest and had been given a complete run of the place on that occasion.

'Is there anything to drink?' Polanski asked.

'Champagne in the fridge,' said Helena. 'You know where it is ... and now, if you'll excuse me, I have to get on with my own work.'

She waited to take a glass of champagne from the magnum of Cristal which Polanski popped, and then left him with the girl. They sat drinking for a few minutes. The young model was apprehensive. She said the last time she drank champagne she was ill. Polanski reassured her; this was good champagne and would do her no harm. She claimed he told her that Nicholson would be arriving soon, knowing full well that he would not; but, it was said later, he

177

was playing on the fact that she desperately wanted to meet him and even have her picture taken with him, so that she could boast to her friends.

'I don't know how much I drank,' the young model was to tell the police. 'I just kept drinking it for the pictures he was taking.' The photographs were posed in various parts of the house. In the kitchen, for example, he had her sitting on the table licking an ice-cube, and in Nicholson's main living room, he photographed her in the bay window overlooking Franklin Canyon.

They moved to the jacuzzi area; the girl was intrigued by the clouds of steam and Polanski suggested she should go topless. He also produced some pills, Quaaludes, which was the fashionable tranquillizer usually taken after cocaine. He took one himself and persuaded the girl to take half. The scenes that followed, ostensibly for photographic purposes, had the girl topless in Nicholson's elaborate jacuzzi, in which she was joined by Polanski. In the middle of this misadventure, the girl's mother telephoned and was assured all was well, though, soon after, feeling the effects of the champagne, the hot jacuzzi and the pill, she wanted to lay down. Polanski took her to what used to be the spare room where he once slept. Now it housed Nicholson's huge television screen and his stereo, with sloppy couches.

'I can barely remember anything that happened with any clarity,' the girl said in her police statement. Polanski followed her into the room and began making love to her almost as soon as she lay down on the couch, first orally, then with vaginal intercourse and finally, anally, when he climaxed. As he did so, there was a knock on the door.

Anjelica had returned home. He called out to her, and Anjelica shouted back, 'Roman?'

He opened the door slightly and Anjelica could see he was naked. She never cared much for Polanski and now she was angry that he should be using Nicholson's house for what appeared to be sexual purposes.

'What are you doing here?' Anjelica asked.

'I'm doing a picture session for *Vogue*,' Polanski replied. Anjelica was not convinced and complained to Helena about allowing him into the house.

Undaunted, Polanski returned to the couch and attempted to

make love again. The girl froze; she wanted to go home. Twenty minutes later, they both emerged from the room, dressed and ready to go. Polanski made some half-hearted attempt to introduce the girl to Anjelica but neither women was especially interested. He took her home and Mary ran straight upstairs to her bedroom, too ashamed, she said, to face her mother. Polanski talked to the mother and said they had done well; he would call back again when the pictures had been developed and printed. Later that night, however, the girl broke down in tears to her boyfriend and elder sister, describing what had happened in the Nicholson house and pleaded with them not to tell her mother. They insisted; the mother, horrified at her daughter's story, called the police.

The following day, Polanski was walking across the lobby of the Beverly Wilshire Hotel where he was staying, unaware of the activity that had unfolded the previous night and earlier that day at the Los Angeles police department. The thirteen year old had made a full statement, describing what had happened in the Nicholson house.

'Mr Polanski,' said a voice quietly as he strode towards the exit doors on his way to a theatre date, 'I am from the LAPD. I have a warrant for your arrest.' Polanski protested loudly and denied everything but was arrested nonetheless.

Two other officers arrived at Mulholland Drive carrying a search warrant just as Anjelica was leaving the house.

'I'm sorry,' she said, 'but I cannot stay ... and anyway I answered questions to a detective earlier when he called about Roman Polanski being here yesterday. It isn't my business, anyway.'

'I'm sorry. It is your business. You live here, don't you?'

'It isn't my house. I have been staying here.'

'Is Mr Nicholson still in Colorado?'

'Yes, I spoke with him on the telephone a few minutes ago. He doesn't know anything about this.'

'Well,' the officer said, taking Anjelica's arm, 'we have court-authorized papers for a search and we have to ask you to step back inside.'

'Where do you want to start?' she asked, resigned now to cooperating with them.

'Your handbag. We'll start there ...'

A half an hour later, Anjelica was charged with possession of cocaine allegedly found in her bag. Detectives also took various items from his house, including a small brick of hashish; the police had already made it known they would like to have the opportunity of taking Nicholson's fingerprints so that they could be checked against those on the hash container. Nicholson remained in Aspen, refusing all approaches from the near-frantic journalistic activity that had blown up around him. His lawyers and advisers told him to stay away from Mulholland Drive at all costs so that he did not become even remotely involved in a public manner.

When he had not returned to Los Angeles by 1 April, police requested a warrant from Santa Monica municipal judge Robert Thomas, authorizing detectives to obtain his fingerprints. Nicholson cooperated by having his prints taken by Aspen police. They did not match those found on the hashish container and on 19 April, the police announced that he was cleared of any suspicion in the case. Angelica, however, still faced possible prosecution over her alleged possession of a small quantity of cocaine, and the newspapers, meantime, continued to have a field day.

Furthermore, when police developed the film Polanski had taken of the girl, they found the pictures were poor quality and certainly unusable in a major magazine such as *Vogue*. But then *Vogue* said that that was never a likely proposition anyway, because they had 'no knowledge' of Polanski being commissioned for the feature. The weeks and months of headlines continued as the story developed through its various stages. Nicholson came back from Aspen but kept a low profile. Anjelica's lawyers negotiated the non-performance of the action against her if she agreed to testify in the case against Polanski, who said there were no hard feelings and, anyway, his lawyers were also in plea-bargaining talks which centred around his admission of having unlawful sexual intercourse with an under-age girl. In the meantime, it had been noted that his friends were putting around stories that Polanski had been set up by the girl and her mother because he refused to give one or the other of them a part in *The First Deadly Sin*, but then the District Attorney was made aware that another of Polanski's under-age girlfriends, Nastassia Kinski, had just arrived in Los Angeles with her mother, Ibrahim Moussa, to begin acting and English lessons which Polanski had promised he would partly finance.

The trial judge, Laurence J. Rittenband, was not swayed by

rumours of a set-up. He even questioned Polanski about Nastassia Kinski and then announced that he wanted him to submit himself to a ninety day custodial order to establish whether or not he was 'a mentally disordered sex offender'. This he agreed to do and on the eve of his surrender to the authorities at the state prison, Jack Nicholson, Kenneth Tynan and other close friends threw a small dinner party for him. He spent forty-eight days in prison and was released temporarily on 27 January while his lawyers made application to Judge Rittenband in chambers prior to final sentencing. Rittenband was unmoved by their pleadings. He wanted Polanski to go back inside for the remaining forty-eight days of the custodial appraisal and seemed intent on extracting from him an agreement for voluntary deportation when he came out – or face a further prison sentence. Nicholson and Tynan were horrified when they learned of Polanski's plight. Faced with this prospect, Polanski telephoned a couple of his friends and then drove to Los Angeles airport where he purchased the last remaining first class seat on British Airways flight L598 to London, departing at 5.57 that afternoon.

From London, he flew on to Paris where he was assured that he would be safe from the law. Back in America, as the headlines of his departure raged, the US Department of Immigration pointed out that as a foreign national who had pleaded guilty to a felony charge and had fled, he would now be denied a visa and would be arrested if he attempted to return. The same threat existed in numerous other countries, including Britain. In France, however, it was viewed differently. He held a French passport and it was never likely that French authorities would allow his extradition on a charge of unlawful sex!

Polanski was safe from prison but barred forever from returning to Hollywood; almost instantly he made a two-fingered gesture intended to show that they could not put him down. He announced he had obtained French backing to make a film adaptation of Thomas Hardy's classic nineteenth-century novel, *Tess of the d'Urbervilles*, a story of lust, sex, rape and murder – plus a few other elements which could have slotted easily into his own recent past. His star was going to be Nastassia Kinski whom the whole world knew by now had been his lover at fifteen – a fact not lost on the *Hollywood Reporter* which in its announcement of the news commented, 'You'd have thought he would have had the good sense to make a war movie or something.' But then a war movie would not have been earned him the new critical acclaim and publicity hype that came with *Tess*. Just to rub their noses in it, he stood at a press conference with his arm around Kinski's shoulder and said to questioning reporters, 'I have never hidden the fact that I love young girls and I will say again once and for all, I love very young girls.' The personal factors that blurred the line between Polanski the artistic genius and Polanski the sexual extremist came into play once again.

Thus ended a disastrous episode in Jack Nicholson's life, though it would never go away. The Polanski affair left a bad taste – in spite of attempts to play down the director's degree of guilt. Although he has never admitted as much, Nicholson was stunned by the sheer volume of publicity and it would affect him deeply in terms of the way he presented himself in future interviews. In the middle of it, he cleared off to Mexico to begin work on his next project, *Goin' South*, in which he was the star and he was directing.

★   ★   ★   ★   ★

Polanski was one thing; John Belushi was another.

They met in August 1977, when Belushi signed a contract to make a cameo appearance in *Goin' South* for $5000, ostensibly hired for five weeks' work. It was the beginning of a friendship between the future cult star of the Blues Brothers and Nicholson which, after a shaky start, lasted until Belushi's death from an overdose of heroin and cocaine in 1982. John Belushi was just one of a number of new actors recruited by Nicholson for the film, and the whole scenario had a decidedly odd feel about it, and seemed to have more to do with Nicholson's determination to direct another picture than anything else. Why he ever wanted to do it in the first place was – and remains – a mystery to Nicholson-watchers in Hollywood. *Goin' South* was built on not much of a story and with no other famous names in the cast to help drag it along, its whole success or failure rested on Nicholson himself, both as director and leading actor.

Why did he put himself in such a position? For a man who had just won an Oscar and whose name was on everyone's lips in

Hollywood – even before the Polanski débâcle – it was a surprising choice of 'next movie' when he could virtually name his role and name his price. He did neither. It was almost arrogant of him to assume that he could, single-handedly, produce a satisfactory product in the style expected of him by his now substantial following of ardent fans. But that was Nicholson then, and now: a bucker of the system and outwardly confident that his own abilities would pull him through. He was also honest enough with himself to realize that a lot was riding on the success of *Goin' South*. He told Mary Rourke, 'If it doesn't work, it is doubtful whether I will be able to direct another film. One unsuccessful film is OK but two and you're in trouble.'

Hollywood has a long memory and *Drive, He Said* was not a commercial success. *Goin' South* was a risk he was prepared to take because he put himself in charge of every aspect. It was a fairly effortless story about a scruffy, smelly cattle thief named Henry Moon who was saved from hanging by an old custom which allowed any single woman to take a condemned man as her husband. The script was one he took from the pile when United Artists finally pulled the plug on *Moontrap*. Nicholson turned to his old friends Harry Gittes and Harold Schneider to coax some finance from Paramount. They, like UA, wanted him in the picture and he agreed, apparently intent on showing his hand as a director.

'Why not?' he replied to questions about his ability to pull it off. 'It didn't hurt Molière, Shakespeare or Pirandello.' He wanted to hire Jane Fonda as his leading lady but she was still fed up with hearing how good Jack Nicholson was, and anyway, she had turned him down on the self same project seven years earlier because she had just done *Cat Ballou* and would not touch another knockabout western tale.

'But it's not like *Cat Ballou*,' Nicholson insisted. 'We don't do gags, we don't play comedy. We play reality and comedy is born of reality.' Miss Fonda remained unmoved. He went to the opposite extreme and hired a completely unknown actress named Mary Steenburgen who, until that point in her life, had failed to land a single screen role and was working as a part-time waitress at Magic Pan by day and performing for no pay at a theatre club by night. When she tested at Paramount, it was the first time she had ever been on a sound stage and at the end of it was so unconvinced that she went down to the pay office to get her expenses to get her home to New York; she was flat broke. 'Forget it,' she was told, 'you're on the payroll.' It was a rags-to-riches tale for Mary, that her first time on a film set should be opposite one of the most sought-after male leads in the land. Ten years later, however, although she was still not what you would describe as a household name, she appeared in *Back to the Future III*. Coincidentally, Christopher Lloyd, the time-machine inventor in all the *Back to the Future* movies also had a role in *Goin' South*, as did Danny de Vito, both of whom had appeared with Nicholson in *One Flew over the Cuckoo's Nest*. Ed Begley jnr., whose name was only familiar because of his famous father, was also in the cast list though with so little to do that he barely rated a mention in the credits.

In fact, though he had never made a film before, John Belushi was better known than any other actor in the picture by virtue of his appearances with Chevy Chase in the American comedy show, 'Saturday Night Live'. Nicholson had enjoyed one of Belushi's most recent routines, in which he did a parody of *One Flew over the Cuckoo's Nest*, with a cruel imitation of Nicholson playing McMurphy and Raquel Welch in the role of Nurse Ratched. He and Nicholson had one other contact in common, a past friendship with Candice Bergen who had appeared in several Belushi television sketches. She joined him in the early days when his humour was wicked, sharp and fresh. Lately, when she came back to do another show, she was disappointed to discover that he relied heavily on drugs to help him through the pressure of his workload. He had become addicted to both Quaaludes and cocaine and his whole personality had become dangerously manic instead of spontaneously and delightfully mad. Nicholson had chosen him for one reason only – he had heard him do a brilliantly comic impression of a Mexican and there was a small part for a Mexican deputy sheriff in *Goin' South*.

Location work was in the central Mexican town of Durango, where seventy or more westerns had been filmed in the past. John Wayne made four there and the set built for *Chisum* in 1969 was the set used by Nicholson for *Goin' South*. It is the sort of place that is famous for its blue skies and breathtaking local landscape of rolling foothills of the Sierra Madres, tipped with pure white cotton clouds. It is also known for its unsavoury tummy bugs, sharp-mouthed mosquitoes, and someone once said the phrase '4000 flies can't be wrong' was invented as a promotional line for some of the restaurants.

They moved down in the early summer, and Nicholson appeared to slide without a hint of schizophrenia between his two roles, though confusingly for onlookers. Dressed in his mangy clothes and bent black hat, he would peer through the camera lens at a shoot-out and then hop in front to become Henry Moon, sleeping in a barn with pigs. His actors were full of praise. 'Most directors feel they have to tell you how to do every line,' says Danny De Vito. 'Jack lets you alone. His style is less direction is better.'

Steenburgen agreed. 'He taught me the art of acting on film down there. He told me to eliminate the obvious and keep it simple and natural. He directs by asking helpful questions and suggesting another way of approaching a particular scene.' He was a seducer of his cast and crew in terms of work, while his own efforts were quite tireless. Not every day was sweetness and light. As the weeks wore on, Nicholson looked tired, and at the end of one long and arduous shoot, he angrily chastized himself, 'I will never direct myself again.'

John Belushi arrived towards the end of August. Nicholson was thrilled but surprised when Belushi agreed to do it; Harry Gittes wished he hadn't. The comedian turned up sweating in city clothes. He was confused and angry, having totally overlooked the need for passports, airline tickets or money. His agent rescued his birth certificate from his mother in Chicago and eventually, John Belushi was brought by plane and car to the Mexican township, depressed and tired after his long journey; he looked dishevelled and his suit was crumpled as if he had slept in it for a week. He complained bitterly about the hotel accommodation they had arranged for him and asked if he could stay at the place rented for Nicholson, a sprawling bungalow up in the mountains overlooking Durango which was had been set out partially as Nicholson's personal accommodation and partially as offices and editing rooms.

'I've gotta get out of here,' Belushi was mumbling to himself inside the office part of the bungalow at which the car had dropped him. 'The hotel is suck-o, man.' Harold Schneider tried to calm him, but Belushi appeared scared and disorientated. He continued to rant and shout, and at one stage picked up a kitchen knife and appeared to be contemplating jabbing the blade into his own heart.

'I don't need all this,' he said over and over again.

Schneider tried to calm him, and then Harry Gittes, who had hired him in the first place on Nicholson's orders, arrived. He was firmer and stronger.

'You are a real asshole. You're acting like a complete asshole,' he told Belushi. 'You're going to put us all in deep shit.'

Belushi slumped into a chair in contemplation, then fell into a deep sleep as if suddenly grasped by an inner force. He was soon snoring and blowing like a tugboat.

'What's this?' snapped Nicholson when he arrived back from the set. 'A crash pad?'

He left Schneider with the task of getting Belushi to his hotel. They were brawling and shouting insults at each other. Schneider, furious, had to be physically restrained from hitting Belushi; Nicholson remained in his quarters, blissfully unaware of the commotion.

Next morning, Belushi arrived on set looking hungover and sheepish. He apologized to Gittes for the trouble. Nicholson had been told. He was the director and had to bawl him out; it was expected of him.

'You asshole. Any other producers would write you out. You only stay in because they're my friends. If Paramount people were here, you'd be kissed off and your career in movies would be totally fucked.'

That said, there followed a frustrating four weeks for Belushi, whose part could be written on the inside flap of a book of matches. Days went by when he and the others were just hanging around while Nicholson and Mary Steenburgen played their scenes; it was their movie. Ed Begley jnr., and Belushi also hit the local bars as they hung around for their time on set, but neither had much contact with Nicholson who returned to his bungalow after each day's work to meals prepared by a housekeeper; others understood that admission was by invitation only. Belushi's contract stipulated he should be available to return to New York to begin filming a new series of 'Saturday Night Live', but by mid-September, he still had not completed his few lines of dialogue for *Goin' South*. He flew up to New York and then back again at their expense to complete his work towards the end of the month. It was a year before the movie was ready for release and it turned out to be a minor disaster for Nicholson. His direction of the film – and especially of himself – was loose and unequal. And since he had to take the blame on two fronts, the critics went for the jugular. Pauline Kael of the *New Yorker*, called him a 'leering leprechaun'. Comparing him with his previous roles and recent dramatic performances, she said, 'Here there's nothing hidden and nothing hell-bent or sinister – he's just a fatuous actor ... [he] keeps working his mouth with tongue darting out and dangling lewdly; he's like an advertisement for a porno film.' Gary Arnold of the *Washington Post* represented a bunch of similarly poor reviews when he wrote, 'Another director would have advised him to put a lid on all the smirking, winking, strutting, grinning, leering, tongue-wagging, growling, cackling, scratching ... ' Several reviewers appeared to be going for Nicholson on a different count. 'He talks as if needed to blow his nose,' said Pauline Kael; 'Nicholson plays the role like the before half of a Dristan commercial, with nasal passages blocked. Why, I don't know, and don't care to ask,' wrote Charles Champlin in the *Los Angeles Times*, while *New York* magazine noted his 'peculiar nasal voice and fogged manner'. To this obvious implication about drugs, Nicholson responded, 'I was merely trying to do my Clark Gable bit.'

John Belushi, for whom the movie and the hanging-around had been a torment, was on screen in the finished version for two minutes and forty-eight seconds, and it was a tantalising taste for more. But the result was that questions were being asked about Nicholson's judgement.

13

Edge of Darkness

We looked over his shoulder in *The Shining* and saw the one line, repeated *ad infinitum*, 'All work and no play makes Jack a dull boy.' Stanley Kubrick worked him harder than any other director ever had while they were shooting this adaptation of Stephen King's best-seller, a gothic horror story of a haunted hotel, and for quite some time Margaret Trudeau claimed she helped him enjoy his off-duty moments to make sure that his life did not become dull.

Never dull?

Bull! said Nicholson when he heard of Mrs Trudeau's version of events, appearing as always to dismiss the love-making claims of the ex-wife of Canada's former Prime Minister, Pierre Trudeau. However, she was quite adamant in her account that they were – albeit briefly – passionate lovers. There had been other lovers since she left Trudeau and their three sons two years earlier, after seven years of marriage, and embarked upon her embarrassingly childish swirl around the world – jetsetting was the 'in' term then – with men several years her junior, ogling Mick Jagger like a love-starved groupie, and standing around at posh people's parties eyeing the local talent. At one of them, she discovered Nicholson. He had arrived in London to work on *The Shining*, for which he had been offered $1.25 million plus a percentage of the gross, which seemed a sure enough bet to earn him more millions, though, of course, he was still not a mercenary actor, we were told by Nicholson himself, and would have done it for less, just for the chance to work with Kubrick. Filming was to start early in 1978, and it was expected to be a long task.

Notwithstanding the salary, producers of *The Shining* provided him with a substantial house in London, rented for £850 a week, which in those days was sufficient to acquire a four-bedroomed, four-bathroomed, four-reception-roomed mini-mansion with a covered garden, on the Chelsea embankment, and put a Daimler with a driver named George outside the front door. For the next eighteen months – with time off for good behaviour and occasional sorties back to Los Angeles – Jack enjoyed stylish London life and was a regular attender of the parties given by the alleged élite of English café society, with their Knightsbridge haunts and reserved entrée to a nightlife populated by poseurs.

Margaret Trudeau met Jack at a party given by man-about-town antique dealer Martin Summers, and his wife Nona. He was alone and, she says, she was immediately attracted by the leering twinkle in his eyes. She was accompanied by a younger rock musician identified only as Tommy from Texas, who had a penchant for staying up all night and eating caviare and drinking champagne in bed; it was he who had introduced her to a sleazy world of drugs and sex. She escaped from him that night by fleeing with Nicholson in his Daimler, crouching in the back so that she would not be seen. That night of their first meeting was also the one when she discovered, as they drove around London behind 'the inscrutable George, just how much room there was in the back of a Daimler'. She ditched Tommy and spent some time with Nicholson. They made love all night, she said and she joined him regularly at his Chelsea home for some 'flirting'. Margaret should have got the message, though. He kept telling her he was in love with Anjelica and gave the former first lady of Canada an unceremonious brush-off when he said one evening with apparent glee,

'Guess who's coming tomorrow?'

It was Anjelica, joining him for the duration in London, and Mrs Trudeau, who for a moment there had visions of a more permanent relationship with Nicholson, settled for a brief encounter and went off to find Ryan O'Neal.

Anjelica was slightly gloomy when she arrived in London, and had been for some months. The Polanski business had left a scar. She did not much care for the kind of sickeningly patronizing people whom she knew would be surrounding Jack at parties. She deserved sympathy, trapped as she was in that phoney existence of famous names and sycophantic hangers-on that had surrounded her like a

strait-jacket since she was a child; few were true friends. Her relationship with Nicholson was back on *terra firma* and he had even asked
her to marry him, which she refused to do because she thought it
was an offer made out of sympathy. Not only that, she was afraid
of marriage. She had seen too many bad ones. She felt her life was
going nowhere. She had no career, no major ambitions and if
she had once become fed up with being described alternately as
Nicholson's 'long-time girlfriend' or Huston's daughter, she now
positively detested seeing these descriptions of herself in print.

If ever that over-used term of 'searching for herself' could be
legitimately applied, it was then for Anjelica. The Huston dynasty
still haunted her, yet drew her to their world. She reacted by
staunchly rejecting the opportunities that came her way because she
was a Huston, and which others in Hollywood would have given
their right arm to have; she saw them as a 'baggage of nepotistic
embarrassment'. Nor could she dispose of the bundle of fears that
had engulfed her since her father forced her into her first acting role
so many years earlier. All this pent-up uncertainty affected her
relationship with Nicholson just as much as his flirtations, for which
he tried to compensate by helping her through the tormented
moments of total disillusionment with her life. He could set up
auditions and lay on film roles; he even offered her a part with
himself and Beatty in *The Fortune*.

Anjelica rejected them. 'Absolutely not,' she said. 'I don't want
hand-outs.' Nepotism again. He tried taking her back to her roots
when they were in Europe, and travelled to Ireland to her former
home. Anjelica had not been to St Clerans since her mother's death.
Her father had sold the castle since then but she wandered the
grounds and talked to a gardener who was there when John Huston
was squire; she and the gardener both cried. Anjelica admitted to a
feeling of being demoralized, almost paralysed. 'When I first met
Jack, I decided I did not want to work for a year,' she said, 'and
then it became two. Before I knew it, I hadn't worked for five years
and when I was living with him it was to all intents and purposes
as a housewife without my own centre. Not that I didn't have a
good time. I travelled a lot on his films but at a certain point I
became thoroughly disillusioned with myself for not having an aim,
and this was merely aggravated by the fact that we were surrounded
by very motivated people all day long.'

There was nothing in London to change her perception of life, either, and once again she had to endure the personality changes that came through the role he was playing in *The Shining*. He was working hard, often not coming home until late in the evening. They seldom went out and on one occasion when they did, they were an hour late for an engagement to meet Princess Margaret. It was all very similar to the time he was filming the traumatic scenes of *One Flew over the Cuckoo's Nest* and he would come home some nights desperately overwhelmed by the demands of that day's work.

This was only enhanced by his appearance, because by then he was into the period of the film where his character was unshaven, unkempt and totally mad. He was the one under pressure now and there were times when he wished he'd never met Stanley Kubrick. There were indeed some very heavy scenes requiring character changes that just could not be easily shaken out of an actor, simply by walking off the set at the end of a day's work.

Kubrick had a reputation for being methodical and meticulous in everything he did, although not everyone shares the view that the end result is worthwhile. That very coherent writer on the cinema, David Thomson, opens his entry on the director in his *Biographical Dictionary of the Cinema*, 'Kubrick is the most significant and ornate dead end in modern cinema ... he is most impressive to the uninformed, speculative visitors to the art.' So at least, there was controversy; it has dogged him through his interpretations of such career milestones as *Spartacus, Lolita, Dr Strangelove* and *A Clockwork Orange* and from that standpoint he and Nicholson looked an ideal partnership. Soon after seeing him in *Easy Rider*, Kubrick called Nicholson out of the blue one day and said, 'I want you to play Napoleon for me.'

'Fine,' said Jack. 'When do I start?'

'Soon,' said Kubrick. 'I'm just putting together a deal now.'

They talked about it for the next five years. 'How's Napoleon?' Nicholson would enquire from time to time. He was still dead.

Kubrick had trouble getting the finance, even with Nicholson's promise of joining him. Perhaps that was the problem. Backers might not readily have seen how that laconic New Jersey drawl, oozing a mixture of mischief and malice that had been Nicholson's forte, could be laid upon a thoroughly European character like Napoleon. Too many people still remembered those awful historical pieces of the Fifties when the likes of Tony Curtis had to say 'Yonder lies the castle of my father' in a thick Bronx brogue.

When Kubrick called, just as Nicholson had finished the script of *Goin' South*, he did not mention Napoleon but asked, 'Have you read Stephen King's new novel?' He hadn't, but got hold of a copy of the book, read it and sent a Yes message to Kubrick back in England, to whence he had retreated from Hollywood mayhem in 1961, saying 'I'll never work in that town again.'

Readers will recall that the Stephen King story is that of an aspiring novelist who gets the job of caretaker at a seasonal hotel in Colorado, called the Overlook Hotel. It is a vast place that is kept closed during winter because of its isolated, inaccessible position in the mountainous snow. It was also built on an ancient Indian burial ground and apparently haunted by the ghosts of past misdeeds in American history. Kubrick achieves an absolute air of prevailing malevolence as the departing staff show the Nicholson character, Jack Torrance, his wife and unknowingly clairvoyant child around the palatial building. When they are alone, the Overlook Hotel becomes a terrifying empire of apparitions, dreams and psychic phenomena which envelopes Torrance, and we see him undergoing the metamorphosis from loving father and perfectly normal ex-schoolteacher, intent on writing a novel, into a raving murderous demon, trying to kill his family with an axe. As an acting task, it was one of the most daunting Nicholson had yet undertaken. He had never experienced the Kubrick style of directing; fifty or sixty takes for a difficult scene was something entirely new to him both as a director himself and as an actor, especially one who came from the Roger Corman school of quick-fire tactics.

'I did not mind that,' said Nicholson. 'Stanley had his way of making movies. But, yes, it was totally new to me, this kind of approach. We all do research, massive research sometimes, but Stanley goes for absolute detail in everything he does. It might be infuriating at the time, but usually it is the better for it.' The scenes that called for some of the most terrifying violence were the ones for which Nicholson had to dig deep; occasionally he brought some personal touches. The most memorable and quoted scene is when Torrance is hacking his way through a door with his axe while his wife cowers on the other side. He cuts a hole big enough for his face to be seen and cries out, 'Heeeeeeeere's Johnny.' The line was not in the script and was not in the book. When Nicholson suggested it, Kubrick did not understand what it meant, having lived in England for so long he had not seen the introduction to the Johnny Carson show on television. It was a line that brought a sudden injection of light relief into a particularly terrifying moment when audiences were being brought to the very edges of their seats.

The other scene written from Nicholson's own experiences, was based on the time he suffered writer's block during his marriage to Sandra Knight. He described it to Kubrick and it was written in. And so it was clear that Nicholson put a great deal into the part though it did attract criticism of the film when it was released, that Nicholson had grossly overacted and was often too camp. He said afterwards it was deliberate and was played just the way Kubrick wanted it; even while they were filming, Nicholson even challenged some moments and said, 'Jesus, Stanley, aren't I playing this too broad?' Kubrick said he was not; he wanted a semi-comical villain who was also essentially very evil.

It was this inter-relationship between humour and horror that most confused the critics because, needless to say, the appearance of *The Shining* brought a major divergence of views. It was to be expected anyway, with two of the most reviewed and reviewable film-makers of the age involved; some were judging Kubrick, some were judging Nicholson, while fans of Stephen King were assessing the overall merit of the film of the book. Too many went for usual analysis of the film, which often gets in the way of a good down-to-earth review, such as What was Kubrick trying to say? Was he trying to tell us that the devil is basically a clown? Those who were prepared to accept the film for what it was, i.e., an epic horror story in which Kubrick had flouted the more conventional expectations of horror, were also able to come to terms with a Nicholson they had not seen before, providing a classic piece of horror-story acting which his friends from days gone by would have applauded.

He was good, and the menace he brought to the part undoubtedly reverberated around cinema audiences throughout the world and still does in living rooms when it appears on television. It was not a critical success, but that never matters in the final analysis, which is the bottom-line figure. As Nicholson always answers when he runs up against a critic of *The Shining*, it got into the top ten of Warner Brothers 'all-time highest grossers'. Nicholson has often pointed out with a greater degree of honesty than some of his arty or pretentious contemporaries, shekels is what it is all about, isn't it? The business of making films is aimed at making money. Anyway, the evil forces in Stephen King's novel had the final say: the set used for *The Shining*, at Elstree Studios in Hertfordshire, mysteriously caught fire and burnt to the ground on the night of 24 January 1979.

⋆　　⋆　　⋆　　⋆　　⋆

Coincidence, as we well know, so often plays its part in the moulding of an image. Kubrick and *The Shining* provided Nicholson with a total diversion from that distinctive array of characters he had played during the last decade, from the alcoholic lawyer in *Easy Rider*, through to the quintessential Nicholson role in *Five Easy Pieces*, the brutal hedonist in *Carnal Knowledge*, the devious sailor in *The Last Detail*, the smooth, sensitive detective in *Chinatown* and the sympathetic lunatic in *One Flew over the Cuckoo's Nest*. *The Shining* gave him the opportunity for the underhand menace, and the theme of violence was to be extended, thus totally confounding casting directors, reviewers and Hollywood watchers, who still felt it necessary to categorize their leading men and give them carefully chosen identities of comparison with past stars. This was more noticeable in Hollywood as the decade turned than it had ever been, and if it meant fairly constant employment, several of the actors themselves went along with that, as illustrated by the words of Clint Eastwood, 'A man's gotta know his limitations.'

Nicholson continued to live dangerously and this was no better demonstrated than by his agreement to appear in films for his friends, which would ultimately mean that *The Shining* would be rapidly followed by three major movies which were all set for release in 1981. *The Postman Always Rings Twice*, directed by his long-time associate Bob Rafelson; *Reds*, for which producer, director and star Warren Beatty had handed him a 6 000-page projection; and *The Border* which another of his director pals, Tony Richardson, was about to bring to the screen. All had built-in risks professionally, not to mention the effect on his work schedule for the coming year, straight on top and overlapping with *The Shining*. It was horrendous. The rewards were immense and he was gleefully receiving box-

194

office reports that *The Shining*, in its third week of release, in June 1980, was second only to *The Empire Strikes Back*.

The coincidence that added one unexpected film to his list and bolstered the new nasty image he was acquiring with *The Shining* was the summary dismissal of Bob Rafelson from the directorship of the Robert Redford movie, *Brubaker*, after ten days of filming the American prison exposé. Rafelson had never been one to hold back in voicing his disagreement with interpretation, or in criticizing a bad script; and when 20th Century-Fox announced they were giving the picture to Stuart Rosenberg instead, he went home for lunch and asked his lawyers to send them an acknowledgement of the dismissal notice, and a $25 million writ for breach of contract.

The phone rang. It was Jack.

'Bob ... since you've got a day or two to spare, why don't we do *The Postman*?'

Rafelson said he did not want to do a remake.

Nicholson replied, 'Jesus, you're the one who turned me on to it in the first place.'

This was true. In 1972, Rafelson had suggested Nicholson should do a remake of Tay Garnett's 1947 hit *The Postman Always Rings Twice*. At the time, Nicholson was with Michelle Phillips, who wanted a career of her own. It was thought they would do a double act, taking the male and female leads. MGM got as far as talking money and then said they would only come in if Raquel Welch co-starred and not Ms Phillips, since the former was a more commercial name than the latter, regardless of her unsuitability for the role as perceived by the novelist James M. Cain. Whereas others would readily have dumped their girlfriend for the chance of climbing all over Miss Welch's body, as called for repeatedly in the script, Nicholson declined their kind offer and there it rested.

He kept it close to the top of the pile and retrieved it when his friend was bounced by 20th Century. Rafelson read it again, then looked at the *film noir* version, director Tay Garnett's classic made in 1946 with Lana Turner and John Garfield. Rafelson talked again with Nicholson, who was convinced that though it had been made several times, *The Postman* still had tremendous potential, partly because the censors had never allowed the book to be accurately portrayed. Also, appealing to Nicholson was Cain's unique approach to thriller writing, in that there were no detective heroes. The protagonists were all criminals. But, above all, it was the sex theme that most attracted Nicholson to it and he wanted to highlight and extend the provocative scenes first made famous by Lana Turner.

They hired the Pulitzer prize-winning playwright David Mamet for the script, and world-class cinematographer Sven Nykist, plus the remarkable new young star, Jessica Lange, to play opposite Nicholson; a fair body of talent, one would imagine, to bring out a great film. Reality has a habit of throwing things off course. But, let's start with Mamet's script — here's a taste:

> He [Nicholson] silences her [Lange] by kissing her. It becomes very passionate. He grabs her by the hair and pulls her face to him. He grabs her crotch and lifts her up on her toes. He bites her lip. She recoils with a slight 'Oh' and then goes back to kissing him.
>
> Their passion ebbs. She holds him off to look at him. She feels the side of her mouth where she was bit. It is bleeding. She examines the blood on her finger. She smears it around Frank's mouth gently.
>
> A beat. Nick [her husband] has stopped singing. He calls from upstairs imperiously . . .
>
> Nick (*vo*): Cora
>
> Frank: You cut it on a glass. You got a glass chipped on the rim . . . '

The story, in a nutshell, is one of passion, murder, mistrust and deceit. Frank, the Nicholson character, is a ex-convict and mysterious drifter in the days of the Depression, hitching across America. He falls upon a roadside café run by a Greek, who befriends him, and his sexy, younger wife, who falls in love with him. Their passion becomes obsessional until they devise a plan to murder the husband and make it look like an accident. A small detail traps them, but a clever lawyer gets them off. So Frank and Cora are together at last, but they begin to grow mistrustful of each other. Then Cora has a freak accident which kills her, and the film ends with police sirens in the distance, leaving us to imagine that Frank is about to be arrested for her murder.

The Rafelson-Nicholson version deliberately packed the story with sex in a way that Tay Garnett was unable to do. They made the sets more in line with Cain's descriptions — a dirtier kitchen table, for example, where Frank and Cora make love; even Jessica Lange admirably agreed to tone down her natural beauty to keep her character more accurately to the slightly tacky Cora in the book.

When it came to playing the sex scenes, Nicholson was intent on making them as realistic as possible – even to the extent of spending forty-five minutes upstairs, away from the crew and fellow actors trying to achieve and sustain an erection, 'a full stinger' to use his own words. He did not normally have any problems on that score, especially when playing with one so attractive at Miss Lange; but he had some difficulty in getting his erection in front of the assembled crew and cast. The scene, he felt, was sufficiently important to virtually portray the sex act and he needed an erect penis – his own – for the full effect. 'They had never seen that before in the movies,' he explained. 'I just knew that odd image would be a stunner.'

Nicholson was obviously pleased with the result and, according to the gossips on set, he retained a personal video of this particular encounter with Miss Lange to take home and show his friends. In an odd sort of way, however, all these modifications and increased sex content actually detracted from the impact. The film turned out to be *not* as sexy, *too* grimy and *too* tacky. Roger Ebert described the movie as a triumph of atmosphere, with dazzling performances by Nicholson and Lange, and encompassed by a crescendo of mounting violence. Yet the film remained empty and unconvincing.

Anjelica Huston had a bit part in the picture, absurdly cast as a German lion tamer, but at last she was working and had done something positive towards bringing a sense of purpose into her life, other than being around for Jack's pleasure and companionship. She had picked herself up and stopped her weepy calls to friends who had turned their telephones off because they no longer knew how to deal with her. The last few months had been bad, and made worse by Jack's day-and-night workload. The moment of decision came while she was convalescing from a car accident at the start of 1980. A drunk driver on the wrong side of the road had hit her car head-on. She had not been wearing a seat belt and went through the windscreen, breaking her nose in three places.

'That's it,' she said to her father. 'I'm going back to it. ... '

She meant acting; he was pleased. While Jack was working, she began to take acting lessons, and her tutor and mentor, Peggy Feury, was as good as a therapist, teaching her to disperse her emotional difficulties which related directly to her relationships with the two difficult men in her life, her lover and her father. Feury built her confidence, helped her stand apart from everything and look back to analyse her life and begin to make some adjustments.

*   *   *   *   *

Jack ploughed on, working as if there were no tomorrow. Workaholics are unusual among the acting profession because of the way the system operates. Nicholson had succeeded in becoming one; he wasn't letting go of any opportunity that appealed to him – but he passed on many that didn't – though it must be said that his policy of going for the off-beat or for self-generated material greatly reduced his earning power. Warren Beatty on the other hand was a model of one-upmanship. He called one day and said, 'Jack, I'm desperate. I'm looking for the right actor to play the part of Eugene O'Neill in *Reds*. Any ideas?'

Nicholson, who had listened endlessly in the past to Beatty's plans for the life story of the author of *Ten Days that Shook the World*, John Reed – one of his two obsessions, the other one being Howard Hughes – replied as Beatty had hoped, 'It's got to be me.'

An interesting comparison could be drawn at that moment between them. Since 1970, Nicholson had completed fifteen movies; Beatty had made five. His last, *Heaven Can Wait*, a whimsical romantic comedy remake of *Here Comes Mr Jordan*, originally released in 1941 starring Claude Rains and Robert Montgomery, was not hugely acclaimed but still took $80 million at the box office. And that was the difference at the time between Nicholson and Beatty. A Beatty movie tended to be a superb exercise in Hollywood aggrandizement, and if the two friends saw themselves in competition in terms of earning ability, there was really no contest.

Beatty's personal earnings from his three most successful movies – *Bonnie and Clyde*, *Shampoo* and *Heaven Can Wait*, only one of which was a very good film – are estimated at $100 million. He could therefore afford to take a breather between projects and view them in a totally different light to the way in which the likes of Nicholson and Bob Rafelson looked at their finances. Not that Nicholson was poor. The millions were clocking up two and three at a time now, and, of course, he was personally viewed as a far better actor than Beatty had ever been; comparisons on that score put Beatty as the lightweight. As a producer and general man about town with a phone sticking out of his ear, however, everything that Beatty did or discussed was in a hugely grandiloquent manner.

There was another difference, best summed up by a friend of both, Peter Fonda: 'Jack sticks to his friends like glue and every one of them knew that if they were in a trouble situation, they could count on Jack. I mean truly count on – and not the famous Warren Beatty "Can I get back to you?" A degree of rivalry was a built-in part of their friendship; it encompassed not merely their professional lives, in which Nicholson was by far the more productive, but also as we have noticed, their love lives. They liked the same kinds of women, they had an uncannily similar approach to women, as in the Chase. They liked a chase but not a long one. They were both apparently anxious to get down to serious matters as soon as possible in a relationship, and both apparently knew instantly whether they were dating someone for a brief encounter, or whether a more long-term arrangement was envisaged.

Their techniques, thereafter, varied; Beatty was always exceedingly polite and well mannered, whereas Nicholson was more casual and relaxed, often adopting a take-it-or-leave-it attitude with a mischievous undercurrent. They are also both highly intelligent men whose tastes and politics were similar, though Beatty tended to be the more active, even powerful, in the latter area.

★   ★   ★   ★   ★

Beatty had been working on *Reds* for ten years, and by 1979, when he was ready to go into production, the projected budget stood at well over $30 million. According to insider reports, it eventually cost nearer $50 million – twenty times more than the production costs of Nicholson and Rafelson movies. Some said Beatty could have put up his own money, but was shrewd enough not to do that; it is interesting to note that the film carried a copyright line which gave the ownership to Barclays Mercantile Industrial Finance Ltd, who came in when the money put up by Paramount Pictures was spent. That was the supreme touch of irony, slapped on a film about a Communist who would have gladly buried the American capitalist system.

It was an all–Beatty extravaganza. He produced, directed, wrote the screenplay (with Trevor Griffiths) and starred in *Reds*, along with some of the finest names around: Diane Keaton, Maureen Stapleton, Gene Hackman and, of course, Nicholson himself who, being a close pal, got caught up in the tailwinds of this much-discussed Hollywood epic – both off-screen and on.

The subject, John Reed, had become Beatty's total fascination. He was the dashing young all-American from Portland, Oregon, who joined the Greenwich Village radical circle of the early 1900s where the talk was of revolution. As a writer, he discovered Pancho Villa's struggle in Mexico and then just happened to be in the right place at the right time to view first hand Lenin's rise to power.

He made himself famous with his *Ten Days that Shook the World* and became more famous as the only American to be buried within the Kremlin walls after his death from typhus at the age of thirty-three. While the politics formed much of the story, there had to be a traditional romantic theme to carry it through, and that was derived from the long love affair between Reed and Louise Bryant, the wife of an Oregon dentist who followed him around the world, through all kinds of adversity, breaking it off only briefly for an affair with the sad alcoholic playwright Eugene O'Neill. Indeed, the heart of the film is the relationship between Reed and Bryant which, coincidentally, was also happening off-screen between Beatty and Diane Keaton, with a gossip column addition of Nicholson to complete the triangle. There was so much of it in the papers that one reviewer chose to focus on this aspect alone, stating that the film was about something far less significant and far less engaging than the romance between Reed and Bryant; it was about the romance Beatty found in Keaton.

To this could be added Nicholson's own enigmatic comments that he'd developed a real crush on Keaton while filming, which he felt bad about because it was his best friend's girl. He let it develop, he said, to help the realism of the film, even to the point of where he handed Bryant a poem – it was one he had personally written for Keaton. It was another mix-and-match love tangle that unsurprisingly gets into the gossip columns at exactly the same time the film is being promoted, and another notch was added to Nicholson's gun in the eyes of the world.

The 'realism' of romantic liaisons apart, the progression of *Reds* from script to film became one of the most talked-of, written-about epics since *Cleopatra*, and the Hollywood establishment chuckled away as reports filtered through that it would be just as disastrous. Headlines about the cost began to surface in the Hollywood trade press, with stories about Beatty and Nicholson flying around in a helicopter while the crew travelled by train, first class, to location in the English countryside. True, Beatty clearly intended to cut no corners and it became a personal fascination of Nicholson's to observe Beatty at work. He called him the Pro. Others were less complimentary as the production lurched on, with its armies and snowstorms and train journeys through several European countries and then back again for location in Greenwich Village.

Beatty, in his first film as director, often seemed unsure of what he wanted. During Nicholson's time on set, he had a lot of private discussions; they would often disappear together, but if Nicholson ever tried to talk him out of the continuous retakes that were occurring, Beatty never listened. Twenty or thirty retakes on dramatic scenes were not infrequent.

Maureen Stapleton, playing the fast-talking anarchist, Emma Goldman, was by 1980 a veteran of so many great parts; she had stood before some of the best directors who ever set foot in Hollywood. Normally, a jovial, happy-go-lucky soul who could – and still does – express herself in quite explicit terms, she became frustrated by being stuck in a series of retakes of a particular scene with Nicholson.

'Cut,' Beatty would shout. 'Let's do it again.'

Take twenty-three. ...

'For Chrissakes, Warren,' said Maureen, 'I don't know how else to play this scene. I've tried every which way. What do you want me to do, take my clothes off?'

'Please,' said Beatty, 'let's try once more.'

Take twenty-eight. ....

'That's great,' said Beatty. 'Terrific.' Everyone relaxed and for a moment they thought they'd got it right, and then Beatty perked up, 'One more time, please.'

To which Miss Stapleton responded, 'Are you out of your fucking mind?' and the crew applauded.

Edward Herrmann who played Max Eastman, described Beatty as '*mysterium tremendum*' because none of the cast except Nicholson and Keaton was shown a copy of the script.

'We could have been filming *Casablanca*,' said Herrmann. 'We'd be given our lines the night before ... when we complained, they said it didn't matter anyway because it was all in Warren's head and he kept changing it all the time.'

At the end of it, Beatty had 130 hours of film which he had to pare down to a final version of three hours and nineteen minutes, which he said was as short as it could possibly be, in spite of the exhibitors' complaints that their cinemas would be able to show it only twice a night instead of three times. Castigated over the costs, and knocked sideways over a flurry of hostile press reports about *Reds*, Beatty became reclusive and refused to give interviews about his masterpiece, which is what some were kind enough to describe it as; by and large reviews tended to be less than kind over one aspect or another, and on the news pages, he had become a current target to be lampooned.

Critics pretty well covered the spectrum of possible comment – Nicholson, for example, was described by Frank Corliss in *Time* as proving under Beatty's direction 'just how resourcefully sexy an actor he can be'. Stanley Kauffmann on the other hand complained that Nicholson's role was blandly written and Nicholson played Nicholson without any colours; he just floated through. That, according to Nicholson, was 'utter crap'. He thought the part was beautifully written, and it would have been criminal if he had not been good in it, given the direction he received from Beatty and the stimulation obtained from Diane Keaton. The Pro, he said supportively, deserved all the credit.

As Beatty became more reclusive, word was around that he was hiding from the embarrassment of producing a flop, and so it became trendy to say that *Reds* was a turkey, when in truth it was eminently watchable. They all learned lessons from that post-production débâcle. Thereafter, Nicholson himself always cooperated with promotional interviews around the time of the release of a film, thus helping the hype or counteracting bad reviews. In 1990, Beatty admitted he had been wrong not to personally come out to promote the film, for which he was criticized by his backers, worried that not even their original investment would be repaid by box-office receipts. 'I realize now that a film has to be promoted by the star. I should have done it with *Reds* and it would have helped; but I didn't and that was a mistake,' he said, as he began his world-wide publicity tour to hype his latest, *Dick Tracy*.

Nicholson remains to this day firmly behind the Pro for his courage in taking on such a vast project, and, as Academy Award time came around, Jack thought it was Beatty's turn. 'In the past the Academy has been a little reticent to give him his due. They think he's a little too pretty and cute.' In fact, *Reds* collected twelve nominations, including best supporting actor for Nicholson. Competition included *Chariots of Fire* and *On Golden Pond*. Best actor and best actress went to Henry Fonda and Katharine Hepburn. *Chariots of Fire* won best picture; Beatty won best director and Maureen Stapleton won best supporting actress, which she deserved for more reasons than one. Nicholson himself received an accolade from a surprising quarter. Soon afterwards, a letter was delivered to him from Eugene O'Neill's daughter Oona, to whom the playwright never spoke again after her marriage at seventeen to Charlie Chaplin. Oona's letter said, 'After a lifetime's acquired indifference I fell in love with my father, thanks to you.'

*   *   *   *   *

For Diane Keaton, the pressure of making *Reds* upon her personal relationship with Beatty was too much; she ended it soon after the Academy Awards. For Nicholson, incredibly, there was one other film to be made ... *The Border*, which he went into the moment he finished on *Reds*. It was overshadowed by *The Shining*, *The Postman Always Rings Twice* and *Reds*. Nicholson agreed to do it more as a favour to an old friend, director Tony Richardson, whom he had known since 1964 and with whom he had a long-standing arrangement to do a film as soon as a suitable script came up. Nicholson enjoyed Richardson's company and his work, notably *The Charge of the Light Brigade* and *Tom Jones*. The money was reasonable, of course, because Jack now had a set asking price from which he would not deter unless it was in an upward direction.

The Border had none of the social glamour of *Reds* or the controversiality of the sex scenes in *The Postman Always Rings Twice*; it was a violent film, in which Nicholson introduced an uncanny artiness as the tough border patrolman engaged in halting illegal immigration into the United States. Richardson had been joined by Oscar-nominee scriptwriter Deric Washburn (*The Deer Hunter*) and it became a docu-drama of occasionally depressing sorts, allied to the character's own personal problems of having a wife who can't stop spending. It was an ethereal subject, dramatic, though like many socio-message pictures, rather boring and never especially appealing to people who are actually spending money to go out for an evening's entertainment. Ever mindful of this thought, the backers, Universal, even tried to cheer up the ending. Jack would remember it for the lesson of being too serious; he was reaching a funny age.

14

Taking Stock

The decade of the Seventies caught up with Nicholson in a sort of concertina effect at the end of it. He stopped for a moment to take a breather and ten years of change barged into him, bringing with it the realization that he was the product of a brief golden era of American film renaissance which was now long gone and further adjustments were probably needed to meet the Eighties. That must have been pretty obvious, if only from the standpoint that the film industry had become swamped by the youth market and edging into the era of $100 million box-office blockbusters – the very word became the symbol of ambition for Hollywood producers, directors and actors – with films like *Star Wars*, *ET* and, at the other end of the adventure scale, *Jaws*.

In a very few years Nicholson had become the most awarded and applauded actor in Hollywood, the most quoted and copied. He achieved what few others had managed, by establishing himself as the champion of both extremes of a critical audience, from the new young radicals through to the smart set. A touch of bewilderment had set in, partly because of this new period of retrenchment within Hollywood and partly because of his own situation. The last four films had earned him a great deal of money but apart from his portrayal of Eugene O'Neill, the critics had not been unanimously enthusiastic either about his choice of roles or about his performances. He has never handled criticism too well, and some of the unkindliness in the review sections, especially of *The Shining* and *The Postman Always Rings Twice*, got his hackles up: 'The Shining has taken $100 million. What more do they want?' Some of the criticism got personal and that touched a nerve.

Whatever else he had achieved in terms of recognition, one other important element cannot be overlooked. Throughout his career, he had taken more risks than any leading man had ever taken in Hollywood, with such a contrasting selection of roles in a very short space of time. What drove him? The money? He said not. His explanation was that he was merely pursuing the policy which he had decided upon from the start. He had stuck to that policy rigidly and he had kept up his study of other people's careers, examining what they did and where they made their mistakes so that he could apply that learning to his own benefit. The risks, however, were not so much that he might upset the people in Hollywood who gave out the contracts and paid the cheques. As far as he was concerned, it was take it or leave it. It didn't matter. There were offers of scripts coming through the post daily. No, the chance he took was in alienating his legions of followers.

He had unquestionably annoyed some of them, for different reasons, with every one of his last four films, discounting *Reds*, in which his acclaim was pretty universal, and *The Last Tycoon*, in which his role was a cameo. In chopping and changing his character with such diversity, he had left a certain confusion amongst his followers. *The Shining*, for example, attracted many of his women admirers to the cinemas but then he scared them to death. *The Missouri Breaks* frustrated Nicholson and Brando fans because it was clearly rushed and not quite right. It was not a bad film but it could have been near brilliant. *Goin' South* proved to be a double disappointment, because he had directed and starred in it; but, like the critics, many of his fans did not appreciate the subtleties and it was largely dismissed as a mediocre, light-hearted romp in which his acting was camp. He admitted that a lot of people thought he had gone over the top in *Goin' South* and *The Shining*, but countered that he was always trying to keep his horizons open, looking to get somewhere new with it.

He also went too heavy for some tastes in the rough sex portrayed in *The Postman Always Rings Twice*, but the group he had most alienated by the switches in character were the academics who were still analysing the atmospherical and metaphorical undertones of *Chinatown*, which was voted in many campuses the best film of the Seventies for the way it had commented on the state of society, as it was told through a story set in the past. They had seen Nicholson as the sophisticate of smooth, clean wit and intelligence.

When challenged on this insistence towards an ever-changing perception, that he was a Hollywood chameleon, he maintained that it was this very fact that kept him fresh; he had to 'fiddle around with the fundamentals to remain sharp'. No one knew what to expect next and anyway, he said, actors like Redford changed often through his characters. There was a difference between the two. Redford was a sex symbol and idolized by women. Nicholson was also a sex symbol, but he was a man's man, as well. Redford never played around with quite such anti-social and controversial topics, nor accepted parts with the kind of frightening physical violence and rough sex with which Nicholson had recently become associated. Nicholson said he had suffered personally because the columnists and pundits had always seemed to have an identity crisis when writing about him, confusing his personality with his screen roles.

He is partly to blame for that; so often he has written part of himself or his own life into his films so that – on his own repeated admission – they became autobiographical moments. It seemed to suit his early pictures, like *Five Easy Pieces*, *Carnal Knowledge* and *The Last Detail*. They all echoed the culture, and he was the epitome of it; but, one day, the culture changed, the mood changed and the requirements changed. The media stopped regarding him in the same adulatory manner in which every move he made was reported with deference and real respect, and if, perchance, someone was going to criticize they usually deeply reasoned why they were doing so.

In 1981, he was forty-four years old; chunkier, with a receding hairline and a face which did not hide the crow's feet; it was the face of a man who had been working hard. He did not try to hide it or repel the signs of age. Like Woody Allen, he allowed the reality of thinning hair and slashed temples to show; it is all part of his style, an overhang from his era of the Sixties, of revealing yourself and mocking images of deception and perfection.

It would have been easy to say that age had caught up with him, and he couldn't play the counter-culture parts anymore, even if counter-culture still existed. What had happened to Nicholson in three years was the same thing that had happened to the previous generation of actors, and the one before that and so on. The new young crowd had taken over, but he had been so busy working, he had hardly noticed; coming up on the rails were the new leading men: Harrison Ford, Richard Gere, John Travolta, Tom Selleck, Tom Cruise and Sylvester Stallone. In fairness, Nicholson had never been a leading man. He had never had to be handsome or heroic and so in that sense Nicholson – perhaps because he was a late starter – missed out on the roles of the type that went to Gable, Grant, Hudson and, in a later age, Brando, Dean, Redford and McQueen. Not being especially goodlooking, he went straight into being a character actor.

The turn of the decade, with the newer stars and the 'blockbuster' syndrome coming in, was a good point at which to stop and look around. Too much had happened in the last ten years, as if he had crammed two decades into one, and life in the Dream Factories had not improved; it was filled with the same kind of uncertainty, indecision and retribution that had dogged the industry for the past ten years. There were also too many casualties lying around Hollywood – some of whom were his friends, and whom he had helped with cash loans during hard times – to remind him that fame and fortune can disappear as quickly as it arrived; his friends were always reminded of his concern for status by one of the objects in his home, which attracted the attention of every visitor. It was a silver platter containing a pile of shredded money, dollar bills of all denominations. It was there to make plain his attitude to wealth: 'It doesn't matter how much you make, you still can't save anything unless you're one of the landed gentry. You just have to remember that John Wayne was broke in 1960 to see just how ephemeral movie money can be.'

Witness also what was happening at that very point in time to his pal, Peter Bogdanovich, who achieved fame at the same time as Nicholson and became the most sought-after film-maker in town. In 1981, he commenced his slide toward bankruptcy and possible oblivion, though for more reasons than a sudden desertion of his abilities. In a darkened room in his Bel Air mansion, he sat morosely alone, indeterminately watching his murdered lover Dorothy Stratten in the film in which she starred for him, *They All Laughed*. When the movie was completed she and Bogdanovich were locked in a passionate affair until, on 14 August 1980, Dorothy was shot dead by her estranged husband who then turned the gun upon himself. If he couldn't have her, no one else was going to either.

Bogdanovich was robbed of his lover at the very zenith of their relationship, and thus mourned her with devouring sorrow.

He wrote a book on her life in which he absolved himself from blame for her death, yet made intemperate remarks aimed at Hugh Hefner and the Playboy system which had discovered Dorothy, claiming that she had been exploited, seduced and corrupted in the Playboy Mansion. Hefner responded by making an hour-long video on Dorothy Stratten and said that her death was in no way due to Playboy, but to the affair she had with Bogdanovich, whom he virtually accused of having under-age sex with Dorothy's sister Louise. The whole business lurched on from one unseemly episode to the next, with mutual friends of the two protagonists looking on incredulously. Bogdanovich married Louise, the film *They All Laughed* was a flop, and the once high-flier who had made millions, saw them all depart – and more – until he was forced to file for bankruptcy with admitted debts of $6.6 million.

Such horror stories of lost fortunes are not uncommon, though rarely as spectacular. They have a sobering effect when the victims are close. In Nicholson's circle of friends, who used the Playboy Mansion like a social club, the Bogdanovich affair was naturally a matter of mutual concern. Some helped him out with loans, though would probably not admit to doing so in Hefner's presence.

Like Bogdanovich, Nicholson, Beatty and many more had been regular visitors to the Playboy mansion, set in five and three-quarter acres of lush gardens on Charing Cross Road, Bel Air. Hefner allowed close friends and show-business people access to the mansion, especially on Friday nights when he gave lavish dinner parties, with a movie and drinks afterwards, followed by a disco or other entertainment. Life at the mansion went on *ad infinitum* and Hefner's personally approved guests could arrive for dinner at nine, or for a two a.m. party or for champagne and breakfast, all based in the heady opulence of the surroundings – pools, exotic saunas, bars, games room and theatre; and, behind the mansion itself, the massive jacuzzi located in an area of Polynesian design with private guest rooms and bungalows. That is what wealth provided for Nicholson – the freedom to choose and the opportunities for involvements in this kind of lifestyle, if he felt so inclined, obscenely flamboyant and carefree though it was. He collected some of the trappings himself, more for comfort and pleasure than display.

His own jacuzzi, which took three years to carve out of the rocks, was his first move towards laid-back opulence. There were also two Mercedes outside on the drive now, a red one and a blue one. There was a Cadillac convertible in the garage, which he hardly ever used; but he preferred to drive his VW convertible. The house had undergone various refurbishment since his purchase. It looked handsome with its white stucco exterior and had an artistic feel to the interior, though still with a lived-in atmosphere, unlike so many Hollywood 'star' homes where the Persian rugs were never walked upon and the furniture looked as if it might never have been used. His living room was beamed and rustic, and it invited his visitors to slump and be comfortable. In winter, aromatic pine logs crackle in the hearth. Long and low sofas are around the walls, and behind them – and elsewhere in the house – he has on view his increasingly interesting art collection ('I'm not so much a collector, I just buy what I like'), which eventually included works by Matisse, Tiepolo, Magritte, Picasso and de Limpicka.

Though he disclaims being a collector, he attends art auctions in London and New York. In front of the sofa, he has an onyx coffee table, edged with silver and trimmed with silver ashtrays and a silver cigar box for his Cuban Monte Cristos. The guest bedroom where Polanski used to stay was long ago turned into the den, with a wall-sized television and VCR, where he will watch favourite movies or basketball. Another wall contains a bank of the best stereo equipment for his vast music collection.

There are two main bedrooms, his own at the end of the corridor with a balcony overlooking the pool, which he had installed to 'give myself an escape route if ever I needed it'. The other bedroom is Anjelica's room; she had been convalescing in Mulholland Drive since breaking her nose in the car accident. He kept to a fairly strict regime while working, though it still did not stop him staying up half the night if friends came to call. New friends, like John Belushi and Ed Begley, jnr., who came into his sphere while making *Goin' South*, dropped by occasionally.

Belushi's life was a mess through drugs and he sought Jack's advice about how much money he should charge per picture. Nicholson had one answer for Belushi, which was not necessarily true for others. 'John,' he'd say, 'just remember this: without you there'd be no fucking picture. Charge them a million and a quarter.' Nicholson admired Belushi's unique comedy talent, and he was known among his circle as being generous with his time in giving others a helping hand or advice based on his own hard-earned experience. When, for example, Mary Steenburgen won an Oscar for her role in *Melvin and Howard*, she made an acceptance speech in which she said she owed everything to Jack Nicholson, who cast her as his co-star in *Goin' South* when everyone else said he was crazy to do so. Mary said it was a good job for her that he was, otherwise she would have gone back to waiting tables in New York. Next day, after the Oscar presentations, Mary received a huge bouquet of flowers from Nicholson, with a message saying 'Dearest Chair ... [his nickname for her because her film character hung chairs on the wall] congratulations on Oscarhood, motherhood and for me, sainthood.'

Sometimes, even friends would not be allowed to disturb the Nicholson routine. Nick Nolte, one of the mavericks of the newer generation, recalled, 'I got there one night and the whole street's locked up. I punched the button on this big iron gate. The lights came on, the cameras started to roll and this automaton voice came out: "Who are you? What do you want? State your name and business." So I say, "Is Jack there, please?" And the voice comes back, "It is four o'clock in the morning. Please state your business." The cameras were still rolling when I left.' Nicholson would blame Brando, who he said was manic about anyone getting anywhere near his place. Though the likes of Nolte, Belushi and, of course, all his more long-standing friends knew they could call at virtually any time, Nicholson jealously guarded his domesticity from unwanted interlopers. He was adamant about knowing who came to his parties and always insisted on learning who each and every guest might bring along. He had a strict rule: there were to be no crashers. He wanted to maintain the atmosphere of a group of people enjoying themselves in a completely private environment. He wanted no gossip column items about what happened at a Jack Nicholson party, and, by and large, he achieved it. In interviews, he himself released snippets to keep the hounds happy, and apart from the Polanski scandal, which attracted some meticulous media key-holing followed by the public scrutiny of police reports, there was only one other occasion when some private detail got out. That occurred when *Washington Post* journalist Bob Woodward began his investigations into the 'life and fast times' of John Belushi, which became a best-selling book.

It was inspired by Belushi's widow Judy, who made contact with Woodward soon after Belushi's death, and she requested all of Belushi's friends to cooperate. Nicholson was among the many whom Woodward interviewed in 1982. Woodward was already famous, of course; admired and hated in equal proportions for his role in exposing the Watergate scandal with colleague Carl Bernstein – portrayed in the film *All The President's Men* by Redford and Hoffman. Nicholson said he did not especially want to talk about Belushi after his death but did so because Judy had asked that he should. He spoke merely about his friendship with Belushi and of his talents; he was less inclined to discuss the comic's drug problems, and he was seething with anger, along with many others, when the book was published in 1984. As he must have anticipated from an investigative professional like Woodward, it was a compellingly chilling book, entitled *Wired*, which, in following his life and brief career, tracked Belushi's astonishing appetite for drugs; the word cocaine appeared in just about every other paragraph. It demonstrated the forces that worked against his wife, friends and managers who tried to stop him, and, in doing so, exposed the extent of the cocaine culture that had gripped Los Angeles, and the entertainment industry, in particular.

Those who cooperated with Woodward found themselves tainted by association with a morbid and awful tale. Nicholson's contribution was a fairly innocuous account of the Belushi he knew, which was accurately reported. Among recollections of Belushi at Nicholson's house was the story of how he turned up before dawn, at about five a.m. 'on a terror and trashing the place'. He took a jacuzzi and then sat around in a bathrobe talking about how he wanted to do a musical with Ken Russell, with himself playing God.

Nicholson's anger over Woodward's work stemmed not merely from the overall tenor of the book itself. Interviews given by others enabled Woodward to put some famous names in a drugs environment, and the passage that stung Nicholson into a rage referred to his ambivalence about his friends using drugs while in his house and claiming that he 'at one time kept two kinds of cocaine – the "downstairs cocaine" for visitors and acquaintances and the "upstairs cocaine" for special friends and women'. Thereafter, Nicholson referred to Woodward in language of the genitalia. 'The man's is a ghoul,' he told Martin Torgoff. 'He's an exploiter of emotionally disturbed widows. I only talked to him because Judy [Belushi] asked me to.'

*   *   *   *   *

Nicholson himself had cancelled 1982. He was tired. He had been telling everyone as he neared completion of filming *The Border* that he had worked virtually every day for the past three years, which was true. He wanted a sabbatical; he wanted to go to bed, get up at the crack of noon, lay on the couch, slumber after a late breakfast, and then go and lay around the pool. When he had done enough laying about, he wanted to go to Aspen to do lots of skiing, and travel again to foreign parts and to the sunshine of the South of France, without having to plug a film or appear in front of the cameras for days on end. And, for the next year or so, the gossip columnists tracked him on his various excursions to fashionable spots, and wrote occasionally of the women he encountered, such as Princess Caroline of Monaco, Cathy Wolff, the seventeen–year-old daughter of Petula Clark, and *Thorn Birds* actress Rachel Ward.

Sometimes, Anjelica turned up at his side and they resumed their apparently open relationship, which allowed them to go their separate ways whenever either of them wished. Both insisted their relationship was better for it.

Anjelica had also come to terms with certain aspects of her life, and the car accident had prompted her into some decisions of her own. She went wholeheartedly towards forging her own career so that she was no longer a side-element to Nicholson's life. She began talking to directors and producers about auditioning, and sought additional coaching to set herself up. She secured small parts in two films in 1982, *This is Spinal Tap*, a satire on a British rock group touring the US, and in another called *The Ice Pirates*. Neither served any other purpose than to give her work experience. She also appeared in television, notably with Penny Marshall and Cindy Williams in their hit television series 'Laverne and Shirley'. She began scouting around for her own house and eventually bought an attractive palm-fringed bungalow not far away, into which she moved – and no, she told enquirers, this did not mean she and Jack were splitting up.

If anything, their relationship had become more stable because they were allowing each other some space, and for once in her life, when the telephone rang she knew it would be for her. 'There is not an area of my life that has not been touched by Jack's influence,' she said. 'He is a very rare and special being, sensible and at home with himself. When I'm with him, I feel as if I've come home. He's family.' The family frequently extended to include Jack's daughter, Jennifer, now nineteen, who had joined him in California from her mother's home in Hawaii to become a student at the University of Southern California, studying fine arts. They had developed what Nicholson himself had described as a very adult relationship, in which he had adopted a 'very open policy'. He had not tried to hide anything from her. She knew he had indulged in marijuana and there were some parts of his life which were easier to understand than others. He explained, 'I felt that we could only have a good relationship if I was totally honest with her about what I'm like and what I do.'

*   *   *   *   *

Ironically, family life was the subject of the movie that brought Nicholson back to the screen after his long lay-off, and it also provided a significant stepping stone in his professional life, more so perhaps than anyone realized at the time. Jim Brooks, better known in television for his productions of 'The Mary Tyler Moore Show', 'Rhoda' and 'Taxi', had been trying to get him on the telephone for ages. He owned the rights to Larry McMurtry's novel *Terms of Endearment* and intended to make a film of it, with himself producing, directing and writing the screenplay. He'd had difficulty in raising the money because the studio people he had talked to all had reservations. It was a first-time big-screen movie for Brooks, and because the story had an unhappy ending they challenged its viability. 'Could it be that we are in danger of doing some original work?' said Brooks with a deserving note of sarcasm. Paramount eventually agreed to back him, subject to cast approval. He had signed Debra Winger and Shirley MacLaine as co-stars and desperately needed a middle-aged male star who would take third billing in a supporting role to play a pot-bellied, slightly balding, hard-drinking, girl-chasing former astronaut, without worrying what it might do to his image. Burt Reynolds had already turned it down.

Nicholson read the script and said instantly that he would do it. 'How many scripts make you cry? I read hundreds of screenplays every year and this one made me think, "Yeah, I know just how this guy feels." It was a terrific play.' Nicholson did not see the film merely as being potentially very good, which would also pay him very good money – $1 million plus profit participation which, it was said, eventually earned him a reported $7 million.

It offered him the very type of role he had been seeking to take him across the threshold from being a thirtysomething renegade from sex and psychopathic activity, into a more mellow style, in which he could grow as a person and an artist. He must have known he had to adjust his image without admitting to having midlife crisis, and *Terms of Endearment* was important because it provided him with exactly that opportunity: 'I could not keep on playing thirty-five year olds. Apart from giving me a more redeeming character to play, I was interested in the transition from a personal standpoint. It's an area of life that had only been explored in sullen lime-green tracts about midlife crises or in situation comedy. Whereas, in truth, it can be different. People have written great novels, for example, during this period of life.'

It could not have been better. The story had a Chaplinesque blend of comedy and pathos in which Nicholson excelled; it was exactly his kind of leery, mischievous humour. He played Gary Breedlove, who had retired from spaceships to a less-than-quiet life in the wealthy suburbs of Houston, Texas – where the squeals and shrieks of his unending parade of one-night stands upsets his neighbour, played by Shirley MacLaine. Her character is the goofy widow, Aurora Greenway, who had remained sexually inactive since her husband died fifteen years earlier. She is first appalled by her obnoxious neighbour and then touched by him when she discovers he has possibilities. This bittersweet romance is second to the main theme of a remarkable mother-daughter story, which flows effort-lessly through their relationships, with ample lighthearted moments of life, quite naturally punctuated by tragedies. It was a warm and enjoyable film which brought excellent reviews. *Terms of Endearment* also won eleven Academy Award nominations and Nicholson became only the third actor in Academy history to do the double. He won the Oscar for best supporting actor to go with his award for best actor for *One Flew over the Cuckoo's Nest*, an achievement matched only by Jack Lemmon and Robert De Niro. Shirley MacLaine won best actress, and *Terms of Endearment* was voted best film for 1983.

Through a non-starring role, which bore an uncanny resemblance to the scene-stealing attributes of George Hanson in *Easy Rider*, Nicholson bounced back with some of the best reviews he had received in years. He sauntered casually to the podium on award night wearing his sunglasses, raised a fist, and, in typical nonchalant style that masked his glee, said, 'All you rock people down at the Roxy and up in the Rockies, rock on.'

Later he went to Europe where the film picked up more awards. France voted him best actor; he always had been a particular favourite of the French. He was jolly and working well in the promotion interviews until the *Sun* newspaper in London upset him with references to his alleged use of drugs, claiming he had had a 'string of drugs busts in America', which was untrue. He had never been arrested in his life, and only once encountered the law when they requested his fingerprints over the Polanski business – and cleared him. He also objected to the *Sun* reporting that he 'liked to get high four times a week'. They had to pay him substantial damages.

The general tone of press coverage in Europe cut deep and when he returned to America he was fed up, 'They blew this drug thing out of all proportion. I gave a press conference and I said some great stuff about the fucking picture, *Terms of Endearment*, and all they wrote about was cocaine which I didn't even say anything about! They said stuff that they just assumed because of my reputation.'

By the time of the accolades for *Terms of Endearment* he was already well into another project, two, in fact. The first was *Prizzi's Honour* which he had agreed to make for John Huston, with Anjelica in a supporting role, and second, he was planning the sequel to *Chinatown*, entitled *The Two Jakes*, with his friends Robert Evans and Robert Towne. The latter provided a minefield of problems which will be examined in a later chapter. *Prizzi's Honour*, on the other hand, gave him a unique opportunity which could probably never be repeated, to work with both the Hustons, whom he dearly loved.

John Huston was seventy-eight years old, and with his health fading through periodic bouts of emphysema he knew well that there would not be many more chances left to make a film with his daughter, an ambition he had held since she rejected his plans for her when she was seventeen. With her own new determination to dedicate herself to becoming a successful actress, Anjelica wanted to work with him, too, and at last overcame her anxieties over the accusations of nepotism. Huston also wanted to direct Nicholson, and the feeling was mutual; they admired each other's work immensely, regardless of having a father-in-law relationship. They were also very good friends. That did not stop Nicholson questioning the choice of script that would finally bring the three of them together.

Huston had taken an option on the novel, *Prizzi's Honour* by Richard Condon, his old friend from Ireland, whose most famous work, *The Manchurian Candidate*, a tense political thriller, became Frank Sinatra's finest film and a classic of its age. Nicholson did not immediately see the new project in the same light and Huston needed to persuade him; without Nicholson it was doubtful if he could raise the money, and the film would probably not have been made.

'I don't understand it,' Nicholson said to Huston after reading the novel and the screenplay, and still not appreciating that the whole tone would be one of satirical black comedy, a parody of *The Godfather*.

'I think,' said Huston, 'We've got the chance of doing something different here.' It was the exactly the sort of film in which he would have placed Bogart and Bacall. Nicholson was not entirely convinced, but said he would trust Huston's instincts, especially as he was so keen to make the picture and give a major role to Anjelica. A fee of $3.6 million provided an added incentive. Once again, he found himself taking on an intriguing, if unattractive, role in which he had to play the Mafia hitman named Charley Partanna with a strong Brooklyn accent and, like Bogart, a stiff upper lip. As usual, his immaculate preparation involved him personally buying Charley's strange wardrobe from secondhand shops in Los Angeles.

Like *The Godfather*, the film opens at a wedding, but there the similarity ends. Unlike the romantic charismatic characters that are liberally cast in that film as the Corleone family, the Prizzi family are a weird and gloomy collection of people whose portrayal upset the Italian community of New York to such a degree that they complained to 20th Century-Fox; they felt that once again their nationality was being shown as Mafia-orientated, which it was not, but worse than that, they all appeared so dumb!

Nicholson, as the Don's grandson, played it very dumb. He was the monosyllabic, implacable hitman who killed without remorse and whose character is so unattractive that Huston wanted Nicholson to wear a bald wig. Nicholson said he would prefer not to do that; he needed to administer his own interpretation, which Richard Schichel of *Time* magazine judged to be 'one of his boldest performances' with a subtlety and nerve that matched Huston's. In the opening scene at the wedding, he discovers a beautiful blonde stranger (Kathleen Turner). There is an instant chemistry between them, not unnaturally, perhaps, because unbeknown to him, she is also a hired gun for the Mafia. As their love affair develops into passionate sex, Charley confides in his cousin and former fiancée, Maerose Prizzi, played by Anjelica Huston, who meantime is scheming to win him back. Ironically, her part had a throwback to her relationship with Nicholson in that she is seen as being seduced, abandoned, shrewish and spinster-like and, finally, an exceedingly efficient woman on her own account. During location work in Brooklyn, they also continued the role off-screen by staying at separate hotels. As usual, Nicholson had become consumed by the part and there was, according to Anjelica, 'too much of the hitman in him when he came home'.

Altogether, it is an odd story that plays with American criminal folklore and attempts to present a group of ordinary people – who perform callous and murderous deeds in pursuit of sex, money and power – as a matter of routine. The message is that organized greed corrupts all, and in composing this somewhat clinical parody, Huston constructed a film that laughs at itself and its characters in a black, almost bleak, way. Some did not see the joke. As Douglas Brodie reported, 'When *Prizzi's Honour* opened, some viewers sat in stunned silence, amazed at what transpired on-screen, a deadly-dull, emotionally empty ... long-winded and unlovable ... bland and boring and eliciting an emotional response from such an audience twice.' The critics were unevenly divided; most awarded *Prizzi's Honour* varying degrees of artistic merit and acclaim, and it provided an excellent topic for critical debate. Some even saw it as one of Huston's best works, in which Nicholson excelled: 'a baroque comedy – like *The Godfather* acted out by The Munsters'. To Nicholson's fans, it was unquestionably another test to their loyalty. He liked it. And he liked Anjelica's performance as the sedate and Machiavellian Mafia princess. So did her father. He called her to tell her she had done well. 'Afterwards, I realized I'd been waiting to hear that from him', she said. After the première, Nicholson said he could smell an Oscar – for Anjelica – and he was right. The Academy awarded her best supporting actress in what was her first major acting role since childhood, and thus the movie industry ensured the continuing Huston Oscar-winning tradition for one more generation. And Jack was jumping gleefully and whooping support for Anjelica. . . .

15

Chinatown *Revisited*

As we have so often seen, true life has a habit of interjecting itself into the dream factories, and turning wonderful hopes and aspirations into shattering disillusionment. It lay abruptly ahead for Nicholson as he moved into what was being billed as his new mellow era. The tenth anniversary of *Chinatown* was the starting point for the first attempt at the making of its sequel, *The Two Jakes*. It became an obsession which captured him for several years to come. The three men who had been responsible for the original, Nicholson, screenwriter Robert Towne, and Robert Evans, former production head of Paramount, formed a new partnership to make the second film of what had been planned as a trilogy, revisiting every eleven years.

Nicholson and his two friends set up a company called TEN Productions (from their initials, Towne, Evans, Nicholson) and were full of high hopes, with a partnership deal which stipulated they would make the film without salaries and take their recompense from a high percentage of the eventual box-office receipts. If *The Two Jakes* became as successful as *Chinatown*, it promised to bring many millions of dollars to share between them. As they planned it, *The Two Jakes* would be their film, owned by the triumvirate and made without interference from elsewhere. This they swore to each other as they sat around the inlaid mahogany conference table in the projection room of Evans' $15 million Beverly Hills mansion in the summer of 1984, when they put their hands together in a bond of trust. There would be no agents, lawyers, deal-makers or outside producers linked to the finance. The idea admirably suited Paramount, who agreed to put up the development money because

220

it would save considerably on the outlay. Work on scripts and the sets went full ahead, with filming planned to start in early 1985.

Nicholson, of course, would star as the detective Jake Gittes. Towne, whose *Chinatown* screenplay won him an Oscar, was to write the new play and direct the film, since Polanski – the original director – was unavoidably unavailable. Evans, who was an actor before he became head of production of Paramount in the Sixties (which he left in 1980) was to be the producer, and co-star in the role as the other Jake, a builder of tract homes in Southern California in the post-war housing boom, named Jake Berman. For the rest of the year and the early part of the next, the three men worked furiously towards their great Hollywood coup, a film of their very own, which had so seldom been achieved. A million dollars' worth of sets were built, location geography carefully mapped out and a rapid initial shoot of a few initial scenes was planned to get, as Nicholson put it, Paramount on the hook.

Somewhere in the sayings of Confucius there must be some advice about starting a partnership of three. Robert Evans became an odd man out as they progressed towards the day actual filming would begin. The story that was handed down in the aftermath was that Towne came to Nicholson and complained that Evans wasn't up to it; he could not cope with the demands of the role. They simply had to tell him he was off the picture, news which Nicholson correctly forecast would not be well received by Evans.

Towne had nothing against Evans personally. In fact, he was once quoted as saying that Evans set a 'standard for every kind of human generosity and one I have yet to see matched in this town'. In the movie business, yesterday's favour is not necessarily a consideration when ruthless deeds have to be done for the sake of the picture. Evans, for sure, would be mortified by what Towne suggested and not the least of his reasons for displeasure was his dire need of money, having just come through the very worst two years of his professional life. Details of his personal problems were already beginning to filter through and even his friends began to question whether or not it was merely the inadequate acting which put him out on a limb with Nicholson and Towne. As far as the two partners were concerned, it might well have been.

Elsewhere in Los Angeles, the name of Robert Evans was being mentioned in a sordid murder inquiry in which the protagonists had links to a consignment of stolen cocaine and, ultimately, connections stretching to the Columbian drugs cartel. How could Evans become involved with such a set of people? Before very long he was asking himself the very same question. Why me? How did it ever come to this? Everybody – literally everybody – in Hollywood was asking the same question because suddenly life looked grim for the former golden boy of a golden era, who was Hollywood's true-life Last Tycoon. Nicholson, who went around to Evans' mansion every weekend he could to play tennis on one of the best courts in Beverly Hills, used to call him 'Mogul'.

Their friendship stretched back long before Nicholson made *Chinatown*. That was just one of a string of successful films produced at Paramount when Evans was in charge. Others included *Love Story* – he married the star, Ali McGraw – *Rosemary's Baby*, *The Godfather*, *The Great Gatsby* and, ironically, *The Last Tycoon*. Some of the less successful included *Darling Lili*, *Finian's Rainbow*, *Paint Your Wagon* and *Urban Cowboy*. Enemies said the successful ones were made in spite of him, because, in truth, Robert Evans had never produced a single picture when he took over as head of production. The cynics and the revenge-seekers ganged up. Bob Evans had it coming to him. Hadn't he just been in the right place at the right time, like the subjects of any Hollywood success stories, fictional and real life?

He was discovered by Norma Shearer who thought he was the image of her former husband Irving Thalberg, and Evans took the role in *The Man of a Thousand Faces*. He then won a part in *The Sun Also Rises*, but after these early successes, he struggled as an actor and was 'on his ass' when he returned penniless to his family home in New York to work in his brother's clothing company. By a stroke of good fortune, the brothers sold the business for $2 million in 1964, and with his share, Robert set himself up as a producer. By another stroke of luck, Charles Bludhorn, the late creator of the Gulf Western conglomerate, had just bought a company which in turn owned the virtually bankrupt film studio, Paramount. Bludhorn knew nothing about the film business and he hired Evans, after reading a profile of him one day in the local newspaper. Six months later, Bob Evans was made world-wide head of Paramount Productions.

In the coming decade, which he described – as he did everything –

as magic, he became the new miracle worker of Hollywood, 'The Man with the Midas Touch', and he made sure that everyone knew it by his continual press conferences. He surrounded himself with all the trappings of great power and influence, including his vast reproduction French Regency mansion, with its thirty-two telephones, countless rooms, a personal bathroom in sheer black marble, a swimming pool with eighteen fountain jets that looked like something off a tropical island and visitors could hardly fail to miss, either, his Etruscan artefacts, all with individual spotlights tuned on their subjects with precision.

At dinner, the food was served on china designed by himself, showing a naked girl riding on a centaur, and after Ali McGraw walked out, he decorated his arms with gold bangles and the latest models. He hobnobbed with the rich and famous. In Hollywood, his party guests were the élite of the profession, especially those from the new wave like Hoffman, Polanski, Nicholson and Beatty. In higher circles, Henry Kissinger and Edward Kennedy were among his friends. His became the supreme success story, which he lived at the highest profile, modelling himself on his hero David O. Selznick, even down to a flirtation with stimulants. In 1980, he pleaded guilty to possession of cocaine and part of the condition of a probation order was that he should make at his own expense a $400,000 anti-drug film, starring Olivia Newton-John and Burt Reynolds.

Quite suddenly, he decided he needed a change and left Paramount. People asked, 'Did he fall, or was he pushed?' as they always do. It mattered not. The mogul had followed the route of moguls past, through the door marked Exit. He wanted to produce his own highly individualistic movie – just as Selznick had done with *Gone with the Wind*, and for him, it was to be *The Cotton Club*, to be written especially by Mario Puzo, with assistance from Francis Ford Coppola – the very same team that had given him *The Godfather*. Richard Gere, the latest male star, had tentatively agreed terms. Evans said it was going to be a masterpiece; but, for once, the super salesman was unable to convince the backers. He was financing pre-production costs himself, running at $140,000 a week and he had sold the last of his Paramount stock to pay his debts.

His search for backers took him into discussions with a variety of possibles, like Adnan Khashoggi, who politely refused. The next development resembled one of those unbelievably coincidental happenings that belong in the movies. His ex-wife Ali McGraw, still a good friend, had happened to mention to her limousine driver one day – Evans incidentally owned the limousine company – that Bob was having difficulty in raising the cash for *The Cotton Club*. The driver, a black actor doing the job while resting, made the fateful connection with a woman from Florida, for whom he had been driving in Los Angeles; she described herself as an importer of jewels and appeared to be exceedingly rich, which she wasn't. Thereafter, followed a long and complicated story of Evans' involvement with the woman and a whole mass of others with connections which tailed back into the seedy drugs world of Florida and Columbia, about which Evans knew nothing at the time.

The upshot of it all was that he went into partnership with a Puerto Rican banker, and an unsavoury New York promoter. Things turned sour, the promoter ended up murdered by contract killers in a row over a missing cocaine consignment. His body was found riddled with bullets in a remote canyon in California and thus, in April 1984, Robert Evans found himself in the middle of what became known as '*The Cotton Club* Case, a trifle unfairly, because the shooting was about the cocaine and not the movie deal.

It took the Los Angeles police force the ensuing five years to investigate, virtually putting Evans' career in suspension and certainly dragging his reputation through the mire as rumours abounded that he would be charged with conspiracy to murder. The District Attorney's office, having first indicated that he might be implicated, failed to produce any evidence to prove it and listed him as a chief prosecution witness. Nevertheless, the Hollywood cold shoulder was applied with vigour and he was outcast by all but a few of his closest friends.

Robert Evans, meanwhile, found other backers for *The Cotton Club*, principally two Lebanese casino owners from Las Vegas, but he lost control of the picture. It also went millions over budget, and he found himself on the wrong end of a nasty writ. The film flopped badly. He blamed Coppola, while Coppola blamed him – and Evans was close to financial ruin, which he hoped to stave off by his partnership with Nicholson and Towne.

When acrimony developed on the set of *The Two Jakes* in 1985, Evans was understandably in no mood to go quietly. He blew his top, as Nicholson always said he would. Towne moved that Evans should be sacked; it was the only way he thought they could save the film from disaster. Nicholson was worried about treating their partner 'like shit' but in the end agreed it had to be done. Evans refused to be replaced and Paramount – by now listening to the jungle drums about Evans' other various troubles – pulled out.

Production of Nicholson's great hope ended before it had even started. A million dollars' worth of sets stood idle and had to be destroyed. The partners were sued by creditors which cost them $3 million and a lot of bad publicity. The three friends who a year earlier had joined hands in a bond of trust and faith, parted in a mess of acrimonious dispute. *The Two Jakes* seemed doomed, for the moment. ...

Nicholson felt especially sorry for Evans, despite the fact that it was his intransigence that had indirectly caused the problem. However, his friend was clearly in dire straits, having to sell his mansion and lease it back to raise some capital on which to live. Towne also suffered. The furore in the press over *The Two Jakes* did his reputation no good at all, and it was almost another three years before he managed to get another film to write and direct, which was the flawed but intriguing *Tequila Sunrise*.

At the end of the day, the story of Robert Evans, reaching Hollywood breakfast tables in piecemeal over a period of time, turned out to be a far more incredible tale than some of the fictional stories he had brought to the screen – including the current one. Fact and fiction became blurred once again, and in that there was to be no better example than Nicholson's next job.

★   ★   ★   ★   ★

Almost on cue as *The Two Jakes* project collapsed, Mike Nichols was looking for a male lead for his film adaptation of *Heartburn*, Nora Ephron's own screenplay from her best-selling novel based on her true-life experience of marriage to a famous journalist. Just to recap, Nora was married to Carl Bernstein, the other half of the *Washington Post's* Watergate duo whose investigative partner, Bob Woodward, interviewed Nicholson in 1982 on the John Belushi story. Nora's tale, as patronizingly seen in *Heartburn*, the movie, was one of a charismatic professional couple who fell in love, had a child, and lived a wonderfully witty life, with nights of pepperoni and show tunes until she discovered he was having an affair with another. The other woman, in real life, was Margaret Jay, daughter of former British Prime Minister James Callaghan, and wife of the man whom the PM sent to Washington as British Ambassador, Peter Jay. But the film was a glossy and glossed-over account of the truth.

In Washington, and eventually London, it was a great talking point because of the personalities involved, and Nora Ephron was so bitter about it all that she sat down to a write a best-seller of a thinly disguised autobiographical nature. And *Heartburn*, the book, was rather different to the eventual film version. A wife scorned so badly writes in blood, Bernstein's. The alleged fictional husband was painted as an insensitive, sex-mad, male chauvinist 'who was capable of having sex with a Venetian blind'. Bernstein said that when he heard about it, he made a deliberate decision to say nothing to fellow journalists anxious to interview him.

He took it in his stride and after his initial anger, nay, white fury, he was man enough to admit that Nora had written a perfect book for the Eighties: 'It is a clever piece of gossip that owed its success to who we were. *Heartburn* is a book of our times. It is prurient and it obliterates everybody's dignity.' He was none too happy when he heard there was a movie in the offing and he telephoned his lawyer. Bernstein was worried that he would become a laughing stock and said, 'From now on I'm going to be hard-assed about this, in terms of what can be in the movie and what can't.' They settled out of court and Nora and the film-makers agreed to give Bernstein the right to see the script and consult with the director, Mike Nichols, on matters which he found distasteful. Nichols and Bernstein were old friends, and when he learned that the director was in charge of Nora's picture, he called and arranged a lunch. Nichols assured Bernstein he would abide by the legal agreement. The result was that script portrayed him in a far more favourable light than the book. Bernstein admitted, 'I was surprised, frankly, that they agreed to these conditions.'

Nicholson came in with a $3.5 million contract, two weeks after filming had started, as a favour to Mike Nichols whose first choice as leading man, Mandy Patinkin, had found the constraints of the legal manoeuvres too much to handle. Nicholson was given specific instructions from Mike Nichols, that he must *not* play Bernstein, whom he had met a couple of times in the past at political events. He had to create the husband character himself and it could not be based upon the real–life husband.

'I probably wouldn't have considered doing the movie,' Nicholson said, 'but I'd never been hired *not* to play someone before. I was hired not to play Carl and I liked the idea. It's a provocative idea for an actor.' He thought the part had been written as an uninteresting sort of a cad, though a likeable enough fellow, which was, for Nicholson, merely the basic ingredient. He reckoned, 'If you play characters for charm it's most often cloying so here was an opportunity where you had to bring a little bit of quality ... make it a little bit showboaty.'

His own personal stock of tricks, such as the way he might enter a room or basic things like getting up out of a chair or putting his feet on a table – plus the revolving eyebrows, a grin for all reasons and the occasional flash of his scary fierceness – are brought into play and at the end of it Carl Bernstein was probably wishing he was more like the character Nicholson created. Meryl Streep found herself pushed to block him from acting her off the screen. His moments were filled with humour and even when he was not in the action, his presence was felt to such a degree that audiences doubtless missed him not being there; never did the audience get the impression of the near villainous snake portrayed in the book.

Nicholson was having fun, as an actor and in his character, but the onus to make the picture work fell to Meryl Streep, the star of the show. She, on the other hand, was guided into playing the real Nora Ephron, and copied her whole demeanour down to her mannerisms and facial expressions; and so, whereas Nicholson was creating a fictional character completely from his imagination, Streep had the constant vision of Nora in her mind. Even so, Meryl Streep did carry the film along and there were some funny moments in which, with Nicholson as the feed, she excelled. These better moments tended to come in scene-length clips rather than hanging together as a whole.

It was also an unfortunate by-product that because so many people – and reviewers especially – were familiar with the characters and their story, which had been well documented in the gossip columns and had been told, every dot, comma and flying saucepan in the book, that it was not quite what they were expecting. The truth is Nicholson really played himself and just happened to be speaking words which were written for him; doubtless, if Mr Bernstein's lawyers had not won such a victory before the film was even started, Jack could just as easily have become the snake that everyone expected of him. Critics gave a mixed reaction and so did audiences; most seemed to think that the actors had been limited by a poorly structured script which went tangentally into other confusing areas, such as the scenes with Streep in the therapy group, with the redoubtable Maureen Stapleton, who personally rescued them from banality by her own performance. The film did not do justice to the book, nor to the actors in it and box-office response was decidedly low key. Streep, Nicholson, Stapleton? It should have been a very good film, and from a project that promised so much, Nicholson scored at best seven out of ten.

In the aftermath of analysis, there was a lot of gossip centred around a certain chemistry which had developed between Streep and Nicholson during the film. Director Mike Nichols had tried to induce it by keeping them apart until the very last minute – they had never met before – but Nicholson spoiled that scheme by barging into Streep's room, looking like something the cat had dragged in, and saying, 'Hi, do mind if I use your toilet?' However, it was certainly obvious in the early scenes of happier times in the marriage that they had quickly established a rapport which brought out the comedienne in Streep such as audiences had never seen. Her cracking wisecrack responses to Nicholson's fairly sizzled. There-after, it fizzled, languishing with a message that the film appeared to be promoting the idea of faithfulness and trust in marriage. This in itself was all rather ironic for Nicholson himself.

Word reached the outside world that underneath the arc lights Nicholson was in love again, totally smitten by Streep who was quite happily married to sculptor Don Gummer. As the film hit the circuits, Nicholson gave an interview to *Vanity Fair* which merely added a touch of spice to the mystery. He often chooses to chat to the mega-media at such vital times as the launch of his new movies. He talked of his 'experience' with Streep and continued ' . . . Meryl is my idol. She was so good [in one particular scene] . . . I was all at sea, floundering around, but I could see that we would be fine because she was doing great. You do fall in love with . . . ' (a weighty pause, a cough) 'with ... certain ... creative situations.'

Read into that what you will, because that is why it is there; it is part of the image and more important than ever, in 1986, because although he denied it when he made *Terms of Endearment*, a psychiatrist might assess that he was showing early symptoms of midlife crisis himself. A life-sized portrait of Meryl was hung in the Mulholland Drive house and Anjelica was so angry that Jack had to buy her a $85,000 bracelet to calm her down, so it was whispered. Was this true desire or was it just that some juicy gossip would give his box-office percentages a bit of a lift? Who knows. One thing was for sure, in an era in which teenage-orientated pictures were all the rage, and which Nicholson did not much care for, he was beginning to feel his age. During a break one night, he went to the movies and watched *Ferris Bueller's Day Off*. He came out feeling 'totally irrelevant, 119 years old and that my days were numbered'.

★   ★   ★   ★   ★

He went home to Anjelica, his ever-faithful and unmarried companion, apparently untouched by the message of fidelity in *Heartburn*, and continued to show some remarkable similarities in his life to that of the character he should have portrayed in the Nora Ephron story (if Carl Bernstein had not stopped him). He made some exceedingly profound remarks about a culture which fears total freedom, and noted that very rigid and specific moral principles relating to sexual fidelity needed adjustment to suit personal situations, like his own, no doubt.

Anjelica drifted in and out of his house and bed, and then back to her own with unconcerned ease; she looked the picture of a relatively contented woman who, unlike Nora, managed to come to terms with the lifestyle of her man, difficult though he was, at times. Another little local difficulty was already on the horizon. Nicholson went to Aspen to relax after *Heartburn*.

At a party one night at his ski-resort home, in February 1986, he met British model and aspiring actress Karen Mayo-Chandler, of whom much more will be heard later, as another tempestuous affair was in the making. The night in Aspen was a fairly typical party for Nicholson, in the Green House, one of the two he owned there. He opened the door personally to the party of six with whom Karen

229

had arrived. He took their coats and hung them in the closet and showed them where to change their snow boots to evening shoes. Some Irish friends were among the guests, including an Irish priest who had known his mother. He played the fiddle and everyone danced and sang. Nicholson, said Karen, was the perfect host; polite and sober. He drank Louis Roederer Cristal champagne, and never to excess. There was a buffet supper laid in the kitchen and guests wandered through the three downstairs room.

Those outside of his circle, Karen observed, might have been surprised to discover that one of the world's highest-paid film stars ran a fairly modest house, relaxed and informal, with few obvious signs of his wealth. He dressed in sloppy clothes which looked slightly dishevelled, but a closer examination would reveal even his baggy sweatpants carried an expensive designer label. Karen and one of her friends from the group with whom she had come to Aspen from Los Angeles were invited back to Nicholson's house the following evening, St Valentine's night. There was a log fire crackling, and the open curtains revealed a stunning view of the Aspen surroundings. More champagne was drunk and Karen claimed Nicholson made a guarded suggestion that the three of them should retire to his room, at which point she said she and her friend decided to leave.

Back in Los Angeles, they resumed where they had left off after a mysterious 'who's chasing whom', scenario in which he virtually snubbed her at Helena's nightclub – which Nicholson part-owned – and then apologized when they met again at a $500-a-ticket charity night at the Hard Rock Café. They eventually came together when she went to his house in Mulholland Drive for another party, at which she was admitted by Dave Stewart of the Eurythmics. Nicholson later showed her off to his friends, taking her to dinner at Robert Evans' mansion and to see a movie at Warren Beatty's. It was *Mona Lisa*. Nicholson and Beatty both loved Bob Hoskins after seeing him in *The Cotton Club*.

Further adventures were in store for Miss Mayo-Chandler. Friends could see what was happening and did not need to ask what this meant as far as he and Anjelica were concerned. It was the same as it had been for the past five or six years, a friendship which allowed him the latitude to continue another life just so long as he did not make a fool of her.

In the spring of 1986, soon after his meeting with Mayo-Chandler, efforts were under way to bring Nicholson and Huston back to the screen in romantic clinches. He had just been offered $5 million to make *The Witches of Eastwick*, which was being produced by a pair of young whiz-kids, Peter Guber and Jon Peters, for Warner Brothers – the same two who, a year later, had the audacity to offer him the part of The Joker in *Batman*. Anjelica was called to do a test for director George Miller, but on the day of her reading, she was unaccountably struck by nerves. She knew as soon as she had completed it that she would not get the part. Cher won the role instead, to join Michelle Pfeiffer and Susan Sarandon for a sex comedy loosely based on John Updike's best-selling novel – a film in which Nicholson played the Devil, in the guise of the satanic Darryl Van Horne, who excelled at the violin and the art of seduction.

For a man of a certain reputation, it was not an unnatural moment to observe, as many did, that it was a role for which Nicholson had been practising all his adult life. He typically threw himself into research for the part by reading Dante's *Inferno* and vast mounds of witch material from the middle ages, to give thought to the nature of evil, and declared to Anjelica that he wanted his audiences to think that Jack Nicholson was the Devil himself. That, she assured him, should not prove too difficult, even without the research.

It was going to be Nicholson's show. Everyone could see that; he was positively drooling in the publicity photographs, and with three beautiful women wrapping themselves around him at every turn of the page, it offered the type of role that best suited him, sexy comedy with a touch of menace – once the producers, with whom he had a devil of a time, decided exactly what sort of film it was they wanted. George Miller struggled to meet the edicts of Guber and Peters, shooting some scenes eight or nine different ways. The three actresses were occasionally near to tears, and were said to have tried some amateur witchcraft themselves to bring down a heavy rash of Herpes to inflict the two producers on the other side of the cameras. 'We all looked forward so much to working with Jack,' said Michelle, 'and then we were reduced to weeping because of the demands of these conflicting forces running the picture. I seriously considered walking off. I might well have done if it hadn't been for Jack.' He provided the shoulder to cry on, and since he only had two, there was always an odd girl out. More often it was Michelle. They had struck up a special kind of rapport and it helped her through the picture.

Nicholson ploughed on, regardless. He was going to have a good time in the role, which placed him in Eastwick, a conformist New England village where he is invoked by three bored wives seeking more pleasurable experiences than the local male population can supply. He buys a big mansion on the outskirts of town and no one knows who he is or from whence he came; the wives who summoned him, meantime, are delighted to discover that he can provide all that they desire of him. The three witches spoke highly of him in the film, and the three actresses were equally complimentary of their co-star off-screen; his well-known generosity towards his fellow thespians was to be invaluable to all three in some especially difficult scenes, and Cher reckoned his contribution alone largely helped to lift the film from average to very good.

The performance of all four sold it, and Nicholson dispensed his usual flair for relaxing his comrades to good effect. Cher was especially grateful: 'I wanted to be in *Witches of Eastwick* because of Jack. He was like the jewel and we women were the setting. I remember getting ready to do the buffet scene on the lawn and for some reason I got an anxiety attack. I could hardly move. I was terrified, and he put his arm around me and said, 'Look, it's free-floating anxiety, nerves. Nobody's gonna do this scene until you're ready.' And the minute he said that, I really started to feel good.'

Left to some uncomfortable moments of fantasia in the plot, it might not have fared as well as it did, becoming one of the great box-office success of 1987, taking more than $125 million. These figures are important, incidentally, not merely to assess the ever-present Hollywood obsession with grosses and box-office receipts, and money rather than art, but because invariably Nicholson has carved out for himself a percentage from which the real wealth – as opposed to the signing-on fee – is acquired. And none would be better in his entire life, past and possibly future, than the offer producers Guber and Peters came bearing at four o'clock one morning on the set of *The Witches of Eastwick*. Nicholson was yawning because of the hour.

'The Joker? In *Batman*?' he repeated incredulously.

'Yeah, Jack, yeah,' said Peters.

'Babe, you've got to be joking. I wouldn't do that even if Warners paid me fifty mill ...'

16

Passionate Nights

He was on television in the early summer, though not voluntarily. Jack Nicholson will not normally appear on television; he never has (apart from a couple of appearances as a struggling actor) and says he never will, and never, never, will he go on talk shows, which he hates. No, the television cameras turned instantly to capture him, head in hands, as the truly mortified fan of a basketball team which had just lost a potential place in history. He has supported the Los Angeles Lakers with an ardour verging on fanaticism for eighteen years, and that night was typical of a thousand. He arrived as the tension was mounting with the capacity crowd at the Los Angeles Forum waiting for the game to begin, and headed towards his two reserved $160-a-night seats in the front row on the side of the court, three seats away from the visiting coach and close to other celebrity fans like his pals John McEnroe and Tatum O'Neal.

A mild cheer goes up as Nicholson and Anjelica Huston arrive, he wearing one of his two dozen pairs of designer sunglasses, a crumpled white suit, black shirt and sneakers, and she more elegant, as usual, in white blouse and casual black slacks, with a silk bomber jacket slung over her shoulders. He waves and claps his hands. They cheer again and he takes his season-ticket seats right on top of the action; in spite of his closeness he has a pair of binoculars hanging around his neck. Normally, he slips in during the National Anthem to avoid a fuss. Then, he shuffles his feet, clears his throat and gets ready for some loud deliveries of support for the home team, or taunts against the visitors or insults for the referee.

This is the Nicholson ritual: a night of devoted, throaty, passionate support for his basketball heroes, whom he watches, work permitting, fifty nights a year. He is their number-one fan and has been for so long that no one treats him any differently to the rest, except for a ribald welcome from the crowd to which he impolitely responds. Visiting fans and officials eye him cautiously. He has a certain reputation in the arena, too. Occasionally he travels with them to away matches, but when he can't make it, either at home or away, they videotape the game for him, and send it express mail the following day to wherever he may be. The Lakers have plenty of celebrity followers, but he doesn't join in the backslapping routine in the dressing rooms. He just tries to be an ordinary fan, without any pretensions, and that means being a highly vocal one.

The tales of Nicholson and basketball are as legendary as him as a womanizer, and just as disputed. One of the best was back in 1980 when the Washington Bullets were playing at the Forum and a lively exchange broke out as the visitors' coach, Dick Motta, began shouting at an official and headed towards the scorer's table. Motta reckoned that just as he passed Nicholson, the star grabbed him by the legs.

'You touch me again and you won't need a frontal lobotomy,' screamed Motta.

'You're breaking the rules,' Nicholson shouted back.

'Say, pal,' Motta responded, 'If you wanna be a coach buy me a team and I'll make you my assistant. Now sit down.'

'Sit down yourself,' Nicholson came back. 'I pay money for these seats and by the way, pal, it'll take somebody bigger than you to make me sit.'

Such repartee has become familiar on the sidelines of some of America's most prestigious basketball events when Nicholson is in attendance. He shouts and argues and sometimes makes physical contact with referees and officials; his outbursts in which surrounding fans – and his own friends – join in have been known to raise the temperature of a game considerably. He has his own selection of gamesmanship tactics which he operates from the sidelines: 1) Save your loudest decibel yelling for drowning out the visiting coach just as he is trying to give crucial instructions; 2) Disguise your voice to make the referee think that the insults you are giving him are coming from the visiting bench; and 3) Make your taunts of the visitors original – so that they'll listen.

His best, or worst, encounters have been with the Boston Celtics.

At the Forum one night, Boston star Larry Bird came close with the ball to where Nicholson was sitting with his godson Nicky Adler, son of Lou, the music mogul, and he turned to the boy and urged, 'Hey babe, bite the son of a bitch.' Bird looked up and winked at the boy. That was good-humoured banter, but sometimes a note of bitterness creeps in. One of Boston's officials described him as 'an embarrassment to the game and a nuisance to the players'. This criticism came after Nicholson was alleged to have dropped his trousers and mooned at the Boston Garden home crowd, and Boston complained about the Lakers' celebrity hooligan – 'there's a difference between being an ass and a fan. And when a guy comes up and moons to the crowd, well . . .'

Since then, Nicholson has been hate material whenever he turns up for a game in Boston. When he flew in for the finals in 1984, he heard there might be a reception committee waiting so he threw fans off the track with an elaborate dodge, by making reservations at every major hotel. One of the local radio stations, WBCN Boston, was urging anyone who had tickets for the game to take a sign reading: 'Jack flew east, Jack flew west, Fly Jack back to the cuckoo's nest'. WBCN said the idea was submitted by a listener and Celtic's fan who was fed up with Nicholson's face and the bad-mouthing he gave the home team and its officials.

When he arrived at the ground, he found T-shirt sellers touting a great new line in slogans, 'Fuck you Jack'. He laughed and bought a dozen to take home. Inside there were more anti-Nicholson posters than pro-Boston signs, reading 'Hit the road Jack' and 'Choke on your coke Jack'. It was all fairly good natured and as he arrived to take his seat, he stood up and held his hand around his throat in the choking sign and made obscene gestures to demonstrate his view that Boston had no chance; he lived to tell the tale. And even in the middle of this sporting hostility, he found a small throng of supporters, all dressed in dark clothing and wearing black sunglasses. When he arrived they held up their own sign, which read 'Nicholson Youth'. The following year when Boston came back to the Forum there was some Nicholson-inspired excitement. K.C. Jones, the Boston coach, had been giving the officials a hard time, and when they came alongside the spot where Jack and his friends sat, he led a loud chorus of 'Fuck You' and a technical foul was called on the Boston bench.

Skiing, playing tennis, watching sport and betting are his major forms of relaxation – 'In my business, sport is the only entertainment I can go to and not know in advance how it ends.' He used to follow football, too, but his enthusiasm was less well received and once someone called the police during a fracas at the Los Angeles Coliseum. When Johny McEnroe was at his peak, he would fly across America to see him in the US Open. He travelled regularly to major fights and bets frequently but sportingly rather than for huge gain. And who else would have an autographed Cecil Beaton photograph of Sugar Ray Robinson hanging next to a Matisse?

★　　★　　★　　★　　★

Meanwhile, Anjelica, in recent months, had come further down the road to establishing herself as a leading actress. An Oscar was fine but she still needed more work to show that it was not merely a one-off role. Francis Ford Coppola cast her in his Vietnam War movie, *Gardens of Stone*, with James Caan, and her father was talking about completing a long-held ambition to film the James Joyce short story, 'The Dead', in which he wanted to involve three Hustons – himself, Anjelica and his son Tony – whom he had already put to work writing the script, in spite of John Huston's own incapacity. He was often confined to a wheelchair and carried a permanent supply of oxygen. Nicholson himself had been planning to slow down his own commitments, but he went back to work because, he said, Anjelica would be tied up in the coming months. He collected another $5 million to star in *Ironweed*, a star-studded film adaptation of William Kennedy's best-seller, which was scheduled for filming in Albany, New York, during the spring of 1987, at the same time that Anjelica would be working with her father on *The Dead*. There was an added bonus – his co-star would once again be Meryl Streep, whom he loved as an actress and, it was said, as a person. There was also one 'family' reunion that did not come off, as hoped by the gossip columnists. Susan Anspach's fifteen-year-old son, Caleb James, who was born after the actress appeared with Nicholson in *Five Easy Pieces*, was down for an audition to play the young version of Nicholson's character in *Ironweed*; dozens turned up for the casting call but Caleb was not among them.

Location filming was in New York and he therefore made it a

condition of his contract that the producers provide him with a house with an indoor swimming pool, where he could keep up a new fitness regime he had recently commenced because his weight had ballooned to over fifteen stone. It often did between films, understandably, perhaps, because he was at that psychological point in life of the Big 5–0, as he called it, and he did not care to be reminded of it. It was only during these periods of working that he looked strictly at his diet, otherwise his food tended to consist of a wide mixture of tastes and styles, ranging from junk food with potato chips to the best Italian food around.

Anjelica flew in to New York for a birthday celebration during the weekend of 18 April, and on his actual birthday she joined the cast on the set of *Ironweed* to toast him in champagne. It had to be a brief interruption because they were shooting until late in the evening, often until the early hours of the morning, largely because Nicholson's contract stipulated a sixty-nine-day shooting schedule with a $70,000-a-day penalty for overtime, a clause which was also doubtless prised from the producers by Meryl Streep's people. Far off and forgotten, it seems, are the days when he'd say, 'I'd have done it for nix just for the chance of working with so and so. ...' Others say it about him, now.

Hector Babenco, famed director of *Kiss of the Spider Woman*, was also an attraction for Nicholson in his personal quest to observe other directors at work while they are observing him. Babenco achieved fame for his classic work on human degradation in the pits of life in Sao Paulo and Rio de Janiero, which made *Pixote* one of the finest films of the early Eighties. Times had changed. Cinema audiences no longer wanted doom and gloom. They wanted bright and breezy, comic-book relief and titillating entertainment. *Ironweed* was a gloomy tale, about alcoholism and drop-outs from society through personal tragedy. Their drink problems became the back-drop to a despairing weight of memory, guilt and hopelessness. It was also an arty film, full of silences and moody locational shots.

The scenes were heavy, but lacked drama or suspense, even though Babenco, it seemed, believed he could extract some kind of Brando-esque performance from Nicholson. There were moments which were as good, if not better, than anything he has ever done. The same applied to Streep. Carroll Baker (*Baby Doll*, etc.), in the supporting role of Nicholson's wife, came through the same training school as Brando, Dean, Clift and Maureen Stapleton, and was as strong as ever. Baker, reflecting on her re-acquaintance with Nicholson, whom she first met back in the Sixties, said, 'We both attended the west coast branch of the Actor's Studio when we were starting out, but I hadn't seen much of him since. If the audience felt chemistry between Jack and me – a special caring and affection – it's because it genuinely exists, and what a joy. Jack is a prince but to me he was and is just as great as when I first knew him.'

It was actually a very good film. It made a little money but why is it that a picture with a budget of $27 million, co-starring the two most sought-after and highly paid actors in the world at that precise moment in time, can drift away with barely a memory of what it was all about? Unlike the days of *film noir* and the Forties message pictures, audiences were becoming disenchanted with films which portrayed intensity and grimness; it is presented in such graphic form almost nightly with television coverage of deprivation and social issues.

Jollity, soap and escapism – almost refined and more expensive Corman-esque – had become the order as was seen by the list of films which made most money in the Eighties. Once a good idea had been ratified, then it was repeated over and over again with the sequels, i.e., *Ghostbusters*, *Gremlins*, *Superman*, *Rocky*, *Beverly Hills Cop*, *Back to the Future*, and *The Godfather*, though the latter became a kind of social art form. Nicholson did not care to be involved in these highly commercial ventures, which is why he was resisting all attempts to get him into *Batman*.

Both Nicholson and Streep received Academy Award nominations for best actor and best actress for their performances in *Ironweed*, but neither won. Miss Streep had by then become somewhat disillusioned by Nicholson. She apparently did not wish to dine with him nor to receive any gifts. She had also reportedly decided that she did not wish to make any more films with him, because she found him rather weird, and thus nothing more was heard of another plan to bring them together in a romantic comedy being written by Pulitzer prize-winning author Michael Cristofer.

In any event, Nicholson could hardly have found the time. He was trying hard to resurrect *The Two Jakes* and there was one other task to be completed in 1987 – a cameo role in *Broadcast News* for

239

his friend James Brooks, who directed him in *Terms of Endearment*. Nicholson played the irascible senior television news anchorman which he agreed to do, provided he received no billing. He explained that it would have been unfair for his fans who might go to the movie on the strength of seeing his name among the credits and then discover it was a brief appearance. He admitted that this unusual step for an actor to remain anonymous was not entirely egoless. He even had a contract forbidding the producers to advertise his participation. The way he worked it out was that it would become a plus for the film, and himself, when it became known. It worked. Audiences actually cheered when he was recognized and it naturally became a focal point of numerous reviews and a topic of conversation among cinema-goers, for whom spotting Jack Nicholson provided an added boost to the success of the film.

* * * * *

Nicholson did not see of lot of Anjelica while he was filming *Ironweed*, and then she herself was tied up with her work with her father and brother. It was during this period, alone and at a loose end, that he began to spend time with Karen Mayo-Chandler, the British actress and model who had minor roles in *Lisztomania* and *Play it Again, Sam* before leaving for Hollywood where she married and separated. She visited Mulholland Drive often that summer and, as she would later describe in detail, he took her on an exciting voyage of sexual discovery with long, passionate nights of love-making – her words. And she loved the messages he left for her on her answerphone, 'Hi babe. It's raining. Come up to my place and we'll do it in the rain.' Nicholson was having fun but Karen took it seriously. She knew that Anjelica was still in the background of his life somewhere, perhaps even he did not know where. 'If he had been married, I would not have agreed to see him,' said Karen. 'And I believed his relationship with Anjelica had become merely a friendship thing.'

Karen insists – using the words 'in all honesty' as if she had vengeance on her mind – that he was going to make some kind of commitment to her. In heated moments when she asked him of his intentions, she pointed out that he was old enough to be her father and that if it was a mere sexual relationship she was seeking, then there were an abundance of younger, more attractive and possibly more virile men around with whom she could find satisfaction. She said she held true feelings for him and she hoped they were reciprocal. It all seemed a bit Mills and Boon, yet in those hot months of the summer and jolly times around the Nicholson pool, if Karen only half-believed that this might be her lifestyle from then on, disappointment would soon loom large.

★　　★　　★　　★　　★

The summer merry-making for Nicholson was interrupted by the sad occasion of the death of John Huston, who had remained active long enough to achieve his earnest hope that he could complete the film of James Joyce's short story, 'The Dead', with his daughter Anjelica in the starring role and with his son Tony writing the screenplay. They had had happy times during the spring and early summer of 1987, and the children felt closer to him than they had ever done in their lives. He had hoped it would be like that, because he knew he was dying and he knew it would be his last film. The subject matter was carefully and poignantly chosen, for he knew that he would be setting up his own epitaph with one line from the Joyce work which Huston reckoned was the finest short story ever written in the English language. It read: '*Better to pass boldly into that other world, in the full glory of some passion, than fade and wither dismally with age.*' A brief description cannot do justice to a James Joyce story and anyone who is not familiar with it is recommended to find a copy; it is the final story in his collection, *The Dubliners*.

Huston could quote it from memory, and it was to be his final grand gesture, not just to his family and his profession but also to his beloved Ireland, as if he was standing up to his full height, opening his arms wide and saying to the world, 'There you are, this is me.' It was a difficult story to film because so much of it consisted of a man's thoughts; neither was it especially successful in the way that Hollywood judges success. It was, however, the best film Huston could possibly have left his audience; he passed boldly on, never looking withered or dismal. The film was acclaimed as a triumph in which Anjelica was also splendid. If there was one unexpected legacy, it was that Anjelica's own confidence was given the last boost she required.

As Tony Huston saw it, their father had spent the last two years of his life in a quest to pass on the knowledge he had acquired in a lifetime. 'It was almost like shift work,' Tony recalled, 'going from one to the other to work in collaboration – first Anjelica, the actress, then me, the writer, and then Danny, the youngest to whom he gave the director's eye.'

To Jack Nicholson, John Huston bequeathed an instruction that he should look after Anjelica. Nicholson promised he would. With director Richard Brooks, Jack served as moderator at the memorial service for Huston arranged by the Directors' Guild and could not hold back the tears as he spoke his tribute. He said he would cry for the rest of his life. In the days following Huston's death he was asked to contribute to many newspaper and magazine articles assessing his life and career.

Coincidentally, a festival of John Huston's films had been arranged in Sante Fé for 16 to 20 September, and it became a memorial to him, instead. Jack, who had stayed closer to Anjelica after her father's death, was to have accompanied her to the festival but at the last minute she decided not to go. Tony and Danny went, along with Lauren Bacall, E.G. Marshall, Zsa Zsa Gabor, Jacqueline Bisset and Brian Keith to talk about Huston and his films. Anjelica herself was due to fly to New York at the end of the month to begins rehearsals for a stage production of *Tamara*, due to open on 12 October. She went to New York, but then dropped out of the play altogether. She had decided to concentrate on films and thus was determined to get on with her life, with or without an accompanying male.

*   *   *   *   *

Throughout these months, there was intense behind-the-scenes activity at Warner Brothers, where it had become a matter of supreme importance that Nicholson be persuaded to play The Joker in *Batman*. Some explanation of their persistence is necessary. He had been the choice of *Batman* creator Bob Kane from the beginning, when it was first being muted as a major movie ten years earlier. In 1979, executive producers Benjamin Melniker and Michael Usland obtained the screen rights from DC Comics, who first launched Kane's *Caped Crusader* in 1937. In those early discussions, Kane had personally selected Nicholson as The Joker, using a doctored publicity photograph of him from *The Shining* to superimpose his image. Worries about the $20 million cost of producing *Batman* as a movie – when it was still being shown all over the world in the form of the long-running television repeats – meant that the project was kept on the back burner until in the mid-Eighties, when it was brought to Jon Peters and Peter Guber, who were coming up on the fast lane among the new, new wave of Hollywood producers.

Their record was already impressive in their solo careers and they joined forces in 1980, establishing Polygram Pictures, whose string of successes included the cult classic, *An American Werewolf in London* and Paramount top box-office earner of 1983, *Flashdance*. They sold Polygram that year and formed a new company, Guber-Peters Entertainment, committed to high-quality, bigger budget pictures which included *The Color Purple*, *Witches of Eastwick*, *Gorillas in the Mist* and *Rainman*.

The old adage that you're as successful as your last picture in Hollywood still applies. Guber and Peters could do no wrong and Warner Brothers committed themselves at last to going ahead with *Batman*. A new young director, unbiased by set ways and too much previous experience, was sought and they found him within the Warner organization – twenty-eight-year-old ex-Disney animator, Tim Burton, who had worked on two recent smash hits, *Pee-wee's Big Adventure* (1985) and *Beetlejuice*, starring Michael Keaton (now to become *Batman*), which earned $100 million in 1988. They were both imaginative, if somewhat oddball. Burton immediately saw the potential and it was his view that the new *Batman* should get away from the Biff! Capow! Holy Crimewave! image of the children's television era. He wanted to take it back to a 'a darker vision, a dark melodrama with almost absurd black humour'.

The recruitment of an actor for The Joker was seen as more important than Batman himself. Peters was given the task of pursuing Nicholson to play the role they reckoned he was born to play, and the pressure for him to succeed was considerable. Those in charge of the finances looked with horror at the projected costs, which had doubled from the original estimate. Warner Brothers executives were pretty well agreed that without Nicholson, it could not succeed. Lines of communication were opened while they were filming *Witches of Eastwick*, and Peters' second approach found the actor still decidedly less than enthusiastic. Had not Brando and Gene Hackman taken a lot of flack for their 'demeaning' appearances in *Superman*? Ah yes, but was not Nicholson's chum Warren Beatty already well advanced with plans to appear as a comic-strip hero, recreating for the big screen the adventures of Dick Tracy? And for Beatty, who had made only three films in the last decade, this was no trivial pursuit.

'At least let me fly you to London to see for yourself what we are doing and what our commitment is,' Peters pleaded. Nicholson agreed and he was taken immediately to view the sets which were already being built at Pinewood Studios. The construction was to be in four stages, the first was already underway and designer Anton Furst showed Nicholson his plans. There were literally hundreds of drawings in existence, sketches of Batman and his armoury, his Batcave and his Batmobile; of The Joker and his paraphernalia. The design of the awesome skyline of Gotham City and its interiors would itself mean the building of the biggest movie set since the multi-million-dollar fiasco of *Cleopatra* in 1963, and would cost well over $5 million.

Nicholson was impressed. He also talked with Tim Burton whom he had never met before, and struck up a rapport; he liked his ideas. He flew back to Los Angeles still undecided. Peters had been told by Warners production chief, Mark Canton, to make him an offer he could not refuse and Warners were talking very big money indeed for what they said would be three weeks' work.

Nicholson was making no commitments, not to anyone. Anjelica was still working hard and they had seen little of each other these past few months, passing like ships in the night on their various travels. On his return, he and Anjelica were suddenly thrust into the headlines when news of Jack's friendship with Karen Mayo-Chandler leaked out. She had been seen on his arm at a couple of high-profile social events in Hollywood recently, including a visit by the Duke and Duchess of York, mostly while Anjelica was away.

On 14 March, they found themselves the subject of gossip column stories around the world when it was widely reported that Anjelica had said enough was enough, and they'd split up, less than a year after he promised her dying father that he would take care of her. She 'finally ditched him after discovering that he had taken Karen skiing' in Aspen three weeks earlier. Anjelica was quoted as saying that she and Jack had had a great time together but she truly now wanted a relationship from which she could achieve the things she most wanted in life, to be a wife and mother. Nicholson was said to be devastated by Anjelica's decision, that he had lost the woman he loved and his best friend; he made repeated telephone calls to try to patch things up. Devoid of any further quotes from either party, 'close friends' were sought to confirm that Anjelica felt her time was running out to start a family of her own, and the discovery of his dalliance with Karen was the last straw.

Two days later, Karen Mayo-Chandler weighed in with the revelation that her affair with Nicholson was already over, claiming she too had called it off. Oh, and by the way, she was prepared to tell all if any newspaper or magazine cared to make an offer for her story at somewhere in the region of, say, $150,000. There were no immediate takers. And, so it appeared that the long-running companionship between Nicholson and Anjelica was over; if she needed confirmation that it was the right decision, she would not have long to wait.

A month or so later, Jack happened to call in at Helena's nightclub, where he was introduced to a new member of staff. Her name was Rebecca Broussard, a resting actress with blonde hair and swimming-pool blue eyes that caught his in a moment. She was exactly half his age and married, but separated from Warner Brothers record producer Richard Perry. What happened next remained a secret between them – or it did, until the *National Enquirer* spotted her driving his black Range Rover in Aspen.

At the moment of meeting him in Helena's there was nothing on the horizon to lead her to imagine she would become famous; she was the living example of that old Hollywood adage – in this town you either eat in the best restaurants or wait on the tables. There was a role in reserve for her and she could not have predicted it in a thousand years.

★   ★   ★   ★   ★

Jack's interest in *Batman* had been whetted and with the customary thoroughness of research and knowledge that he approaches any task, he checked the library and did some homework. He then invited one of the movie's three screenwriters, Warren Skaaren, to

Mulholland Drive to discuss the part. Skaaren noted later, 'He was like an encyclopaedia of culture and history and art. I threw out a line from Nietzsche and Jack jumped on it and he threw out a line from Nietzsche.' From these initial discussions, the role became extended and far from a mere three weeks' work, it would run to one hundred days. Warners were getting far more than they believed possible from the star and it was developing exactly the way Peters had hoped, making it a true Batman versus The Joker scenario. Some said Nicholson had made a takeover bid for the picture, and had succeeded by his sheer presence; given his time on-screen, he must have had a pretty good idea that he would steal the show.

It was a hijack. Serious talking about money had been going on in the background and he eventually put his name to a contract for a $6 million fee plus a percentage of gross box-office receipts, a cut of record royalties, merchandising and other trinkets released with the film. The amount of cash that this deal would eventually generate was seen when *Batman* took $200 million in America alone in the first four weeks of showing, and children and adults were scrambling for *Batman* souvenirs. In total, Warners estimated that they would be paying Nicholson somewhere between $30 million and $90 million. At the last count, it had reportedly reached $60 million.

He also gave his nod of approval to the casting of Michael Keaton in the starring role of Batman, which sparked off such a storm of controversy world-wide. Keaton well known but not exactly famous; he was an unorthodox choice, well away from the muscle-bound mould of previous comic heroes and Warner Brothers received 50,000 letters from 'Batman' fanatics all over the world, protesting at the choice and the exclusion of Robin. 'I knew there were dissenters,' said Peters, 'but I also knew that casting Michael Keaton as Batman would automatically make the film twice as interesting and original than if we cast a traditional hunk. Batman is not your usual hero and Keaton is not your usual actor.'

The producers began to get worried as the protest movement grew loud and threatened to damage the picture's reputation, even before it was released. Though *Batman* had been filmed in intense secrecy, Warners took the unprecedented step of releasing a trailer which was aimed firstly at quelling the fears of 'Batman' fans and secondly, providing an excellent marketing exercise in pre-release hype. A documentary was also made during shooting, called *The*

Making of Batman, in which most members of cast appeared – except Nicholson. He knew it would end up on television and he still does not do television for anyone, not even the suppliers of what was probably going to be the largest pay cheque for a single actor in the history of Hollywood.

Otherwise, he threw himself into the production with devastating energy. Tim Burton found him a model of co-operation and clearly Jack's portrayal of The Joker had been the subject of meticulous planning and adjustment on his part, even down to personally selecting the wardrobe of clothes he would wear during the film, costing $30,000. But who wouldn't for that money? Burton said, 'Jack gave the entire cast the confidence and courage – that's not an overstatement – to make this film. He was terrific. I had heard people talk about him before, but to watch him work was a pure education in the true art of film-making.' In an instant, he could amend his performance at a particular time to give more menace, or less, as directed.

Everyone who saw it has their own opinion of *Batman*; some loved it, some hated it. At the première which attracted many of his peers, Eddie Murphy largely summed up their thoughts: 'He was brilliant. Nobody can mess with that guy.' Reviews were mixed about the film, but most were complimentary about Nicholson's creation of The Joker. Tom Green, writing in *USA Today*, was typical of the praisers, 'Combining incendiary demonics with an impish harlequin flourish, Nicholson's nifty nack for over-the-top performances reaches a zenith in The Joker, cementing his reputation as the best actor working in Hollywood today.'

In London, reaction was similar. Shaun Usher of the *Daily Mail* remarked, 'Lulls develop during his absences', while Ian Christie at the *Daily Express* observed that the success of the movie was down to two words, Jack Nicholson. The London listings magazine, *Time Out*, never afraid of offending anyone, went further: 'The plot is an unmitigated disaster ... [The Joker] was cackling, dancing, killing for sheer humour value and hogging the best one-liners. Jack Nicholson's Joker makes *The Witches of Eastwick* seem restrained, and pulls off the greatest criminal coup of the decade, stealing a whole movie.'

Nicholson himself was said to be underwhelmed by the movie, but said during and after filming that he thought it was one of his own best performances. Would he appear in the sequel – which there would surely be at one time or another – if only to re-use the multi-million-dollar sets gathering rust at Pinewood? During the coming winter, when there was much talk of him starring again in *Batman II*, he was asked point blank as he walked into a Lakers game in Los Angeles.

'The Joker's dead,' snapped Nicholson. 'Didn't you see the movie?'

The question was: Does dead mean buried?

No one was saying.

17

Nobody's Pawn

It is early summer, 1989 and lines of kids are waiting excitedly by the roadside on the news that Jack Nicholson is coming. They are gathered on a run-down industrial zone of Los Angeles and as his limousine comes into view they start shouting, 'Joker! Joker! Joker!' He steps out, wearing jet black sun glasses, of course. His hair is combed back, parted slightly in the middle though it is thinning and less controllable. Almost instantly beads of perspiration appear on the high forehead from which the hair has receded, as the hot Los Angeles sunshine beats down from a cloudless sky, only slightly hazed by smog. He's wearing a grey check suit, carrying the coat over his arm, the slacks look rather old fashioned, a smart pale blue shirt and a tie that is also slightly Forties-style. But, wait a minute, that's not The Joker. Isn't that guy whats his name, you remember – the detective? Jake Gittes.

There was not a child in the group of cheering children who would remember Jake Gittes or *Chinatown* or even Jack Nicholson's last movie before *Batman* because Jack Nicholson had come the full circle and this year had added to his ranks of followers the last bastion of audience that had remained untouched by his characters over the years: the children. He had given them, with parental guidance, the face to frighten them in their dreams, just as he had given their elder brothers and sisters and their parents faces and characters to remember him by. It was also ironic; in that month, almost to the day twenty years earlier, he stood watching audience reaction to *Easy Rider* at the Cannes film festival and he said to himself, 'I'm a star. I'm a movie star.' He knew it because of his performance as George Hanson, the alcoholic lawyer. What he did not know was the scope that lay before him nor could he have possible judged the new mood in society, the new attitudes to politics, the renaissance of the American film, all coming together to thrust him forward. The circle was completed at the beginning of the year when finally he pulled all parties together and reached agreement to start filming *The Two Jakes* again.

Past troubles had been set aside but not resolved. Robert Evans languished still under the cloud enforced by the LA District Attorney's office over *The Cotton Club* Case but all this time after the event, no evidence had been brought forward of his involvement in the murder. Robert Towne, the screen writer, who was the one who wanted to sack Evans, the actor, in the first place was himself no longer to take an active part in the direction of the picture which was originally to have been his job. Depending on which press statements one read, he was either unwanted by Paramount as its director or too busy with his own commitments. From that original partnership of three friends good and true who shook on the deal and swore no-one would come between them, Nicholson stood alone, although all three still stood to benefit financially but to a far lesser degree than might have been the case back in 1984 when it was all planned. On his shoulders fell not just the leading role but the task of directing, too because that was the only way he could get the picture made. Other directors had been approached including Mike Nichols, Bernardo Bertolucci and the late John Huston. They even considered trying to bring Roman Polanski back. In the end, it rested upon Nicholson to decide and he insisted that he would not let it die, even if it meant directing himself. There were those in Nicholson's inner circle who were brave enough to remind him of what he said after *Goin' South,* that never again would he direct and star in a picture.

Was he casting a rod for his own back? One of more widely quoted self-assessments of his career was that an actor should immediately discard what he had been successful with. Why then was he returned to old ground, especially at a time when some sequels to other first time hit films had not done so well? Furthermore, *Chinatown* became a classic of its age because it reflected in its content one of the most horrendous examples of political corruption of modern times. Where could it pick up a decade and a half later? For Nicholson personally, it was like a good book that he could not put down and, as Anjelica had once said, an obsession. The characters were the same, or at least Gittes is. He is still a detective and a upright member of the community, a war hero and member of the local country club, set in 1948 and eleven years on from the events in *Chinatown*. The elements of sexual infidelity, betrayal, greed and the lust for power are still there, overlaid on to the new scenario in which Gittes is placed which is one of disillusionment with life. Having said that, Jack and Robert Towne never wanted it to be seen as an updated copy of *Chinatown*. It was not a sequel in the sense that it was *Chinatown II* under a different name. *The Two Jakes* had to have a life of its own and come out to be just as unique as it predecessor. It was, said Nicholson, a very difficult film to make because the script did not accommodate in words the undertones he was trying to convey. It all had to be done by implication. This perhaps may explain why it took him such a long time to complete the work, and get it the way he wanted it after filming was complete. Nicholson had to be involved at every stage right through to the delivery of a final print and he was not letting it out of his hands until he was satisfied it was the best it could be.

All the problems of the actual shooting had come to him. He had to handle the hundred crew and direct his actors, guide them, cajole them and nurse them. He had to give the producers his requirements to meet the allotted $19 million budget. He personally had to check locations after the scouts had been out and ensure to the finest detail, as is always the case in a period piece, that nothing came into shot which identified it as a later setting. On one morning, for example when they were shooting a scene using original cars of the era, Packard, Chevrolet, Nash and Hudson, many of which had to be post-war vintage, he suddenly noticed in the background a car park full of modern vehicles.

'That wasn't there yesterday,' said Nicholson, angrily. One of his assistants plucked up the courage to tell him that it wasn't in the shot yesterday but it was there; it had become visible because the city parks department had unexpectedly trimmed the trees overnight. The same thing happened at another location, an important one, of orange groves which had been there when they scouted the locations but which had been cut down by the time they came to film them. And then having done all that, and looked through the camera lens at the shot in front of him, he had to dash behind to the other side of the glass and position himself, shout Action! and let the cameras roll, focusing largely upon himself. Yes, now it reminded him of *Goin South*! It was damned hard work and worrying too. Who was going to tell him if he needed more violence or less, or a bigger grin or a lesser one? No one, except perhaps the forthright Eli Wallach, another from the old Method crowd of the Actors' Studio, vintage 1948, in New York – he was in the same class as Brando, Clift and Stapleton – and still knew when to speak his mind.

Nicholson had some old friends around. Robert Evans with whom his friendship had never really faltered, in spite of the difficulties, was listed as associate producer. Jack had also personally asked for Vilmos Zsigmond, the cinematographer he had worked with him on *Witches of Eastwick*. There were others like Jeff Morris in the cast. He always liked a buddy among the actors and Morris was here again, just as he was in *Goin' South, The Border* and *Ironweed*. He dismissed the studio moaners who would say, 'Jack's bringing his cronies in again'. These people, he said, like Morris and Harry Dean Stanton, another of his regulars, were part of his life. He had known them and worked with them for twenty years or more and when he took them into a picture, he did so because they were good. Whether the same could be said about Rebecca Broussard, only a viewing of the film will tell. The actress with whom he had been seen a lot of late was given a small role and because of that she was always around the set, or out on location. Thus, she had quickly achieved what all of Jack's longer terms companions had, with the exception of Michelle Phillips who refused; they all appeared with him on the big screen.

Rebecca made herself scarce when Anjelica showed up. She and Jack were 'friends' again; sixteen years of relative togetherness could not be ruined by the meaningless fling he had with Karen Mayo-Chandler. Whether she was also aware of Miss Broussard's presence was another matter on which she has remained silent. She was well aware, however, what *The Two Jakes* meant to Nicholson and on occasion she turned up during location work at the bungalow Jack was using as his base during the filming of scenes at the country club, bringing a hamper of food and flasks of iced tea to ease the gruelling twelve-hour day shooting schedule he kept up for almost four months. There was one other member of the 'family' now involved who, unlike Anjelica, had no particular qualms about nepotism. Nicholson's daughter Jennifer – who is the same age as Rebecca – having come through her course at the USC, was now a fully qualified production assistant with no aspirations towards acting. She and her father were firm friends; she spent a lot of time at Mulholland Drive over the past few years and now had her own place in West Hollywood.

Filming *The Two Jakes* was wrapped up in the late summer of 1989 and Jack had maintained a degree of secrecy over the film; he had given virtually no publicity interviews and he had kept writers and photographers well away from the set. In the few public observations he allowed himself on *The Two Jakes,* he spoke of his hope that the film would carry an extremely human story which would carry an underlying comment about Californian and American society.

'I never thought we'd get the damn thing made,' he said. 'There were so many twists and turns getting this on film than there were in the script. Tell you one thing, I want this to be better than *Chinatown* and that was a damn classic.' Then, he disappeared into the cutting room at Paramount Studios in late September and did not surface again for months. Originally scheduled for a Christmastime release, *The Two Jakes* was pushed back first to May 1990 and then to later in the year. Everyone concerned said that the delay merely reflected Nicholson's insistence on producing a final print that would do the movie full justice. The fact that it was not released until the summer suggests that there was plenty of work to be done, and when finally it came to the previews, many were thoroughly disappointed with the result. A patchwork of reviews complained of the film's slowness and that it lacked the magic of *Chinatown*; another period of reflection was undoubtedly necessary before he decided upon his next move, because Jack, as a director, had once again failed to deliver the sought-after 'blockbuster'.

During the latter stages of editing *The Two Jakes*, there were other diversions to distract him, however. In October 1989, it was revealed that Karen Mayo-Chandler had sold her story to *Playboy*. She would be appearing in the December issue. Then came another bombshell on 26 October – a gossip column printed a whisper that Rebecca Broussard was pregnant. Another whisper said Jack was the father and that he had installed her in a house he had bought for $385,000 in Benedict Canyon. Neighbours had seen her jogging and they had seen Nicholson arriving and leaving. Anjelica was naturally outraged by this news which was made all the more hurtful by her own ambitions of motherhood. She drove straight to Paramount studios where Jack was still working.

'Is it true?' she demanded. It was true. She slapped him across the face and screamed, 'That's it. Finished.' And she stormed out leaving Nicholson speechless, silent and apparently in shock. When the news broke, Jack moved Rebecca up to his house at Aspen away from the avalanche of press people who were trying to get her story. Worse was to come.

The December issue of *Playboy* landed with a thud. Karen Mayo-Chandler, a lover scorned was doing a Nora Ephron, though not with anything like the same style, panache, wit or reason. But then she did not have the material to work on; she had no 'life with Jack' to reveal nor the betrayal of a scheming, two-timing husband. Hers was the classic hit-and-run, kiss-and-tell made famous in days gone by and *Playboy's* presentation of her in scant attire, telling her tale of sex and woe seemed almost a parody of those once popular but long forgotten excursions into the bedrooms of the rich and famous when Victor Lownes and Hugh Hefner were past 'victims'.

Unlike *Playboy's* normal style, the story of Nicholson's passion for Karen used a certain colourful, cliched, tabloid language under a quotation headline: 'He would hold me down, rip off my clothes and make incredible, mad, wild, wonderful love to me' which of course made Miss Mayo-Chandler an instant three-minute star and the required guest of chat show hosts across America. In England the *News of the World* and the *Sunday Mirror* vied with each other for the story and she stood to collect a pretty penny. Actually, to begin with it all sounded like an illuminated address from the Jack Nicholson Appreciation Society of woman the world over he had loved: 'Jack is the most fantastic lover who had ever lived. He is not selfish, he's not just interested in satisfying himself like so many men are. He really ought to write a book about it and call it *How to Make Love to Women by Jack Nicholson*. It would be a best seller.'

So had Miss Mayo-Chandler done him the biggest favour of his life by disposing of that awful image of male chauvinism and sexual malpractice that had hung around since he played Jonathan in *Carnal*

Knowledge? If Karen had stopped there, it might have done. In fact, she went on to paint a picture which only served to enhance the old image: 'I don't mind admitting that I learned everything I know about life, love and sex from Jack. I did things with him that I had never done with any other man,' said the twenty-eight-year-old star of *Strip To Kill II*. 'I was trembling like a child when he first carried me up to his bedroom; but he was very gentle, very loving, very romantic. He kept right on kissing me deeply, undressing me all at the same time. We did not sleep a wink that first night. He has amazing stamina and self control and we just kept on making love. He's a guaranteed non-stop sex machine.'

Now, in a kiss-and-tell, as writers and readers of such parables of the past will well know, the description of one romantic scene becomes much the same as the next, exhausting hours of sex between the green silk sheets of his superking sized bed or thrashing about naked in the jacuzzi with only a breather to crack open another bottle of Cristal and a quick Marlboro. Karen, however, was able to vary her version by virtue of the sexual variety she claims Nicholson introduced into her life. In certain moods, he was a 'horny little devil'. That sounded promising and more in line which what his male admirers had come to expect of him, a touch raunchy and possibly even a little rough. That was next in Karen's account of her 'nights of torrid passion' when Jack wasn't watching basketball or sports on television. Out came the implements of fun which he kept in a black bag along with a Polaroid camera for some saucy snaps. Kinky sex games, naughty pictures; whatever next ... spankings? Of course. Jack loved to dish out a good smack across the bottom and sometimes, she said, lovemaking became painful. He, meantime, grunted, groaned and moaned because he was a very loud participant of these events and loved to give and receive vocal encouragement. He didn't have many bad points, except that he snored loudly and ate peanut butter and jelly sandwiches in bed.

Nicholson shuddered when he read it. It was supposed to be a fun story; the whole tenor of the piece made it that way and it was presented as the epitome of a vigorous interlude in the much-discussed, much publicized sexual adventures of Jack Nicholson, movie star. It had to happen. He must have known that, on the law of averages, some time or other a woman would go to the news-papers and tell all and perhaps at any other time, it might have merely been seen as a further light-hearted addition to his reputation which he has himself carefully nurtured over the years. The timing was right for Karen in view of the other things going on in his life, and made hers a more valuable story. It was one more problem for Nicholson and he was desolate.

Why did Karen spill the beans? Money? Notoriety? Revenge? It was a mixture of all three influences although she said initially that she was fed up with being tagged as Jack Nicholson's former floozy and 'just wanted to put the record straight'. It seemed an odd thing to do, because she – as much as Nicholson – would have her linen washed in public and since the affair was over long ago, she was by then a virtually forgotten member of the clan. She actually telephoned him before allowing British journalist Kenelm Jenour to release the story to *Playboy* and British and European newspapers.

Jack could, one supposes, have attempted to buy her off – in the old days of the protective cordon thrown around their stars by the studios, she would have been given a new car with the glove compartment filled with dollar bills and told to drive off into the sunset, stay silent and keep out of his life. Jack did not even attempt it. He told her bluntly: 'You must do what you have to do' in the full knowledge that her story could be a trifle damaging, coming as it did alongside his other personal traumas. But it is a fact that he has always maintained this openness. Once a secret corner has been exposed, he has seen no point in trying to hide it, with the possible exception of the events surrounding his own birth.

He has remained unwilling to talk about that and says he wants to write about it himself some day. His reputation as a womanizer came as much from his own mouth, with admissions during the publicity interviews he gave in the early days, as it did from the gossip columns who have endlessly charted his dates and one-night stands. He has never sought to deny them. He has also been honest about his drug usage to the point that it became a bore to him even to discuss it and sometimes, has regretted his frankness. Anyway, he gave up drugs – apart from the occasional socially smoked marijuana cigarette – in 1983 when he began having weight problems. He has been less successful in giving up smoking which he has tried a couple of times although he now hardly drinks, other than champagne and not to excess and when he is seen these days coming from some nightspot at four or five in the morning, it is not some night of debauchery that has detained him.

More likely he has been sitting up a corner somewhere listening to the music, smoking and imbibing modestly, bending someone's ear about the meaning of life. The reputation of the past now arrives ahead of him. It was helped by remarks from people like Robert Evans who once told a reporter that not even Beatty had been so successful with women as Nicholson and that one quote has appeared in every other story written about Jack Nicholson's private life. He is more realistic; if only half of the adventures he is alleged to have had were true, he might well look considerably older than he does; but let that not detract from the fact that women have played a very large part in his life, and even that half represents a vast number of encounters.

Occasionally, if the moment requires it – for publicity purposes, for instance – he has helped the cause along a bit with what the papers call a knowing wink here and a weighty cough there, as he has talked to his interviewers in all frankness about his past. Careful research also disclosed that these interviews are only ever granted at the very moment another of his films is about to be released. He does a good double act with his press agent Paul Wasserman and has become, in the latter part of his career, one of the finest manipulators of the media — better even than Beatty himself who stayed silent and reclusive too long and by refusing interviews damaged the publicity potential of his last two or three pictures. Beatty realizes this now and no-one could have failed to notice that as the release date for *Dick Tracy* came up, he was beginning to appear on the front cover of magazines and colour supplements around the world, and giving interviews for selected mainstream writers, speaking more candidly than he had ever done about his life and times and the colour of his bed sheets. He even gave television interviews and exchanged superbly relaxed banter with Britain's Barry Norman.

★   ★   ★   ★   ★

Having accepted that Karen Mayo-Chandler was going to have her say, and there was nothing he could or would do to stop it, he just stood back and let the fur fly. Rebecca was different. There was nothing he wanted less than to have her plastered all over the newspapers and she did not want that kind of publicity either. She was carrying his baby, an event which after the initial shockwaves had subsided, he began to look forward to with an enthusiasm. Because she was with child, his child, he threw protective arm around her and tried to shield her from some of the media glare that he knew would follow. Rebecca was stunned by the media reaction world-wide. Newspapers in every language had been telephoning and writing stories about her. She was getting the kind of publicity normally reserved for Elizabeth Taylor, and all she had done to get it was to become pregnant by a famous actor. Jack promised her than when the time came he would take the burden of publicity and indeed when their baby daughter was born on 16 April, six days before his own fifty-third birthday, he adopted the stance of British royalty which is to allow a photographer or two in, let them take the pictures for worldwide distribution and then, hopefully, they'd leave them alone. He posed with Rebecca and the baby whom they called Lorraine – after his aunt – and he spoke of his proudness at being a father. They looked supremely happy and said they were.

Clearly, Rebecca has become someone special in his life and one suspects that, given her own willingness, their relationship will become long-term. She has the aura and intelligence to keep up with him and she has come into his life at the time, when through age his opportunities, or even desire, for the chase are diminishing by the day. 'I can't get interested anymore,' Jack said. 'It's getting to be too much of an effort.' He brushed aside obvious questions about marriage. Rebecca was available. Her divorce from Richard Perry was finalised in May 1989, but even his closest friends would not be prepared to place a wager on whether or not he marries her and it is noticeable once more that he has set up the arrangement of a two-house relationship which gives them both a good deal of space. The media camped as close as they could get to Mulholland Drive but found little to write about on the spot.

They were back again the following month to observe the continuing saga of life in the compound which this time focused once again next door at the Brando household, scene of many domestic upheavals in the past. Police arrived to arrest Christian Brando following the shooting of his sister Cheyenne's lover Dag Drollet. Later, when Marlon Brando was desperately seeking to get his son released on bail, Nicholson came to his neighbour's aid by writing to the Los Angeles court to state that he had known Christian for fourteen years and could give reference to his character.

*   *   *   *   *

Anjelica kept well away. Mutual friends feel she deserves considerable sympathy for the way she has ended up, without Nicholson, without a child and a touch wistful about what might have been. At Christmas she said bitterly, 'Jack Nicholson has given me the worst two Yuletide presents I have ever received in my life.' She is finished with him in terms of their romantic relationship and now seeks company elsewhere. She still speaks of motherhood as a remaining ambition, 'Personally, I'd love to have a child. I'd like to have a husband and a child,' she said just before Jack's new daughter was born. 'It is not something I have immediate plans for because there is simply no-one on my horizon but it is something that certainly has to be considered. And also, I'd like to feel calm and happy.'

She has gained new strength from her career and in April 1990 was at the Academy Awards once again, having been nominated best supporting actress for her role as Dolores, the put-upon, pill-popping mistress in Woody Allen's *Crime and Misdemeanours*. She also won best supporting actress award from the US National Society of Film Critics for that role and immediately signed to appear in another excellent movie, Nicolas Roeg's *Witches*, based on the Roald Dahl story. As far as Nicholson is concerned, she saw the debacle of Karen Mayo-Chandler followed by the revelation of Rebecca's pregnancy, as her own 'public humiliation' by the man with whom she has spent the last seventeen years of her life, give or take the occasional separation. She was undoubtedly furious with him but she will not discuss it, and indeed refuses to. She said, 'It's been a long relationship and it is between us – I don't feel that it is for public scrutiny. If you are dealing with two very volatile people – such as we are – you go through many changes every day. The relationship is a fact of my life and there is not an aspect of my life that has not been touched by him. He is a soulmate and I hate to think of a world without him. It would be dismal.'

*   *   *   *   *

What is his magical power that he has over people that no-one can stay mad at him for long? If there was a courtroom specially set aside for feminists to bring charges against men who have sinned against the rights and dignity of women, someone somewhere could make some charges stick against Jack Nicholson. He would put up a stout defence, of course, intelligently reasoned, eloquently argued and resolutely denying anything other than a total fondness of them spiritually, sexually and in terms of pure and simple friendship. There is too much evidence against him: chasing stray pussy with anyone who would join him (self-admitted), skunk-spotting with Beatty (self-admitted), having a young model fly 10,000 miles for a weekend of sex (undisputed), smacking the bare bottom of a young actress during love-making (not challenged), not to mention a few dozen broken hearts. 'So I'm sexy. Is that a crime? I know I am sexy, but only in the eye of the beholder. It's a simple as that.' And once the dust had settled, he actually appeared to be revelling in the latest fillip to the Reputation. In the spring of 1990, he and Beatty were together one night at the Roxberry, one of Hollywood's trendiest nightspots, gathering female companionship for a party that was to be staged that night at Jack's house.

'How about a night out with Spanking Jack?' he said with his usual mischievous grin to Sylvester Stallone's recent ex-girlfriend. Not long afterwards, he called Karen Mayo-Chandler to say he had forgiven her. So nothing changes. But enough of Nicholson and women; a book could be written on that topic alone but it would be fairly pointless. The subject is just one part of him, and of a whole mixture of other equally interesting parts that go to make up the whole: a man who, in spite of his anti-establishment beginnings, has turned into an American institution.

He still regards Brando as number one and chooses to believe that, as Beatty put it, when Brando goes everyone moves up a place. He has continued to show a total disregard for what is expected of him, and especially in his choice of roles and more especially in his odd choice of directors with whom he has worked. In pure economic terms, there is no one to match him anywhere. His last decade of films alone have brought him conservatively around $130 million, which in his non-mercenary days of sixties philosophy he would probably have adjudged to be obscene wealth reserved for the establishment. The US treasury takes a good slice yet he remains 'exceedingly financially viable' – his words – to the degree that he could if he so desired retire totally from acting and concentrate merely on direction. That decision is one which he will make when reaction to *The Two Jakes* has filtered through and box-office returns counted. One suspects, however, that if he continues acting, the title of number one – which he modestly disputes but against which he does not put up too fierce an argument – is one which attracts him, as a natural and eager recipient of accolades, that desire does not lessen with age.

He fervently believes himself to be without an enemy in the world, which is probably true. Even Anjelica has forgiven him, though still bitter about the humiliation. On the other hand, he is never averse to speaking his mind which is filled with the by-product of thirty years of such diverse and intense reading matter that he is able to call down a quotable quote to suit any occasion, or in other circumstances a plain, simple and exceeding offensive expletive. Having said that, he is now seldom overtly public in his views about anything other than his current films and long ago wisely stopped promoting his opinions on the revision of the drug laws, doubtless moved to silence by his own dimishing interest and by the explosion of narcotics trafficking emanating from South America in the Eighties. His politics were naturally liberal to begin with and he supported McGovern in the 1972 campaign. He was outspoken about the evils of Nixon's reign, despaired at Ford, laid a few choice remarks at the door of Ronald Reagan and eventually, like Beatty, gave his backing to Gary Hart and then saw the chances of having a friend in the White House scuppered by the kind of scandal normally reserved for himself or Beatty.

Unlike Beatty, he has never attempted to fling his influence into political areas and just gets on with his own life. Billy Wilder once said of him when standing talking to Nicholson and Sam Spiegel at a party, 'You know Jack, what the public likes about your characters is that you're always playing the guy who has this tremendous ability at any given moment to say, "Why don't you go fuck yourself". And that's what people love because they can't do that.'

There was another party, stacked to the doors with the Hollywood big-time, simply everyone who was anyone was trying to look intentionally conspicuous and important; a sickening sight. Nicholson was standing on the edges behind his black sunglasses hoping that no one would see him, bored and looking at some of the guests with extreme derision as he peered at them occasionally over the top of his champagne glass, blowing smoke rings in their direction.

Jim Brooks, the director, came over and leaned his head towards Nicholson's as if he was going to make impart some secret information and from the corner of his mouth, he said in usual attempt at disdainful irony, 'You got the feeling that somehow these people own you?'

'Own me? You've got to be joking.'

He thought for an instant and chuckled, then his face went serious. 'I'm one of the few people alive – not just in this room – but alive, for whom that question isn't even hypothetical,' he said.

'I'm a pawn in nobody's game.'

That is true, and there is more than just the obvious reason. A few years ago, a magazine headlined an article on Nicholson as follows: IS JACK NICHOLSON HIDING SOMETHING? Their search was, of course, for the real Jack Nicholson – the one who he himself claimed in his *Playboy* interview he had hidden with a smokescreen of confusing statements and observations.

The truth is, he is hiding nothing.

Select Bibliography

Baxter, John. *Hollywood in the Sixties*; International Film Guide Series, A.S. Barnes, New York, 1972.

Brodie, Douglas. *The Films of Jack Nicholson*; Citadel Press, New Jersey, 1987.

Downing, David. *Jack Nicholson: A Biography*; Stein and Day, New York, 1983.

Gitlin, Todd. *The Sixties: Years of Hope, Days of Rage*; Bantam, New York, 1987.

Harris, Martha. *Anjelica Huston: The Lady and Her Legacy*; St Martin's Press, New York, 1989.

Keyser, Les. *Hollywood in the Seventies*; A.S. Barnes, New York, 1981.

Leaming, Barbara. *Polanski: His Life and Films*; Hamish Hamilton, London, 1982.

Marriott, John. *Batman: The Official Book of the Movie*; Hamlyn, London, 1989.

Norman, Barry. *Talking Pictures*; BBC/Hodder and Stoughton, London, 1987.

Palmer, William J. *The Films of the Seventies: A Social History*; Scarecrow Press, New Jersey, 1987.

Osborne Robert. *The Oscar: The Official History of the Academy Awards*; Abbeville Press, New York, 1989.

Polanski, Roman. *Polanski*; William Morrow, New York, 1984.

Springer, John. *The Fondas: The Films and Careers of Henry, Jane and Peter*; Citadel Press, New York, 1970.

Woodward, Bob. *Wired: The Short Life and Fast Times of John Belushi*; Simon and Schuster, New York, 1984.

Nicholson and the Oscar

Nicholson has had nine Academy Award nominations, three for best supporting actor, winning once, and six for best actor, also winning once.

Note: * indicates Oscar winner.

1969: BEST SUPPORTING ACTOR NOMINEES
Rupert Crosse in *The Reivers*
Elliott Gould in *Bob & Carol & Ted & Alice*
Jack Nicholson in *Easy Rider*
Anthony Quayle in *Anne of the Thousand Days*
*Gig Young in *They Shoot Horses, Don't They?*

1970: BEST ACTOR NOMINEES
Melvyn Douglas in *I Never Sang for My Father*
James Earl Jones in *The Great White Hope*
Jack Nicholson in *Five Easy Pieces*
Ryan O'Neal in *Love Story*
*George C. Scott in *Patton*

1973: BEST ACTOR NOMINEES
Marlon Brando in *Last Tango in Paris*
*Jack Lemmon in *Save the Tiger*
Jack Nicholson in *The Last Detail*
Al Pacino in *Serpico*
Robert Redford in *The Sting*

1974: BEST ACTOR NOMINEES
*Art Carney in *Harry and Tonto*
Albert Finney in *Murder on the Orient Express*
Dustin Hoffman in *Lenny*
Jack Nicholson in *Chinatown*
Al Pacino in *The Godfather Part II*

1975: BEST ACTOR NOMINEES
Walter Matthau in *The Sunshine Boys*
*Jack Nicholson in *One Flew over the Cuckoo's Nest*
Al Pacino in *Dog Day Afternoon*
Maximilian Schell in *The Man in the Glass Booth*
James Whitmore in *Give 'em Hell, Harry!*

1981: BEST SUPPORTING ACTOR NOMINEES
James Coco in *Only When I Laugh*
*John Gielgud in *Arthur*
Ian Holm in *Chariots of Fire*
Jack Nicholson in *Reds*
Howard E. Rollins, Jnr. in *Ragtime*

1983: BEST SUPPORTING ACTOR NOMINEES
Charles Durning in *To Be or Not To Be*
John Lithgrow in *Terms of Endearment*
*Jack Nicholson in *Terms of Endearment*
Sam Shepherd in *The Right Stuff*
Rip Torn in *Cross Creek*

1985: BEST ACTOR NOMINEES
Harrison Ford in *Witness*
James Garner in *Murphy's Romance*
*William Hurt in *Kiss of the Spider Woman*
Jack Nicholson in *Prizzi's Honour*
Jon Voigt in *Runaway Train*

1987: BEST ACTOR NOMINEES
*Michael Douglas in *Wall Street*
William Hurt in *Broadcast News*

The Joker's Wild

Marcello Mastroianni in *Dark Eyes*
Jack Nicholson in *Ironweed*
Robin Williams in *Good Morning, Vietnam*

Filmography

CRY BABY KILLER (1958)
Starring: Harry Lauter, Jack Nicholson, Carolyn Mitchell, Brett Halsey, Lynn Cartwright
Director: Jus Addis
Producer: Roger Corman
Screenplay: Leo Gordon and Melvin Levy

LITTLE SHOP OF HORRORS (1960)
Starring: Jonathan Haze, Jackie Joseph, Mel Welles, Dick Miller, Myrtle Vail, Leola Wendorff, Jack Nicholson
Director: Roger Corman
Producer: Roger Corman
Screenplay: Charles B. Griffith

TOO SOON TO LOVE (1960)
Starring: Jennifer West, Richard Evans, Warren Parker, Ralph Manza, Jack Nicholson
Director: Richard Rush
Producer: Mark Lipsky
Screenplay: Lazlo Gorog and Richard Rush

STUDS LONIGAN (1960)
Starring: Christopher Knight, Frank Gorshin, Venetia Stevenson, Carolyn Craig, Jack Nicholson, Robert Caspar, Dick Foran, Jay C. Flippen, Kathy Johnson
Director: Irving Lerner

Producer: Philip Yordan
Screenplay: Philip Yordan

THE WILD RIDE (1960)
Starring: Jack Nicholson, Georgianna Carter, Robert Bean
Director: Harvey Berman
Producer: Harvey Berman
Screenplay: Ann Porter and Marion Rothman

THE BROKEN LAND (1962)
Starring: Kent Taylor, Dianna Darin, Jody McCrea, Robert
   Sampson, Jack Nicholson, Gary Snead
Director: John Bushelman
Producer: Leonard Schwartz
Screenplay: Edward Lakso

THE RAVEN (1963)
Starring: Vincent Price, Peter Lorre, Boris Karloff, Hazel Court,
   Olive Sturgess, Jack Nicholson, Connie Wallace, William Baskin,
   Aaron Saxon
Director: Roger Corman
Producer: Roger Corman
Screenplay: Richard Matheson

THE TERROR (1963)
Starring: Boris Karloff, Jack Nicholson, Sandra Knight, Richard
   Miller, Dorothy Neumann, Jonathan Haze
Director: Roger Corman
Producer: Roger Corman
Screenplay: Leo Gordon and Jack Hill

THUNDER ISLAND (1963)
Starring: Gene Nelson, Fay Spain, Brian Kelly, Miriam Colon, Art
   Bedard, Antonio Torres Martino
Director: Jack Leewood
Producer: Jack Leewood
Screenplay: Jack Nicholson and Don Devlin

ENSIGN PULVER (1964)
Starring: Robert Walker, Jnr., Burl Ives, Walter Matthau, Millie
Perkins, Tommy Sands, Kay Medford, Larry Hagman, Gerald
O'Laughlin, Sal Papa, Al Freeman, Jnr., James Farentino, James
Coco, Diana Sands, Jack Nicholson
Director: Joshua Logan
Producer: Joshua Logan
Screenplay: Joshua Logan and Thomas Heggan

BACK DOOR TO HELL (1964)
Starring: Jimmie Rodgers, Jack Nicholson, John Hackett, Annabelle
Higgins
Director: Monte Hellman
Producer: Fred Roos
Screenplay: Richard Guttman and John Hackett

FLIGHT TO FURY (1966)
Starring: Dewey Martin, Fay Sprain, Jack Nicholson, Jacqueline
Hellman, Vic Diaz, Joseph Estrada. John Hackett
Director: Monte Hellman
Producer: Fred Roos
Screenplay: Jack Nicholson

THE SHOOTING (1966)
Starring: Warren Oates, Will Hutchins, Millie Perkins, Jack Nich-
olson, B.J. Merholz
Director: Monte Hellman
Producer: Monte Hellman and Jack Nicholson
Screenplay: Carol Eastman writing as Adrien Joyce

RIDE IN THE WHIRLWIND (1966)
Starring: Cameron Mitchell, Jack Nicholson, Millie Perkins, Tom
Fuler, Katherine Squire, George Mitchell, Brandon Caroll
Director: Monte Hellman
Producer: Monte Hellman and Jack Nicholson
Screenplay: Jack Nicholson

HELL'S ANGELS ON WHEELS (1967)
Starring: Jack Nicholson, Adam Rourke, Sabrina Scharf, Jane
  Taylor, John Carwood, Richard Anders, I. J. Jefferson
Director: Richard Rush
Producer: Joe Solomon
Screenplay: R. Wright Campbell

REBEL ROUSERS (1967)
Starring: Cameron Mitchell, Jack Nicholson, Bruce Dern, Diane
  Ladd, Harry Dean Stanton
Director: Martin B. Cohen
Producer: Martin B. Cohen
Screenplay: Abe Polsky, Michael Kars and Martin B. Cohen

THE ST VALENTINE'S DAY MASSACRE (1967)
Starring: Jason Robards, George Segal, Ralph Meeker, Jean Hale,
  Clint Ritchie, Frank Silvera, Joseph Campanella, Richard
  Bakalyan, David Canary, Bruce Dern, Harold J. Stone, John
  Agar, Jack Nicholson
Director: Roger Corman
Producer: Roger Corman
Screenplay: Howard Browne

THE TRIP (1967)
Starring: Peter Fonda, Susan Strasberg, Bruce Dern, Dennis Hopper
Director: Roger Corman
Producer: Roger Corman
Screenplay: Jack Nicholson

HEAD (1968)
Starring: The Monkees, Victor Mature, Annette Funicello; featuring
  Frank Zappa, Carol Doda, Sonny Liston, I. J. Jefferson
Director: Bob Rafelson
Producer: Bob Rafelson and Jack Nicholson
Screenplay: Bob Rafelson and Jack Nicholson

PSYCH-OUT (1968)
Starring: Susan Strasberg, Dean Stockwell, Jack Nicholson, Bruce
  Dern, Adam Rourke, Max Julien, Henry Jaglom, I. J. Jefferson

Director: Richard Rush
Producer: Dick Clark
Screenplay: E. Hunter Willett and Betty Ulius

EASY RIDER (1969)
Starring: Peter Fonda, Dennis Hopper, Jack Nicholson
Director: Dennis Hopper
Producer: Peter Fonda
Screenplay: Peter Fonda, Dennis Hopper and Terry Southern

DRIVE, HE SAID (1970)
Starring: William Tepper, Karen Black, Michael Margotta, Bruce
   Dern, Robert Towne, Hanry Jaglom, June Fairchild
Director: Jack Nicholson
Producer: Jack Nicholson and Steve Blauner
Screenplay: Jack Nicholson and Jeremy Larner

FIVE EASY PIECES (1970)
Starring: Jack Nicholson, Karen Black, Lois Smith, Susan Anspach
Director: Bon Rafelson
Producer: Bob Rafelson and Richard Weschler
Screenplay: Carol Eastman writing as Adrien Joyce

ON A CLEAR DAY YOU CAN SEE FOREVER (1970)
Starring: Barbra Streisand, Yves Montand, Bob Newhart, Larry
   Blyden, Jack Nicholson
Director: Vincente Minnelli
Producer: Howard Koch
Screenplay: Alan J. Lerner

A SAFE PLACE (1971)
Starring: Tuesday Weld, Jack Nicholson, Orson Welles, Philip
   Proctor, Gwen Welles, Dov Lawrence
Director: Henry Jaglom
Producer: Bert Schneider
Screenplay: Henry Jaglom

CARNAL KNOWLEDGE (1971)

Starring: Jack Nicholson, Candice Bergen, Art Garfunkel, Ann-Margret, Rita Moreno, Cynthia O'Neal, Carol Kane
Director: Mike Nichols
Producer: Mike Nichols
Screenplay: Jules Feiffer

THE KING OF MARVIN GARDENS (1972)

Starring: Jack Nicholson, Bruce Dern, Ellen Burstyn, Julia Anne Robinson, Scatman Crothers, Charles Lavine, John Ryan, Sally Boyar
Director: Bob Rafelson
Producer: Bob Rafelson
Screenplay: Jacob Brackman

THE LAST DETAIL (1973)

Starring: Jack Nicholson, Otis Young, Randy Quaid, Clifton James, Carol Kane, Michael Moriarty, Luana Anders
Director: Hal Ashby
Producer: Gerald Ayres
Screenplay: Robert Towne

CHINATOWN (1974)

Starring: Jack Nicholson, Faye Dunaway, John Huston, Perry Lopez, Diane Ladd, Darrell Zwerling, John Hillerman, Roman Polanski
Director: Roman Polanski
Producer: Robert Evans
Screenplay: Robert Towne

THE PASSENGER (1975)

Starring: Jack Nicholson, Maria Schneider
Director: Michelangelo Antonioni
Producer: Carlo Ponti
Screenplay: Mark Peloe, Peter Wollen and Michelangelo Antonioni

TOMMY (1975)

Starring: Ann-Margret, Roger Daltry, Oliver Reed, Elton John, Keith Moon, Jack Nicholson, Eric Clapton, Robert Powell, Tina Turner, The Who

Director: Ken Russell
Producer: Ken Russell and Robert Stigwood
Screenplay: Ken Russell

THE FORTUNE (1975)
Starring: Jack Nicholson, Warren Beatty, Stockard Channing
Director: Mike Nichols
Producer: Hank Moonjean
Screenplay: Carol Eastman writing as Adrien Joyce

ONE FLEW OVER THE CUCKOO'S NEST (1975)
Starring: Jack Nicholson, Louise Fletcher, William Redfield, Will
Sampson, Brad Dourif, Marya Small, Louisa Moritz, Sydney
Lassick, Scatman Crothers, Danny DeVito, Dr Dean Brooks,
Christopher Lloyd
Director: Milos Forman
Producer: Saul Zaentz and Michael Douglas
Screenplay: Lawrence Hauben and Bo Goldman

THE MISSOURI BREAKS (1976)
Starring: Marlon Brando, Jack Nicholson, Randy Quaid, Kathleen
Lloyd, Frederic Forrest, Harry Dean Stanton, John McLaim
Director: Arthur Penn
Producer: Robert M. Sherman
Screenplay: Thomas McGuane

THE LAST TYCOON (1976)
Starring: Robert De Niro, Ingrid Boulting, Robert Mitchum,
Jeanne Moreau, Jack Nicholson, Tony Curtis, Donald Pleasance,
Ray Milland, Dana Andrews, Theresa Russell
Director: Elia Kazan
Producer: Sam Spiegel
Screenplay: Harold Pinter

GOIN' SOUTH (1979)
Starring: Jack Nicholson, Mary Steenburgen, Christopher Lloyd,
John Belushi, Veronica Cartwright, Richard Bradford, Jeff
Morris
Director: Jack Nicholson

Producer: Harry Gittes and Harold Schneider
Screenplay: John Herman Shareer, Al Ramus, Charles Shyer and
    Alan Mandel

THE SHINING (1980)
Starring: Jack Nicholson, Shelley Duvall, Danny Lloyd, Scatman
    Crothers, Barry Nelson, Philip Stone, Joe Turkel
Director: Stanley Kubrick
Producer: Stanley Kubrick
Screenplay: Stanley Kubrick and Diane Johnson

THE POSTMAN ALWAYS RINGS TWICE (1981)
Starring: Jack Nicholson, Jessica Lange, John Colicos, Michael
    Lerner, John Ryan, Anjelica Huston, Jon Van Nees
Director: Bob Rafelson
Producer: Bob Rafelson and Charles Mulvehill
Screenplay: David Mamet

REDS (1981)
Starring: Warren Beatty, Diane Keaton, Jack Nicholson, Edward
    Herrmann, Jerzy Kosinski, Paul Sorvino, Maureen Stapleton,
    Nicolas Coster, Ian Wolfe, Bessie Love
Director: Warren Beatty
Producer: Warren Beatty
Screenplay: Warren Beatty and Trevor Griffiths

THE BORDER (1981)
Starring: Jack Nicholson, Valerie Perrine, Harvey Keitel, Warren
    Oates, Elpidia Carrillo, Shannon Wilcox
Director: Tony Richardson
Producer: Edgar Bronfman
Screenplay: Deric Washburn, Walon Green and David Freeman

TERMS OF ENDEARMENT (1983)
Starring: Shirley MacLaine, Debra Winger, Jack Nicholson, Jeff
    Daniels, Danny DeVito, John Lithgrow, Kate Charleson, Lisa
    Hart Carroll
Director: James L. Brooks
Producer: James L. Brooks
Screenplay: James L. Brooks

PRIZZI'S HONOUR (1985)

Starring: Jacl Nicholson, Kathleen Turner, Anjelica Huston, William Hickey, John Randolph, Lee Richardson, Robert Loggia, Michael Lombard
Director: John Huston
Producer: John Foreman
Screenplay: Richard Condon and Janet Roach

HEARTBURN (1986)

Starring: Meryl Streep, Jack Nicholson, Jeff Daniels, Maureen Stapleton, Stockard Channing, Richard Masur, Catherine O'Hara, Steven Hill, Milos Forman, Natalie Stern, Karen Akers
Director: Mike Nichols
Producer: Mike Nichols and Robert Greenhut
Screenplay: Nora Ephron

WITCHES OF EASTWICK (1987)

Starring: Jack Nicholson, Cher, Susan Sarandon, Michelle Pfeiffer, Veronica Cartwright, Richard Jenkins, Keith Jochim, Carel Struycken
Director: George Miller
Producer: Neil Canton, Peter Guber, Jon Peters
Screenplay: Michael Cristofer

BROADCAST NEWS (1987)

Starring: William Hurt, Albert Brooks, Holly Hunter, Robert Prosky, Lois Chiles, Joan Cusack, Peter Hackes, Jack Nicholson
Director: James L. Brooks
Screenplay: James L. Brooks

IRONWEED (1987)

Starring: Jack Nicholson, Meryl Streep, Carroll Baker, Michael O'Keefe, Diane Venora, Fred Gwynne, Margaret Whitton, Tom Waits, Jake Dengel, Joe Grifasi
Director: Hector Babenco
Producer: Joseph H. Kanter, Denis Blouin, Rob Cohen
Screenplay: William Kennedy

BATMAN (1989)
Starring: Jack Nicholson, Michael Keaton, Kim Basinger, Jack Palance, Robert Wuhl, Billy Dee Williams, Pat Hingle, Jerry Hall, Michael Gough, Lee Wallace, Tracey Walter
Director: Tim Burton
Producer: Jon Peters and Peter Guber
Screenplay: Sam Hamm and Warren Skaaren

THE TWO JAKES (1990)
Starring: Jack Nicholson, Harvey Keitel, Meg Tilly, Madeleine Stowe, Eli Wallach, Frederic Forrest, Richard Farnsworth, Ruben Blades, David Keith
Director: Jack Nicholson
Producer: Robert Evans and Harold Schneider
Screenplay: Robert Towne

Index

277